Iron Rice Bowl

A MEMOIR BY TOM KWOK

Cover design by Peter Cobcroft

ISBN 978-0-9942792-3-1

Published by Rainbow Works Pty Ltd, Pottsville, NSW
Printed and bound by Lightning Source Australia

Dedicated to my loving family

DISCLAIMER

In this story, real names of the people are used as they are remembered. The places and situations are also real. Dialogue has been reconstructed as accurately as memory permits. However, some names are made up because the author could not recall them. Any similarity of fictional names to real people who had no involvement in this story is purely coincidental.

ONE

‖‖

MY GRANDMOTHER'S PROMISE

MAY 1954

Grandmother Do Shui Ying is leaving Hong Kong. She is going to Australia. We all go to say goodbye.

I am excited to be able to explore a huge ship. I run on the open deck, from one end of the ship to the other. Grandmother takes us down to the lowest deck, where she will stay for the fifteen days of her journey. It is packed with cargo. Part of it is cleared and set up with rows and rows of two-tiered bunks where the passengers sleep.

When the hooter sounds to remind all the non-passengers to leave the ship, I begin to cry.

"Don't be silly, and stop crying," my grandmother says. "I'll bring you over to Australia to join me soon."

Will I meet you when I come to Australia, Father? I want so much to get to know you.

♋♋

It was spring. I was seven. I didn't often have outings, so I was wildly excited to be going down to the docks to see my paternal grandmother off on her voyage. Do Shui Ying was her maiden name. My brother, Lu Kee, and I called her Ah-por[1] .

My grandmother was born sometime in November 1905, in the Year of the Snake. According to Chinese astrology, those born in the Year of the Snake are self-composed, gentle, and philosophical; even profoundly deep-thinkers. They display wisdom, courage, warmth and understanding. They are inquisitive and cautious and show perseverance. Snakes can also be imperious, judgemental and haughty.

Ah-por was born shortly before the 1911 revolution. After the revolution, the one-thousand-two-hundred-year-old Chinese custom of binding the feet of young, wealthy girls was abolished. Foot-binding was an excruciatingly painful process in which a young girl's toes, except the big toe, were crushed and tucked under the soles of her feet. Year after year, the feet were bound with a long cotton bandage, stunting their growth. The feet only grew to three inches long and were known as 'golden lilies'. These girls were crippled for life. It was considered necessary if they were to marry into wealthy families, because bound feet were symbols of wealth and beauty. Women with unbound feet were from poor, peasant backgrounds and rarely permitted to marry into wealthy families.

Although she was born before the revolution, my

---

[1]   Por, ah-por and por-por are Chinese terms that mean old woman or grandmother.

grandmother's feet were not bound. At the age of six, she was probably considered not yet ready for the process. She was able to walk normally. Girls with big feet were often married off at fifteen or sixteen as child brides. Ah-por was just sixteen when, as was traditional, she entered an arranged marriage to my grandfather, Kwok Lin Cheong. As was customary, astrological details were checked to ensure they were compatible with each other. The Chinese believe this is important to ensure the everlasting happiness, prosperity and longevity of the couple and their descendants.

Raised in the traditional way, my grandmother was skilled in cooking, sewing and looking after the household. She was a very capable person, despite having little formal education. Healthy, with no physical deformities, she was of average build, well proportioned and not too short; but not a woman of extraordinary beauty. She was brought up to be a dutiful wife and a good mother; to look after her parents-in-law and the affairs of the family.

My grandfather died in 1933, aged thirty, leaving the twenty-nine-year-old Ah-por widowed with four children. The burden of running the household and the family-owned rice paddies fell upon her. Although uneducated, she was able to read — unlike many other women in China who, during that era, could neither read nor write. When her parents-in-law died, a few years after the death of her husband, Ah-por took over running the household and the rice production with absolute power and authority.

During the Japanese occupation of China in the 1940s, Ah-por displayed wisdom and courage in bringing up four children on her own. She was resilient, with a strong personality. No matter what happened, she always managed to pick herself up. Perhaps she was born with that strength, or she might have developed it during the civil war between the Nationalists and Communists, and the war between China and Japan. Adversity toughened her.

My father's family had been landlords, and well-off. Although life was hard for a young widowed mother, Ah-por was fortunate to be financially secure. In 1950, our family wealth was confiscated by the Communists and redistributed among the peasants. It seemed to me, at age seven, that we must be quite poor.

Understandably, my awareness of our home and lifestyle was quite limited. I understood that I had no father. I didn't know why. That made me different from my peers. I was painfully aware that I was different in other ways, too.

I lived in an apartment in Lockhart Road, Wanchai, Hong Kong. Eleven other family members and a servant shared a small space in a huge four-storey building, fed by ten stairwells that led to apartments on the second, third and fourth floor. The ground floor was taken up with a variety of shops and businesses. There was a grocery shop from which, for some reason, Leung-por[2] never bought groceries. Three or four women sat peeling raw prawns in

2   Por, in Chinese, means old woman or grandmother. I call my maternal grandmother "Leung-por".

front of the shop next to it. It always smelled fishy around that building.

All the apartments were the same: rectangular-shaped shoe-boxes, with their length two-and-a-half times their width. The occupants divided the space into rooms according to their needs. Timber-panel partitions divided into four: three bedrooms and a living area.

My mother, brother, youngest aunt and I shared a bedroom that had wall-to-wall bedding. A female servant slept on a folding stretcher at the bottom of our large bed. Two other bedrooms were occupied by my grandparents, Leung-gong[3] and Leung-por, and by my second and third aunts. Four uncles slept in two double bunks on the entrance side of the apartment.

By the window facing the road was a dining and living room. A circular dining table with four seating stools stood in the middle of the room and a four-seater settee, bookcase, glass cabinet and refrigerator lined the walls.

Past the bedrooms, the width of the apartment reduced to half, with a narrow balcony, just wide enough for one person to walk through, which led to the kitchen and a single toilet right at the back. A set of triangular-shaped metal brackets fixed to the edge of the balcony supported half-a-dozen bamboo rods on which washing was hung to dry. Often, washing from the floors above dripped onto the laundry of the lower floors, causing neighbours to argue.

---

3   Gong, ah-gong and gong-gong are Chinese terms that mean old man or grandfather. It is our village custom to distinguish the maternal grandparents by adding their surname. My mother's maiden name is Leung. Thus, I call my maternal grandfather "Leung-gong".

I saw little of my mother, who worked long hours as a sales assistant and had only one full day off, on Monday, every two weeks. Leung-por saw to my care. She took me to the doctor and nursed me to recovery when I contracted diarrhoea. She was kind to me. Leung-por cared for me when I was scalded one evening running toward the kitchen. A servant was coming through with a bowl of hot soup. We collided. She lost her balance. The soup spilled over the top of my head and down the left side of my face. There were no painkillers for me to take, but Leung-por calmed me. She went to the chemist shop to purchase some cream to apply to the burned area. She told me not to touch it with my fingers, as it would be even more painful if the skin ruptured.

Except for attending school, I had little social life. Life was devoid of small-boy adventures like tree-climbing and water play. I suppose I was over-protected. My mother's parents were anxious people who seemed to feel a great weight of responsibility for our welfare. They kept us from joining in social gatherings for fear we might mix with the wrong crowd. Their protectiveness made me quite afraid, so I avoided any form of play that might result in physical hurt.

I went to afternoon school from one-thirty until six-thirty in the evening. My brother, Ah-kor[4], attended an all-day school five days a week, Mondays to Fridays. We were together on Sundays and school holidays, but we only

---

4   My brother's name is Lu Kee. Kor is a Chinese term meaning older brother. I call Lu Kee, Ah-kor.

occasionally played together. He was the quiet type, and not much interested in me.

Each day after lunch, I reluctantly descended the stairs dressed for school and tried valiantly to heed Leung-por's warnings not to loiter about the shops below our apartment. Directly below was a motor service and repair shop. Two shop spaces were taken up by a shop that printed everything from primary school text books to traditional Chinese invitation cards with golden embellishments on a glossy red surface. A rice shop sold all kinds of rice, and also peanut oil for cooking. I ordered rice to be delivered to our apartment, and I bought peanut oil for my grandmother.

Another store sold firewood. Most households used wood stoves, as kerosene was expensive and kerosene cookers were dangerous. I often watched the shopkeeper, in the morning, chopping wooden logs into pieces to deliver in the afternoons.

In a furniture shop people worked with cane and rattan, weaving chairs, small tables, carry bags and suitcases. They wove rattan into sheets to be used as bed linen in summer, because rattan didn't absorb heat, and it cooled quickly. Were it not for Leung-por's cautions, I might have been tempted to stand and watch the weaving. The activity fascinated me.

My favourite shop sold sweets, chocolates, tins of biscuits, soda water, ice blocks and small buckets of ice cream. I seldom had money to buy anything from it, but I loved to look.

I suppose I was loved and cared for, but my childhood was far from carefree. At school, I was somehow a misfit. I didn't know where my father was. I talked to him often — imaginary conversations in which he tried to reassure me sometimes, and to ease my troubles, but he never told me where he was or why he wasn't present in my life. My mother refused to answer questions about him. When I asked, her standard answer was "You shouldn't ask questions like that."

Now, my father's mother, Ah-por, was going to Australia. I assumed then, that my father must be there. Perhaps our family had somehow fallen on hard times and he was trying to make a new start in a land of opportunity? Ah-por planned to send for me to come to Australia. Things would be better then.

Surely, then, I would finally meet my father.

TWO

‖‖‖

LAUGHING STOCK

SEPTEMBER 1951

I start kindergarten this morning, Father.

Leung-por gives me a zippered shoulder bag made of cotton. It holds a small hand towel, a bottle of water, and a plastic container full of food.

"Where are we going?" I ask.

"To kindergarten, where you will learn and play with other children," she says.

The kindergarten is in walking distance, on the second level of a four-storey apartment building. It is small. There isn't much space for children to run or play. Animal pictures are pinned on the wall: horse, cow, dog, cat, rabbit and elephant. There are also pictures of a fire-engine, police car, ambulance, ship and aeroplane. A toy box holds cars, trucks and aeroplanes for the boys and dolls, cooking utensils and a tea set for the girls. Rag dolls sit on shelves.

We have lessons, singing, play, lunch, a sleep, then more play. Then it is time to go home.

I don't join in the play much. I stand and watch other children, joining in only when the teacher says I must. I'm not used to playing with other children. I don't know how to make friends.

කර

A few days after I start kindergarten, I notice a part of my right chin and neck is a little swollen. It isn't painful. When the teacher notices, she tells other children to stay away from me. She says I have mumps, and others can catch it just by touching me.

I stay at home for a few days.

Leung-por says I won't be going back to kindergarten, Father. I don't know why. I feel sad that I can't go.

Later, I wonder if Leung-por didn't have time to take me to kindergarten and collect me every day. Or perhaps the teacher upset Leung-por by telling her she did wrong to bring a sick child to kindergarten. Maybe my mother simply couldn't afford the fees?

SEPTEMBER 1952

I am to start school today, Father. I hope school might be like kindergarten, with lots of things to play with. Maybe I will make some friends.

Leung-por takes me to school. It is a ten minute walk. We enter through the back gate and she asks for my Primary One teacher and introduces us.

"Don't lose sight of the teacher," she says as she prepares to leave.

Two playgrounds are separated by a single-storey assembly hall. My teacher tells me to play in the playground for Primary One to Three students and not to go to the one for the Primary Four to Six students.

Before classes start, the whole school gathers at the assembly hall to listen to the principal's address. Afterwards, students go to their classrooms. Our teacher leads us to our classroom. I don't know any of the other thirty-nine students, and I am embarrassed that I am among the youngest and smallest. I am so skinny.

All sorts of pictures are stuck on three classroom walls, while one wall is all windows. Twenty twin desks with seats are divided into four rows. Children sit in pairs — a girl and boy at each desk. When the teacher enters the room, we must show respect by standing up and bowing, before sitting down.

Our teacher is a young woman with deep brown eyes and a big smile. Her voice is soft and sweet, but firm. I liked her until —

"Students," she says, "when I call out your name, put your hand up and answer me with 'Yes, Teacher'. I want to see who you are and put a face to your name."

She calls the names of children, not in any particular order. They all answer promptly.

"Kwok Loo Shang," she calls.

"Yes, Teacher," I answer softly, and without hesitation. My right thumb is jammed in my mouth, muffling my reply.

"I can't hear you, Kwok Loo Shang," the teacher says. "Pull out whatever you have in your mouth and put your hand up."

I pull my thumb out of my mouth and raise my hand.

"Only a baby sucks his thumb!" one of the students shouts. Everyone laughs loudly.

"Loo Shang sounds like a girl's name," says the teacher. "You are not a girl."

"Are you a boy or a girl?" the girl beside me asks, laughing uncontrollably. Another round of hearty laughter follows.

What is so funny about my name, Father? Nobody ever told me my name is for girls. I don't like school. The teacher and students make fun of me.

∽∾

After roll call, the teacher asks questions to test our knowledge. Students who know the answers raise their hands and hop up and down in their seats to draw her attention. I don't know many answers, so I try not to draw her attention.

"Kwok Loo Shang," she calls out suddenly. "If you are facing east, which direction is your back?"

I shrug my shoulders.

"West, stupid!" a student exclaims. The class bursts out laughing again.

"It is not nice to call people stupid," the teacher says. "Now, Kwok Loo Shang, tell me which is your left hand?"

I hesitate, then slowly raise my right hand.

"No, that is your right hand."

Again, the whole class laughs, and I squirm in my seat. A burning sensation rises up my neck. The teacher continues her questioning, and I again try to be inconspicuous.

After testing our general knowledge, the teacher says, "It's time for me to hear what your father does." She focuses on one girl and asks, "What does yours do?"

"My father has a business," she replies.

"My father is a fireman," says another, full of pride.

"My father works for the government," says the girl who sits next to me.

This goes on until every student except me has related their father's occupation.

"Kwok Loo Shang, what does your father do?"

"I don't know," I reply. The whole class erupts into laughter again.

"Be quiet students," she says, then turns back to me and asks, "Why don't you know?"

"I have never met him. No one has ever told me anything about him."

"A bastard!" one older student shouts.

Silence.

Mouths open wide. Hands of older students fly to cover their mouths. Students my age are staring at me. Perhaps, like me, they don't know the meaning of the word.

"I'll be very angry with you if I hear that word again." The teacher's tone is authoritative. She seeks to defend me, but she is to blame. She should not have asked me those questions.

What do you do, Father? And what's a bastard? Am I one? It seems like it's a very bad thing to be.

☞☜

I stop sucking my thumb after that first day at school. My mother and Leung-por are glad that something has finally cured me of the habit, but I never tell them how I suffered that day. They never ask.

The teasing continues. A boy with a girl's name who doesn't know anything about his own father? What a joke! They never again call me 'bastard' to my face, but one student tells me that others often say the word behind my back.

It would be many years before I understood the meaning, and longer still before I truly understood that I wasn't one, and why I had no father.

☞☜

School days in Primary One are predictable. After my first two weeks, Leung-por no longer walks to school with me. She cautions me not to loiter, but I have a little welcome freedom at the start and end of each school day.

We practice writing on a slate with a slate pencil, pushing a damp cloth up and down to clean it. The slate dries quickly, and we can practice some more.

For homework, we write in an exercise book with a lead pencil. The book has large squares in which to write Chinese characters. It is hard to keep my characters within the boundaries of these squares. We do sums in an exercise book with small squares. Near the end of my first year of school, there is an exciting event: Coronation Day.

2ND JUNE, 1953

Today Father, Princess Elizabeth officially became the Queen of England. Before classes began, the whole school went to assembly and the principal addressed us. He told us we are to address the Princess as 'Her Majesty Queen Elizabeth the Second.' Every classroom has a picture of her high up on one wall.

All the students received a gift from the newly crowned Queen, in commemoration of the special occasion. We queued up, and we had to behave ourselves while waiting to collect our gift.

It was exciting. Students were guessing what the gift might be. I have never had anything of value. A gift from the Queen! It was unbelievable.

I received an aluminium mug with the Queen's profile engraved. It was inscribed on one side: Queen Elizabeth II

Coronation 1953. I have something of value now, far more valuable than my collection of bottle tops and ice-block sticks. I couldn't wait for school to finish so I could proudly show my mother my new and most valuable worldly possession.

When I need a drink, I climb up on the big concrete water tank in the kitchen and balance on my stomach on the edge to scoop water out with my mug.

I go to sleep with my mug, and I take it with me to school. Some of my fellow students reckon that I'm crazy to carry it around. There must be hundreds of thousands of them around. Every Government school student has one. But I don't care that they think it cheap and worthless.

To me, my mug is priceless.

THREE

─────────────────────────

I'M YANG FIRE DOG, BUT NOT A LEADER

It's the first week of my school holidays, Leung-por calls, "Loo Shang, what are you doing?"

"Playing with my toy fire-engine." My fire engine is my pride and joy. It's the only toy I have ever bought for myself. It cost thirty cents, and I treasure it.

"You'd better pack up and get ready. I'm taking you with me to do some shopping at the departmental store in the Central District. It's nine o'clock now. We'll be leaving in five minutes."

"Yippee!" I'm getting out of the house. At age seven, this is a rare treat. "Can we ride on the upper level of the double-decker tram?"

"Only if you are careful when you walk up the stairs."

It's a twenty-minute ride to the Central District, but the wait at the tram stop seems interminable. When the tram finally arrives and the door slides open, I rush up the stairs and drop onto a double seat next to a window. Waving at my grandmother, I call, "Hurry up," concerned that another passenger might take the empty seat beside me.

"Sit still!" Leung-por cautions.

"I can't see very much while sitting down. Is it okay for me to kneel on the seat?"

"All right then. Kneel on the seat. But don't put your head or hands outside the window."

Now, the whole world is passing by underneath me.

The tram stops right outside the six-level Wing On Department Store. It is the sister company of Wing On Textile in Shanghai, where my great-grandfather worked as the treasurer.

"You go up to the toy section and entertain yourself for a few hours," Leung-por says. "I'll come and get you later this afternoon... about two o'clock. Here's fifty cents for you to get some lunch at the canteen on the ground floor. Don't break anything."

I carefully put the fifty cents in my pocket, and run off towards the lift, managing to squeeze myself into it just before the door closes. *How should I spend the money? There are so many choices.*

"Fifth floor," I say to the lift operator. I've been to the store before, and I know where to find the toys.

When the lift door opens, I rush out. The lift door closes behind me. To my horror, the toy section has disappeared. I run around frantically, searching for it, but there is no sign of it.

I'm supposed to wait for Leung-por in the toy section, Father. I don't know where she is spending the day. I can't do anything wrong, or Leung-por won't bring me ever again.

Walking back to the lift, I blink seeing a huge number '4' on the wall.

"Silly me. I'm on the wrong floor," I whisper.

I hop back into the lift and repeat, "fifth floor." This time there's no mistake. The toy section is still on the fifth floor, and I gasp with delight entering this magical space.

Half the floor space is filled with toys, Father.

I hardly know where to begin, so I set out to explore what is new since my last visit, a few months ago. I play with toys. For a while, I stand watching model trains going around and around the miniature countryside. Then I put on a fireman's hat and ride on my beloved paddle fire engine.

At about one o'clock, I decide to have lunch. Checking that the fifty cents is still inside my pocket, I go down to the canteen and queue up to be served. I would have loved a roast pork bun, can of soft drink, ice cream and some chocolate, but with only fifty cents I can only have two of my favourite foods. I buy a bun and a drink.

After lunch, I go back to the fifth floor to wait for my grandmother to catch the tram back home. It was a wonderful day out. The tram ride was fun.

☙❧

In my second year at school, in Primary Two, students are selected to put on a show for parents in the evening.

I am to take part in a play called The Three Little Pigs, Father. It is a popular fairy tale about three little pigs who are old enough to leave home to live on their own. Mother Pig warns them about the big bad wolf. The first little pig, being lazy, decides to build his house with straw, because it is easy to build and won't take long. The second little pig decides to build a stronger house with sticks thinking it will be harder for the big bad wolf to push over. The third little pig, being the wisest, decides to build his house with bricks. It is hard work, but he builds a house that the big bad wolf will not be able to push over.

A girl and I play the part of the brick walls. We stand a pace apart, facing each other, holding each other's hands. Our bodies will be covered with a cape and hood painted like a brick wall. The boy who plays the third pig stands inside, between our hands, as if he is living inside the brick house. We have to stand still while the wolf pushes against the wall.

We rehearsed the play a number of times, Father. It's easy for the children representing the straw and stick houses, because they are to fall down when the big bad wolf pushes them. A couple of times, we fell down accidentally during rehearsals, because the boy playing the wolf pushed us too hard.

On the night of the play, the assembly hall fills with parents waiting anxiously to see their sons and daughters perform. While the straw and the stick house are walking up the stage, my brick wall partner points out where her parents are sitting. I crane my head to see if my mother or Leung-por have come. I can't see either of them.

There is lots of laughter from the audience. They must have enjoyed our performance. The applause, when the curtains closed, was deafening. Our teacher is proud of our effort. She congratulates us. But neither my mother nor Leung-por came.

Nobody came to share my moment of glory, Father. Would you have come if you were here?

JUNE 1954

Ah-por has gone to Australia. I wonder when she will send for me?

For many days, after her departure, I am distracted by excitement and secret plans. I dream about meeting my father. But as the days pass, I realize that it will be some time before Ah-por can send for me. I fall back into a dull and frustrating routine.

Near the end of my second school year, when everyone is looking forward to the long summer break, our Primary Two teacher announces that the class will spend the second-last day of school at the Botanical Gardens.

I'm so excited, Father. There will be lots of interesting things to see.

My excitement quells when the teacher announces that each child must be accompanied by a parent. My mother will be at work and won't be able to go. My hopes are dashed. I am unable to hide my disappointment.

"Kwok Loo Shang," my teacher says, noticing my sadness. "You can come along, and your mother doesn't have to accompany you. I'll look after you during the day."

Students, parents and teachers left the school this morning. It took thirty minutes for the two buses to reach the entrance to the Gardens, Father. Students were talking over one another, many yelling excitedly. Nobody seemed concerned about the noise. Parents and teachers carried on with their own conversations.

The Gardens are beautiful and peaceful. The central attraction is a fountain with water jets that shoot high up into the air. Lots of people are taking photographs in front of the fountain. A military band plays popular British military tunes. They also play popular tunes, and encourage spectators to sing and clap along. The band is barricaded in a circle. Adults and students stand five-deep outside the barricade, listening.

At lunch time, everyone is given a brown paper bag containing a roast pork bun, a coconut bun, a small cake and sweets. Some parents give their children money to buy a small bucket of ice-cream from a street vendor riding a bicycle.

⚯

I was too young at that time, to appreciate the many different species of plants in the garden. I spent my time running around and playing hide and seek in the bamboo garden with other students. Lunch was a wonderful treat. Such delicacies were rarely available in our household. I envied the other children their ice-cream, but it was an unforgettable day.

⚯

I conversed with my father often. Unlike my mother, he was always — in my imaginary world — available. To speak with my mother, I had to time my approach precisely. Her day began at nine-thirty in the morning. She spent half an hour bathing, making coffee, dressing, and putting on make-up. Then she went to work until eleven at night. The only opportunity to talk to her was while she was having coffee. It took her only five minutes to drink it, so my conversation had to be quick and concise.

Looking back, it seems the only time my mother took much interest in me was when I presented her with my school report card. I was a poor scholar — performing well below average. I never had much confidence in my ability, and for the first few years, I was close to the bottom of my class. My nickname was 'useless'. I could never do anything right.

At times, I wished I could prove to other students that I was good at something, but my school results were always poor. My mother yelled as she signed my report card. "You could have done better! You're just lazy, lazy, lazy. What is the point of sending you to school? What a waste of money. After you have completed primary school, see if anyone will take you on as an apprentice. If you can't study, you might as well go and get a job to earn some money."

The first few times, this reprimand upset me greatly. Later, I became immune to her criticism; it didn't bother me a bit.

SEPTEMBER 1954

Leung-por lets me leave for school earlier now that I am eight and in Primary Three. I can escape the confinement of our small apartment and run around the school yard before class starts.

I cross two roads on my way to school: Lockhart and Hennessy. I try to get there by one o'clock — half an hour before class starts — to seek out whoever will accept me into their games. I am a small and skinny kid. Unlike most kids, I don't have a special friend. I merely tag along with anyone who'll accept me. I try to fit in, but the group always rejects me.

Today, a group is kicking around a small plastic ball in the school yard. Pang Kwok Choy, the leader of the pack, suggests, "Let's play a game of soccer for half an hour before the class starts," he said. "There are twelve of us here, so six to a team. I'll pick five and Chen Lou, you pick five."

I know Chen Lou is a good friend of Pang Kwok Choy. Both are much older than me — probably by three to four years. I know I'll be last to be picked. I wait patiently.

"Kwok Loo Shang is the only one left. You have to take him," says Pang Kwok Choy.

"No, I'll take Wong Ti Sun. You take Kwok Loo Shang."

"No, I don't want to take him." says Pang Kwok, pointing at me.

"Why did you have to pick first? If I had picked first, Kwok Loo Shang would have ended up in your team," says Chen Lou.

"Okay, let's settle this. Next time you pick first."

"He's no good in any ball game. He's useless. It's not fair. I don't want him on my team. He can't stop a ball with his feet. He misses kicking it most of the time. It's better not to have him at all," Chen Lou cries.

I look from Pang Kwok Choy to Chen Lou, wondering who will relent.

"No, I'm not going to have him. We'll play with five instead of six," Chen Lou says.

I can't believe this is happening. I am blocked out of a game again.

"You can't do that," Pang Kwok Choy protests. "If you lose the game, you'll say you only had five, not six, in your team."

"Okay then. I'll have him but we won't pass the ball to him and we'll make sure he doesn't touch the ball at all," Chen Lou says.

Chen Lou is right, Father. I'm hopeless in any type of ball game. Why am I so clumsy? I'm not a sporty type. I don't mind being picked last, as long as I eventually belong to a team and get to have a bit of fun.

But no one will pass the ball to me. Maybe they think I'm odd because I only have a mother and don't know who my father is. I can't understand why I need to have a father when I am living with my mother, grandparents and all her seven siblings.

NOVEMBER, 1954

There's a small red-purple patch on the skin on the inside of my right calf. It's been there as long as I can remember. I must have been born with it. Its shape resembles a Chinese junk in full sail.

"What's this?" asks one of the students, pointing.

"I don't know. It's a red patch, but I can do magic on it," I reply.

"Don't believe you."

"If you press hard on it and let go, the red patch will turn to skin colour and gradually will turn back to red."

"Can I try?"

It's true. It happens.

"Let me tell the other students so that they can all have a go," says the student.

Before long, there are students surrounding me taking turn to press my red patch. I now have something that no other student has — a magic red-purple patch. While I enjoy being the centre of attention, an older student comes along.

"Don't go near him!" he warns. "Only bad people have marks on their bodies. It is a sign to warn others not to associate with that person. Don't touch it! How do you know it's not contagious? You might end up getting one. Then you'll be branded as a bad person."

All the students surrounding me start to disperse. My five minutes of fame has vaporised. I'm sure it's not contagious, because it doesn't cause me any pain and hasn't spread to any other part of my body. But who am I to argue? No one in the class has ever taken any notice of me.

Later in life, I learn this deep red-purple patch is called a birthmark. According to some myths, birthmarks are caused when an expectant mother experiences a sudden fear. Perhaps my mother was afraid when my father disappeared?

Although this permanent birthmark poses no long-term health problems, having it affects me emotionally. It's yet more fuel for primary school students who want to tease me.

As well as a birthmark, I have a scar between my groin and the bend of my upper left thigh. When I was eighteen months old, there was a growth there. It grew to the size of a quail egg. I had an operation at one of the hospitals in Skak-Kee. The operation was successful. The growth was not cancerous. My mother apparently considered the operation minor. She never spoke to me about it. It was my grandmother who told me about the operation.

Leung-por told me that, as a baby, I was often sick. My mother never produced enough breast milk to feed me. Women from poor backgrounds who are capable of producing milk often sell their milk to feed wealthy families' babies. These women, known as nai-mah (milk-mothers), are very close to the children they feed. Often, children have better relationships with their nai-mah than with their own biological mothers.

I didn't need a nai-mah because, back then, my family could afford to give me powdered or condensed milk. It seems that when I was a baby, we were wealthy enough to afford such luxuries. I asked Leung-por what had happened to make our family poor. She told me our fortunes changed when our family fled China for Hong Kong. I was three years old at that time. She told me some of China's and our family's history.

16th December, Mintkuo 35th year, was the day of my birth. According to the Western calendar, it's 7th January 1947. Mintkuo 1st year was established in 1912 by Sun Yat-sen, the father of modern China, who ignited a revolution in October 1911. His political party, the Kuomintang (Chinese Nationalist Party), was ruled by Chiang Kai-shek after Sun's death. Early in 1912, the last Emperor abdicated, bringing the Manchu dynasty to an end, after 267 years of rule from 1644 to 1911.

Before he abdicated, the Emperor appointed an army general, Yuan Shih-kai, to be commander-in-chief. Yuan controlled the north from the capital Peking; Sun, in Nanking, controlled the centre and south. Sun feared that a terrible civil war would break out, so he unselfishly resigned, making Yuan the President of a United Chinese Republic. In 1916, Yuan died suddenly, leaving China in as uncertain a state as it had been back in 1911.

After Yuan's death, regional military commanders and other local strongmen set up autonomous regimes, and the period 1916 to 1927 was the period of the warlords. To make matters worse, with Western powers occupying during World War I (1914-1918), Japan seized the opportunity to invade China. Their attempt was unsuccessful, because the United States intervened.

The Chinese people's hopes for a better life after the revolution disappeared as China entered a period of chaos. They continued to endure hardship, due to the ruthless regimes of the warlords. In these unstable times, the Chinese Communist Party, led by Mao Tse-tung, emerged in 1921.

The second revolution, from 1916 to 1927, witnessed a power struggle between the Kuomintang and the Communist Party. In 1937, Japan invaded China again. The Kuomintang and the Communists temporarily put aside their differences and partially cooperated to resist Japanese aggression. Meanwhile, Europe and elsewhere was embroiled in World War II. The war was brought to a sudden end by the dropping of atomic bombs on Hiroshima and Nagasaki in August, 1945.

In 1946, fruitless negotiations between Communists and Nationalists merely gave the Communists more time to consolidate their position. It was a year of great unrest, and it was to be followed, in 1947, by the outbreak of another civil war.

The 16th December, Mintkuo 35th year is also the Year of the Dog in the Chinese calendar. My birth was two weeks before the Chinese New Year.

I was born into one of the wealthiest families in the village of Jyuk-Sou-Yuen (Bamboo Garden) in the District of Skak-Kee, County of Chung-Shan, Province of Canton, in China. It was also the birth-place of Sun Yat-sen.

Because there was no hospital in the village, children of the village were born in the traditional way — at home, delivered by a midwife. Hours before my birth, the midwife was already at our house, on stand-by for my arrival. The village midwife had no formal medical training, but having witnessed and assisted in a number of deliveries, she was considered competent. It was due more to good fortune than to her midwifery skills that her previous deliveries were without complications.

My first cry was followed by sighs of relief from all family members — my grandmother, my mother, my big aunt (older sister of my father), my little uncle (younger brother of my father) and my little aunt (younger sister of my father). My older brother, who was only two and half years old, was too young to understand.

It was not the first occasion that my family experienced a birth like mine. My little aunt was also born without knowing her father. He had died a few months before her birth.

According to Chinese astrology, I am a Yang Fire Dog. Yang represents the masculine principle and light as opposed to Yin which represents the feminine principle and darkness. Fire, metal, wood, water and earth are the five elements of the universe, and everything in the universe has a relationship with these five elements. Fire makes heat which either warms or burns. People born under the element of Fire are leaders. The Dog is one of the twelve animals that appear on the Chinese Zodiac calendar. Dog people are loyal, affectionate, sincere and honest. They live righteous lives, care about disadvantaged people and fight injustice. Whether the prediction will hold true or not, in my case, only time will tell.

My birth was supposed to be a joyous occasion of double happiness — not only does the family have another male to carry the family name, but also it heralds the Chinese New Year. Yet everyone was sobbing quietly because my father was not present.

My paternal grandmother named me Loo Shang.

FOUR

|||||||||||||||||||||||||||||||||||||||||||||||||||||||||||||||||||||||||||

LONELY AND AFRAID

I can't recall what I learned in the first two years of schooling, but Primary Three school work was harder. Disinterested in school work, I often got into trouble with the teachers for not paying attention.

This year Father, we are learning to write Chinese characters with a brush. The writing pads are made of ink-absorbing paper and faintly ruled with vertical and horizontal lines forming squares which we have to write in. We all have our own brush and a small plastic circular box containing a cotton patch saturated with black ink. We dip the brush into the black ink patch and then write on our ink-absorbing paper. The teacher demonstrates, to a group of four students at a time, how to make strokes. Afterwards, she goes around to each student to ensure they are holding the brush correctly and writing characters properly. She helps me by standing behind me and holding my hand with the brush to write within each square of the paper.

I find it difficult to make the transition from writing in pencil to brush. I am unable to keep within the squares. When my characters go over into the next square, I compensate by writing the first character leaning towards the left-hand side of the square and the next towards the right. Instead of all the characters being in the centre of squares and straight down in a vertical line on the page, my characters are left and right, left and right, zigzagging down. I also get into trouble for smudging the paper with black ink.

The teacher walks around the class looking at students' calligraphy. She holds mine up in the air.

"This is the worst I've ever seen," she says. "There isn't a single word written within the squares and also the page is smudged with black ink. This is not how you write characters with a brush." Then, she posts my work on the wall as an example of how not to do it.

This year, we also started to learn English. We began with learning the alphabet and later we tried to pronounce simple English words. We use Chinese characters to transliterate, phonetically, the syllables of the English words. It's sounds ridiculously 'Chinglish'. I already have enough problems learning Chinese characters, and now I also have to deal with English words.

On Wednesday afternoons, we go to the assembly hall for cultural and physical activities. Teacher Choy is in charge. Every student participates in singing, playing in our band and physical exercises such as games and ball sports. I enjoy these activities. I sing, even though I am not good at it, but because Teacher Choy tells me to. For a while, I play the triangle in the band. I get to participate in all the games and ball sports we play because the teams are decided by Teacher Choy, not by some headstrong students who exclude me.

I'm glad not to be sitting inside the classroom. Nevertheless, Teacher Choy is my main concern. I think he dislikes me. I've lost count of how many times I've had to stand facing the corner at the back of the hall on my own, for twenty-five minutes, for 'misbehaving'. Although my misbehaving is generally instigated by other students, I'm the one who gets the punishment. Standing facing the corner, at the back of the hall and out of sight, is not as bad as parading in front of the whole class while holding my earlobes with my thumbs and first fingers and my head down. Having students point and laugh at me is so humiliating!

Today, I have to stand in a corner at the back of the hall again. Students are talking at the top of their voices. They sound like people bartering at a market place. Something is not right. Teacher Choy would never allow students to behave like that. I turn around to see what is going on. Teacher Choy is not in the hall. Some students are pushing and pulling one another. Some are fooling around and laughing. As soon as Teacher Choy re-enters the hall, he yells, "Be quiet everyone. Kwok Loo Shang, go and stand at the back." I am confused. The whole class begins to laugh.

"Why are you laughing?" Teacher Choy asks.

"Kwok Loo Shang is already standing at the back," several students answer in unison.

The whole class starts laughing again. I laugh with them.

There's no doubt in my mind, Father, that I'm the one getting all the blame. I don't know why he dislikes me. I don't consider myself to be so bad in the class that I warrant punishment more often than all the other students added together. It seems to me that school is a very unfriendly place.

WANCHAI MARKET

Today is Leung-gong's 50th birthday. Leung-por is preparing a birthday dinner for the family. She asks me to accompany her to the market to shop. She wants to use me as a carrier so her hands are free to pick and choose goods.

Wanchai Market is only a couple of minutes walk from where we live. As a small child, I am seldom allowed to venture outside the apartment, except when accompanied by a closely-related adult. I am always excited when an opportunity arises to escape from the apartment.

On the way to the markets, I see a boy carrying a small wooden box full of shoe polish. He isn't much older than me. He asks people to pay him ten cents to polish their shoes. He walks along the footpath seeking customers. When he finds one, he squats down and asks his customer to put a foot on the box's foot-shape handle. Then he starts shining one shoe at a time. Maybe, like me, he goes to school in the afternoon and has time in the morning to earn some money. It would be good if I was a shoe-shine boy. I wouldn't have to do small household chores. I could wander about exploring the neighbourhood every morning, while earning money at the same time.

While I am dreaming of freedom, Leung-por says, "See that kid over there shining shoes for people. If you don't study hard and do well at school, you could end up like him. You'll be poor and never able to get ahead. Do you understand?"

I nod silently. A minute before, I had been thinking that shining shoes was a dream job, but now I think differently because it seems that only poor kids do this type of work.

Is it a bad job to have to do, Father?

As we continue along Lockhart Road, a local shopkeeper tips leftover food scraps into the footpath gutter. The food scraps will smell and attract flies.

A beggar, wearing filthy, torn clothes, crawls on his knees towards the gutter to forage for food scraps. He picks up the food scraps with his fingers and puts them into his mouth. He is too weak to sit up. He just rolls over and lies on the footpath. People look at him, but without interest in his plight. Due to his body odour, they walk around him with their hands covering their noses. No one seems to have any sympathy for him. As we walk around him, Leung-por says, "If you don't work hard and earn a good living, you'll end up like him — eating from the gutter."

It is awful that a person can be so hungry that he is willing to eat food scraps from the gutter. I wish I could run home to the kitchen and take whatever leftover food is there and give it to the beggar.

I hope I'm not going to end up in his situation, Father.

♋♋

The Wanchai Market has three sections: vegetable, seafood and meat. All the produce is fresh. Meat, poultry and seafood are sold under cover inside a big, ugly, single level concrete building. The vegetables are sold out in the open.

Chinese people believe everything should be eaten as fresh as possible. Shoppers expect the produce to be fresh and in season. Women haggle and bargain for whatever they purchase. Bargaining is the Chinese way of doing business. A Chinese will always ask the question, "Is this fresh?" Without fail, the answer from vendors is, "Of course, it's fresh!" Other questions and comments follow such as, "Is this in season?" or, "Too dear. It's not worth that much" or, "Have you given me the correct weight? Is your weighing scale correct?"

The ground of the vegetable section of the market is wet because the storekeepers periodically douse water onto the vegetables to maintain freshness, and also to put a few grams of extra weight onto their goods. Because the market stalls have limited space, they can only store a limited amount of stock. One vegetable stall sells no other vegetable except various types of cabbage. Another sells root vegetables such as potatoes, sweet potatoes, yams and carrots. Fruit stalls sell whatever is in season, but also with limited varieties.

The fish stalls are full of fish crammed into wooden water-filled tubs. It's impossible for them to swim. They are kept alive in the water for freshness because shoppers are reluctant to buy fish that are already killed and gutted. Shoppers indicate the one they want, and the storekeeper places it flat on the stainless steel bench. The fish thrashes around.

I watch as the man takes out a razor sharp knife. Within a blink of the eye, the belly of the fish is sliced open and the fish is gutted. The fish's mouth is still opening and closing as it gasps for oxygen. The man then pulls out the fish's guts and tosses them into a bin. He scrapes off the scales, making them fly like a hundred pieces of scattered glass. The fish is still fighting to survive and flips while being de-scaled. When it is truly dead, a narrow strip of rattan twine is pulled through its mouth and knotted together. It is then handed over to the shopper to carry away.

Live prawns swim in aerated water tanks, and lobsters lie lazily at the bottom of the tanks. Live crabs, with their claws, crawl on top of one another inside a small wire cage. Shoppers find female crabs more desirable than male ones. Live eels are kept in separate tanks.

Water sloshes all over the floor as the storekeeper uses a net to catch live prawns from tanks. The floor of the seafood section is wet and slippery, so grandmother and I have to walk slowly and carefully to avoid slipping.

The butchers' stalls have no refrigeration. The wide range of meat cuts — mainly beef and pork, and internal organs — hang from hooks on racks. Shoppers want to buy fresh meat because they believe that refrigerated meat is not fresh enough. The tools of trade are sharp meat cleavers and bone choppers. Cattle and pigs are slaughtered in the morning, chopped and sliced into various cuts and the meat hung from hooks. The butcher slices off whatever shoppers want from the hanging meat.

Chickens and ducks, quails, pigeons and geese are sold in poultry stalls. Some shoppers prefer to purchase a live bird and keep it alive for a day or two before consuming it. The storekeeper ties the two feet together with twine for the shoppers to carry the bird upside down.

Other shoppers choose a live bird and ask for it to be killed and its feathers plucked.

Until purchased, live birds are crammed in crates made of rattan and cane, hardly able to move. The smell of the poultry section is overwhelming, particularly on hot days, when the odour of poultry faeces is intense. One wouldn't enter the section without a firm intention to buy.

To add weight to ducks, the storekeeper force-feeds them with rice husks by pushing a funnel straight down the neck into the stomach. The purchase always includes the bird's internal organs. The seller kills the bird by slitting its throat, tying its feet together and hanging it upside down by its feet to let the blood drain out into a bowl.

After plucking feathers and cleaning the bird, it is hung by its neck on a hook ready for pick-up. The storekeeper then ties the two feet together with twine for the shoppers to carry the bird upside down.

In the middle of the walkway, in the marketplace, is a man. It isn't the first time that I've seen him there. He is pale and thin, of small stature, with a slight hunch back. There are marks of tears on his cheeks. No one can tell his age. His eyes are dull, as if he has not slept for days. They look haunted and have dark rings of tiredness surrounding them. Filthy long hair frames a sickly-looking face. His feet and hands are black, as if he has been crawling on a layer of black coal. His black finger nails are filled with dirt. Clothed in filthy rags, his unbearable odour is apparent from several feet away. He crawls on the ground and pushes a small empty tin can in front of him as he moves forward.

Because his whole body is on the ground, people steer away from him as he approaches. He extends his hand out and asks for money. One can see he is struggling to even extend his hand for someone who is generous enough to give him a five or ten cent coin. He tearfully whispers, "Help me, help me." People ignore his plight and carry on as if he is invisible, hurrying by without a backward glance. On rare occasions, someone drops a coin into his tin. Hearing the clinking sound, he raises his head to glance at the person. It is his way of showing appreciation. He is too weak to do anything else.

Leung-por turns around and stares at me walking behind her, carrying groceries, then looks at the beggar.

Without her saying a word, I know what she wants me to understand.

Outside the market, street vendors sell their goods on the footpath. The street hawkers sell an amazing variety of things. They spread their goods on a cloth on the footpath. Some sell fruits, and they carry the produce in two large woven baskets attached to bamboo shoulder poles. Each vendor sells only one type of fruit, such as apples, oranges, mandarins or pomeloes. They do not sell fruits which could be bruised or damaged easily, such as bananas, custard apples or grapes. There are always a lot of browsers, but few buyers. I wonder how they can possibly make a living.

Police consider the street hawkers nuisances because they block the pedestrian traffic on the footpath. If caught, they are often closed down by the police and have their goods confiscated, and they are dragged into the police wagon and taken away. To catch illegal vendors, the police seldom put on the siren as their van comes down the road. This is to ensure they catch some of the illegal vendors without any warning.

A vendor who sells cheap imitation jewellery has his merchandise spread on a four feet square table cloth lying on the footpath. Today, while he is busy trying to complete a sale transaction, someone yells out, "Police!" Before he has a chance to pack up, the police van stops near him. He has no choice but to surrender.

I feel disturbed by what I've witnessed today, Father. I've seen a dying man so hungry he eats food scraps from the gutter; a beggar crawling and begging for money; and a street vendor whose goods have been confiscated by the police.

The world can be a very harsh place, but I don't think that school is the answer for me. I wish you were here to give me advice.

ॐॐ

WOLF CUBS

It is Saturday, the alternative week morning school session.

One of the students from my class is wearing a soldier's uniform instead of the usual school uniform. His beige coloured short-sleeved shirt has two front pockets, and around his neck he wears a colourful twisted scarf with a woggle. Olive coloured shorts have two side pockets and two hip pockets. A brown belt is finished with a badge buckle. Dark green knee-high socks, a pair of polished black shoes, and a tight-fitting green cap with yellow stripes and an emblem at the front complete his smart look. I imagine myself in that uniform.

"Why are you wearing this uniform instead of the school uniform? Aren't you going to get into trouble? Are you a boy soldier?" I ask.

"This is a Wolf Cub uniform. I'm not a boy soldier. I'm a Wolf Cub. The school allows me to wear this every Saturday that I have a Wolf Cub meeting after school," he replies.

"What does a Wolf Cub do?"

"We do a lot of fun things such as going to sport meetings, playing or going to ball games, the zoo, the museum and many other places. We learn to do lots of things."

"How can I become a Wolf Cub?"

"You can join me in the Wanchai District. We have an hour-and-a-half meeting every Saturday afternoon. Wolf Cubs are only for boys aged from seven to twelve. After you turn thirteen, you can join the Scouts."

I am nine, the right age to join. I couldn't stop staring at his uniform and imagining all the fun Wolf Cubs must have.

"I'd like to join," I say.

"You can be in my Six and be my buddy. You're allowed to wear the uniform before you become a member, but the scarf and woggle will be presented to you at a ceremony. My parents turned up at my ceremony and watched the leader present the scarf and woggle to me. Wolf Cubs do a lot of outdoor activities as well, like rock climbing, camping, bush walking and learning traditional scouting skills like tying knots and using a map and compass. We might also go to big events with thousands of other Wolf Cubs. We could also go camping for a week in summer and stay in a cabin or tent."

I begin to daydream about climbing trees, swimming in waterholes, catching fish, bush walking in forests — all the activities my grandmother considers dangerous and won't permit. I've never had any friends. Surely, if I joined Wolf Cubs, I'd have a lot of friends. I'd learn new things and visit exciting places. It would be much more interesting than school.

"Are you listening to what I am telling you, or are you daydreaming?" he asks.

I am daydreaming all right. I can't wait to become a Wolf Cub.

"Wolf Cubs can set challenges for themselves to earn special badges to put on their uniforms showing their achievements in Arts, Nature, Science, Sports and Our World," he says.

I had never achieved anything to be proud of. I was called 'useless'. Here was an opportunity to set myself some challenges and to show off my achievements by earning special badges. Others would realise that I'm not useless after all.

"Listen. You're wandering off again," he says.

"Okay, I'm listening."

"Now, I'll show you the Wolf Cub salute. It's a distinctive two-finger salute. You join the second and third fingers of the right hand; holding the fourth and smallest fingers down with the thumb and touching the extended fingers to the forehead. The two fingers represent the head of the wolf with its ears cocked. Show me, and I'll see whether you can do it."

I follow his instruction and salute.

"Hmmm," he approves. "Another thing, because I'm of higher rank, you have to salute me first and then I acknowledge you by saluting back. This is a mark of respect. Do you understand?"

I nod.

༄༅

"What?" says my mother. "You want to become a Wolf Cub. I don't have the money to buy you the uniform and to pay for all the activities. Do you understand? Don't bother me. I am already running late. Let me get ready for work. I don't want to talk about it. Don't bring it up again. I don't have the money."

I feel so disappointed, Father. I have no friends. I'm not allowed to do anything outside of school. I don't have a chance to achieve anything that I can be proud of, or to win badges or certificates that I can show off to others. I'm sure I'm not entirely useless. I just never get a chance.

༄༅

A WEALTHY FRIEND

I live in an apartment and seldom have the opportunity to venture outside the four walls. I'm never allowed to invite other school friends over to play. A new student in my Primary Four class made friends with me. I was surprised, because no student has ever wanted me as his friend.

Perhaps he doesn't know much about me and is unaware of the names other students call me. He invites me over to his place to play. His father's chauffeur picks me up in a car and drives me to his home.

An amah opens the door to let me inside. Amahs are older female domestic servants. They seldom cut their hair, which they plait, making them easily recognisable on the streets. They live in a tiny servant's room, just big enough to hold a single bed butting hard against two corner walls and leaving barely enough space to get in and out of the bed. Their duties include cooking, minding young children, cleaning the house, buying food, laundering and serving at table. My new friend's amah wears a white smock and black trousers. Her hair is twined into a pig-tail.

My friend's apartment is at least ten times bigger than ours. The furniture is matching — rosewood chairs padded with cushions and a dining room set comprising a table with a marble top and eight seats. The wall cabinets are carved with dragons and phoenixes and filled with ancient artefacts. Hand-painted silk scrolls depict China's well-known regional mountain landscape in black, grey and white and Chinese calligraphy. The lounge room contains a television set. My new friend has his own room, full of toys. I have a great time watching the cartoons on television and playing with his toys.

Leung-por must have told my mother that night about my visit. The following morning, my mother says, "You're not allowed to go to your friend's place any more. They are wealthy, and we are poor. If you break some of your friend's toys, I don't have the money to replace them. Do you understand?"

I nod.

I just have to play with my own treasures, Father. I keep them in a shoe box: a few marbles, some plastic soldiers, soft-drink bottle tops, empty thread reels and ice-block sticks.

I am now old enough to do some local shopping for Leung-por on my own, Father. I feel happy when I spend time wandering around the streets in Wanchai. I treasure these brief outings to explore the world. Many times, I get into trouble for being away far too long, especially when I have money in my pocket.

I watch the rickshaw pullers and wonder how they are able to pull and dodge the traffic. They seem to know how to avoid colliding with motor vehicles and trucks causing accidents. I want to experience the ride. I negotiate with a rickshaw operator to take me for a round trip to anywhere in the neighbourhood, for the kingly sum of fifty cents. He agrees to give me the ride of my life for fifteen minutes.

Although the wooden seat is padded with a cushion, it is still very uncomfortable. Without any good suspension system, every time the wheels run over sunken manhole covers, divots, or across the tram lines, I bounce up and down.

The rickshaw is zigzagging in and out of the traffic to avoid hitting any moving vehicle. It's a hair-raising experience, and it seems just a matter of time before we are run over by a motor vehicle. Setting off and stopping is a big struggle for the operator. To set off, he leans forward, his hands holding onto the long handles, and sets his legs in motion. The pace is slow to start with, but soon he gets into a rhythm and maintains reasonable speed. Then he leans his body slightly backward, pushes the handles backward and gradually slows down until he stops the rickshaw.

When travelling downhill, I fear toppling over. I need to hold onto the seat. When travelling uphill, I lean back. At the end of the ride, I am not sure whether the man has tried to frighten me or to get me all excited. I have mixed feelings about the experience. I was thrilled, yet I do not wish to take another ride. It's dangerous dodging the traffic and breathing in the vehicle fumes. It made me feel nauseous and dizzy—as if I was about to vomit.

FIVE

THE COURT JESTER

By Primary Four, I thoroughly dislike school work. My mother, maternal grandparents, uncles and aunts consider me lazy. I complete my homework quickly because I do the minimum just to get by. Because I don't learn my lessons, I don't do well in tests and examinations. My academic results are, at best, erratic. I am always below average, and often near the bottom of the class.

I'm no scholar, Father. Although the family seems to be concerned about my school work, none of them has taken the time to help me. I know some students whose parents help them with their work, and some of them even have private tutors.

During the last class period for the day, a number of parents stand outside the classroom door. They are waiting to pick up their sons or daughters. They can't help looking in to see and hear how their sons and daughters behave in class or how smart they are, answering the teacher's questions. Students with parents standing outside try to impress them by raising their hands to answer questions. The teacher never fails to pick the students who are sure to give the correct answers. I am never picked, because the teacher doesn't want to embarrass herself by picking a student who gives wrong answers most of the time.

When the bell rings today, the teacher gives permission for us to pack up and leave. Students can't wait to rush out of the classroom. I am in no hurry. While I collect all my books, shoving them inside my school bag, I see my teacher approaching me. As she comes closer, she says, "Kwok Loo Shang, stay back. I want to talk to you."

I panic. I try to think of something I might have done wrong, and pray I am not about to get detention. I'll be in serious trouble if I'm not home by seven o'clock.

"Does anyone help you to do the homework?" the teacher asks.

"No, Teacher."

Why would anyone help me to do my homework?

"What about your mother?"

"She works all day. She leaves home about half-past-ten in the morning and doesn't return until around eleven o'clock at night. By the time she gets home, I'm already asleep. I see her for a few minutes in the morning, while she gets ready to go to work."

"Do you have any older brothers and sisters to help you?"

"I have an older brother who goes to an all-day school. He does his homework during the evening. I don't like to bother him. Besides, he is going to Australia soon to study."

Lu Kee and I are not at all close. He is a quiet sort of person, and even in the holidays we seldom do things together. The school he attends is considered better than mine. His is a fee-paying school and is run by a Christian religious order, whereas mine is a government school. Perhaps our mother can't afford to send both of us to fee-paying schools. In any event, I don't feel comfortable asking for his help with my homework.

"So you're on your own in the house after your mother leaves for work in the morning?"

"No. My maternal grandmother is home. I live with lots of people: my maternal grandparents and my mother's seven brothers and sisters."

"Do any of your uncles or aunts help you with the homework?"

"They're all working, except the youngest uncle who's still in high school. He also does his homework and study during the evening."

"I see. Now I know why I haven't met your mother at our parent-teacher meetings. I've checked with your former class teachers and they haven't met your mother either."

"I don't know why she hasn't turned up for the meetings."

I burn with a sense of injustice. My mother thinks I'm lazy, and yet she has never come to the school to find out how I'm performing. She could have. Why hasn't she?

"Kwok Loo Shang, you're not dumb, but you need to put more effort into your work," the teacher says, patting my head.

I couldn't believe what I was hearing, Father. Kind words from a teacher's mouth! I lowered my head to look at the floor, not saying a word. No one at school has ever thought that I'm clever. Some older students have set out to deliberately intimidate me and make me feel worthless, and that is exactly how I feel.

My self-esteem has left me and my self-confidence is zero. I'm no good at anything: reading, writing, school work, homework, cultural activities or ball games. With all these negative comments from my peers about me, I can't help but put myself down. Sometimes, I act stupid to draw attention.

I'm convinced I'm stupid, useless and worthless. I just wish I could achieve something to prove I am just as good as others. No one wants to be my friend. I'm unable to do anything that my peers consider acceptable. They think I'm stupid—like a court jester, here to make them laugh—but the teacher says, "You can go home now, Kwok Loo Shang. Remember, you're not as dumb as everyone thinks. You need to work and study harder in order to get a good report."

I hurry out of the classroom as quickly as I can. If I am late home, I'll be in trouble with Leung-por for being in school detention again.

I am glad that the teacher didn't ask about you, Father. Maybe she already knew, by talking to my former class teachers, that I don't know anything about you. With such an unimpressive family background, I'm uncomfortable talking to people, especially when the subject of my family comes up. I dislike it when students talk about the outings and fun they have with their parents. It is embarrassing when my schoolmates ask me about my father, and I have to say I do not know.

I have learned to walk away when such conversations come up. I try to protect myself from suffering more anguish and agony. I am nine years old, and I still have my old fears of losing my mother and being placed in an orphanage.

SIX

FAREWELL MY BROTHER...

My school work didn't improve much after my Primary Four teacher told me that I was not a dumb kid. She didn't recognize the effect of the teasing I was getting from my fellow students. Parents can nurture their children, but it is other children who decide whether they are socially acceptable. Kids use shy and withdrawn people like me to boost their own self-confidence and self-image.

I had a gentle nature, and lacked the skills either to make friends or to defend myself against bullying. A boy with a girl's name; a skinny, little kid; a useless, bad luck boy; a bad boy... These were just some of the names I was called.

As I grew older, I found myself getting used to it. By Primary Five, I knew how to deal with the verbal abuse, bullying, humiliations and intimidations. I took it on the chin, then took a deep breath and walked away. I tried to ignore the abuse, reminding myself not to let it consume me. I was too small to fight back, so I learned not to retaliate, but to grow a thick skin and hope that, one day, the bullies would tire of teasing me.

Although the Primary One Teacher had told the students not to call me 'bastard', I have occasionally overheard them saying it behind my back. I now know the meaning, Father. It means 'illegitimate child'. Am I? I long to be just like the other kids. Why must I be different? Why can't they understand that children from broken families are just trying to live normal lives?

∽∾

JUNE 1957

I am surprised to see Ah-kor at home this morning.

"Are you sick?" I ask him.

"No, I'm not sick."

"How come you're not at school this morning?"

"I don't go to school anymore."

"Why not? Has the summer holiday already started in your school?"

"I'll be going to Australia soon. There is only a week left of the school year. There is no point spending the remaining week at school. Besides, who is going to take me shopping?"

"When are you going?"

"In about three weeks' time."

"So soon! How come I didn't know about this? If I hadn't asked you, I still wouldn't know."

"Three or four months ago, mother told me that Ah-por had made application for me to study in Australia. She also told me not to tell you until everything had been finalised and a date set for my departure."

"What about me? When will I be going?"

"I don't know! Ah-por might get you over there one day. I go first and you come later. Ask mother. She might know."

"I don't want to ask her. She doesn't tell me anything."

I decide to just accept the fact that I have to stay in Hong Kong. But Ah-por promised she would take me to Australia. Ever since she left, she has been trying to find a way to get Ah-kor and me there. She believes we will have better opportunities in Australia. I suppose my turn will come.

"How are you going to get there?" I ask Ah-kor.

"On a ship similar to the one Ah-por caught back in 1954."

"Are you scared to go on your own on a large ship?"

"No. I'm not going on my own. I'm going with Goo-mah and her three children, our cousins. They are to join up with Goo-mah's husband, Uncle Shek Chor, who is in Australia."

18TH AUGUST 1957

Today, my brother departs for Australia to continue his education. We travel by taxi to the ship terminal. It is a special treat for me to ride in a motor-car. It doesn't happen often—perhaps once a year.

Leung-gong sits in the front seat, next to the taxi-driver. Our mother and Ah-kor sit on the back seat. I half sit and half stand between my mother and Ah-kor.

The two luggage bags are placed inside the boot of the taxi. One bag is full of Ah-kor's personal belongings and the other is packed full of dehydrated food: mushrooms, shrimps, scallops, salty fishes, fungus, sea weeds, Chinese teas and herbal teas for curing sickness such as minor colds and coughing.

The ship is a cargo ship—not a passenger ship—and there are no designated storage compartments for the luggage. Each passenger is responsible for his own, which is placed next to his bed.

There are people everywhere at the so-called terminal, which is just an open space inside a huge shed. One can tell that the best-dressed ones are travelling, and the rest are here to say goodbye to their family members, relatives and friends. I am anxious to get onto the ship, remembering the great time I had at Ah-por's farewell, three years ago. I ask my mother, "Can I go down to the ship now?"

"No, you can't! We have to wait here until your Goo-mah and her children get here, and besides, all your other uncles and aunts want to say goodbye to your brother. You might get lost on the ship, and we don't want to get into a panic and run around looking for you. You just stay here and be patient."

I notice our mother constantly wiping tears from her eyes. She must be really upset to see her elder son off, with no idea when he will be back. I am showing no sign of being upset. In my excitement, I don't appreciate the implications of this separation, but it must be heart-wrenching for my mother.

Soon, Goo-mah and her children arrive and meet up with us. One by one, our mother's siblings turn up to farewell Ah-kor and Goo-mah. Before I have a chance to ask if we can go onto the ship, Goo-mah says, "We have to wait here, because I have some friends and distant relatives coming. If we get onto the ship, they won't be able to find us."

"Yes, we have to wait here because I have some school friends coming to see me off as well," says Lily, Goo-mah's eldest daughter.

Finally, Lily's school friends and the distant relatives all turn up. "You children wait here with the adults while I'm checking-in," says Goo-mah, and she asks three of the distant relatives to help her carry all the luggage bags.

Ah-kor is the centre of attention. He is surrounded by Leung-gong and our mother's siblings, all giving him a last minute talk that I can't hear. Our mother remains silent. She might be too upset to say anything to Ah-kor. She keeps wiping tears from her eyes. I am getting impatient and anxious, because time is running out for me to get onto the ship.

Goo-mah comes back with the three distant relatives. It has taken a long time. She looks around the people and says, "We are going to say goodbye here instead of on the ship". My mother bursts out crying. She mumbles a few final words to Ah-kor, which must be well wishes and something encouraging. She then pushes me gently in front of Ah-kor, Goo-mah and our cousins and tells me to say goodbye to them one-by-one. I am upset. Is it due to Ah-kor leaving, or not having a chance to get onto the ship?

☙❧

With my older brother gone, I am on my own during the summer holiday at the end of the Primary Five year. There is no one around to play with. I have no toys, so I make my own entertainment and become very creative. I use Leung-gong's empty cigarette packets and Leung-por's empty thread reels. I become obsessed with collecting bits and pieces and inventing things out of scraps. I also love to make things out of soft drink bottle tops and ice-block sticks, the odd tooth-paste box and rubber bands. My greatest treasures are toys bought in a shop—a handful of marbles and some plastic soldiers.

Fear of all crawling insects—cockroaches, crickets, grasshoppers and the like—make me disinclined to trap them and to keep them in a jar or box as other boys do. I borrow my school friends' comic books to read. Sometimes I buy a comic book at a second-hand book shop. More often, I read the comics at the book stores, standing there for a long time, reading, while the storekeeper becomes very annoyed, because it is clear I have neither the intention nor the money to buy anything.

Looking back, I realize that material things were of little importance. What I lacked was that abstract thing that kids need most: a sense of security.

Why does my mother never talk about you, Father? What happened to you? I dream often, that I have a real family that does things together. When I see a small child with his father, I wonder what it would be like to sit on your shoulders with my legs wrapped about your neck and hands holding on to your forehead. It must be scary to be so high up off the ground. What would happen if I were to lean backward? Would you be able to grab both of my legs to stop me falling? What would it be like being chased by you in a park or playground?

I help my grandmother with grocery shopping, chopping the firewood into smaller pieces, dusting the furniture and mopping the floor. I am happy to do all these odd chores to kill the boredom. Occasionally, she gives me ten cents for my efforts. I also help her to assemble plastic flowers and make bead necklaces. There are many small manufacturers in Hong Kong and some of them produce plastic flower parts such as petals, leaves and stems. Instead of employing their own workforce for the assembly of these parts, they outsource the task to anyone who wants to earn some extra money. Leung-por is good to me. When she is paid, she always gives me extra money for helping her.

SEVEN

///

A FRESH START

JULY 1958

My school work doesn't change much. Primary Six is
the final year of primary schooling. Students graduating
this year, in July 1958, need to enrol in another school to
continue their education.

The Hong Kong Education system consists of six
years of primary school—Primary One to Six—and five
years of secondary school—Form One to Five. There are
two years of a matriculation course—Lower and Upper
Form Six—for students who wish to sit for the entrance
examinations to universities in Hong Kong.

I couldn't wait to walk out of that school and enter a
new one for a fresh start. At the new school, I will be able
to tell others that half of my family is in Australia, and one
day my mother and I will join them.

POVERTY

For two weeks, in August 1958, the newspaper headlines are about a fire destroying all the shanties on one of the hills in Hong Kong. It started accidentally, and it has left hundreds of people — or maybe thousands — homeless and without their possessions.

There is so much poverty in Hong Kong, Father. Many people are desperate, trapped in appalling conditions. Some live in shanties made from building materials scrounged from rubbish piles. These makeshift houses are isolated and without public utilities.

There are no roads to these shanties. Dirt tracks lead to slum areas. Children live in poverty and are undernourished and hungry, because their parents are trapped in the poverty cycle. These people feel so defeated and isolated that it seems impossible to escape.

There are also homeless people sleeping on the street and in the lane-ways separating apartment blocks. These narrow lane-ways run from one street to another, one apartment block long and about five feet wide. They form the back way thoroughfare for all the ground floor shops, just wide enough for two people to walk abreast.

It's not just single men who are homeless, Father. Sometimes there are whole families. Some live in the slums and on the hill slopes and streets, but others live on the rooftops and stairwells of the apartment buildings. I've seen young children and their parents building a makeshift home on the rooftop of our apartment building.

Quite a number of families live up there. The size of each dwelling depends on the number of people living in it, but they are no more than ten feet by ten feet. Families make their shanty-dwellings out of whatever materials they can find: large pieces of timber board, cardboard, canvas and rusty iron sheets nailed together. I can't figure out how the shanty stays put on the concrete surface.

Of flimsy construction, the shanties have no chance of withstanding typhoons and torrential rain. None could survive fire. Occupants are on full alert at all times. If a typhoon threatens, they need to collect all their possessions and evacuate down the stairwell within minutes. They remain inside the stairwell until the worst is over. It is worse when there is a fire. Rooftop people live with the daily risk of fire engulfing their makeshift homes, because they cook in the open with kerosene stoves which easily tip over.

There is no water. Water is scarce in Hong Kong. Supply to apartments in our building is only for a few hours each day. Each floor has a supply for about an hour. We store water for cooking and drinking in a large tank in the kitchen. Laundry is only done after drinking and cooking, if there is enough water left. But the shanty-dwellers have no water supply at all. Their drinking water is contained in large plastic bottles. Where do they get the water from?

Without electricity, a kerosene lamp is the only source of light at night. There is no toilet or bathroom facility, and it puzzles me where they go to do their business. How often do they clean their bodies? The children are at risk, due to poor hygiene. It is tragic to see them living in such appalling conditions.

There is a family of four — father, mother and two boys aged about eight and ten — living on the roof just outside our apartment stairwell. Their home is about fifteen feet square and just like a box. It has a timber frame with timber board on the outside and an old rusty corrugated roof. The mother cooks in the open air over a small kerosene stove. I wonder where she does the cooking when it rains? There is a kerosene lamp nearby. Because she has only one burner, she can only cook one thing at a time: rice first, then she stir-fries a small dish of meat with some vegetables in a small wok. Another dish is steaming away inside the pot while the rice cooks. Their dining table is a square board placed on a small wooden box, and two small stools serve as chairs for the parents, while the two boys sit on two rattan mats on the hard concrete rooftop.

My family gives them leftover food sometimes. When I go up to deliver it, the two boys' faces light up in smiles. The older one rushes to get an empty plate to transfer the leftovers onto. He is polite and thanks me for the food. There are other children there too, wanting to share in the leftovers, which are barely enough for one. Those who miss out lick their lips with their tongues and saliva nearly drips out of their mouths. Their eyes are so sad.

Do these two boys attend school, like me? They might be shoe-shine boys during the school hours. Perhaps the whole family needs to work extremely hard with the hope, eventually, that they will be able to afford to rent a small room and end the constant fear of losing all their possessions in bad weather or fire.

Men and women who live on rooftops and in the lane-ways spend their day doing low paid jobs or hard physical work, while older children look after younger siblings. Some children even have to prepare the meals for when their parents come home to eat.

The lane-way behind our block of apartments has always been a 'no-go' zone for me. When I was younger, I was always warned, "Don't walk into the lane-way. It's too dangerous. We don't know what sort of homeless people are hanging around there. Besides, it's filled with filth and rubbish." Now, at the age of eleven, having built up enough courage, I've decided to venture into this 'no-go' zone to look.

Immediately I enter the lane-way, I realise that I can't walk straight in. The lane-way is full of rubbish that has piled up outside the rear entrance of the shops. It is dim, because sunlight can't shine through down there. The smell is repellent. It seems the lane-way has never been cleaned. Rats, cockroaches and feral cats run amok.

Street people have set up their beds permanently on the lane-way and have taken up nearly half of its width. It is hard to walk through. People sleep on permanently set up, wooden collapsible and foldaway beds with canvas tops. All their utensils are packed in boxes and their personal belongings are in old and worn-out suitcases that fit underneath their beds. The roofs above their beds are made of rusty old corrugated iron sheets.

There is a queer looking man standing in the middle of the lane-way, blocking others from getting through. He is filthy and smelly, as if he hasn't cleaned himself for days. He is just skin and bone, as if he hasn't had anything to eat for a long time. His stare is daunting. I hesitate and decide not to go past him to walk through the full distance of the lane-way. Leung-por is right. This lane-way is too dangerous.

> *These homeless people are so desperate, Father. Trapped in a cycle of poverty and hopelessness, it's impossible not to feel worthless and depressed.*

Although I live in a cramped apartment, I consider myself fortunate to have a full stomach, a warm bed and a roof above my head. I am grateful to my maternal grandparents for letting the three of us live with them, and for providing us with a safe environment. Without their support, we could end up living on an apartment roof too. I don't know what happened to my father, but we are lucky. Although I do poorly at school, I am determined to work hard so that I'm never poor or hungry. I don't want to fall into that vicious poverty cycle.

PRIVATE SCHOOL

> *I'm eleven, and I've finished primary school, Father. Now, I'm to go to one of Hong Kong's most prestigious Catholic Boys'*

Schools, St Louis English School. My grandmother—your mother—has recommended that my mother send me there. She wants me to have a good grounding in the English language before going to Australia.

My mother works hard as a sales assistant and earns very little, but she is willing to pay for my schooling despite the financial difficulty. The fees amount to a quarter of her monthly wage, so it's a huge sacrifice for her. My mother has no high expectations of me, unlike most Chinese parents who want their children to be doctors, lawyers and other highly paid professionals who will attain a high status in society. These parents can have 'face' and be proud of their children's achievements. My mother probably realises that she can't expect too much of me, as I am not particularly good at anything.

St. Louis School is run by the Salesian Fathers of the Roman Catholic Church. It was founded in 1864 by the Fathers of Catholic Mission. They turned a small building into a school with twenty boys enrolled. The boys were to learn a trade such as carpentry, shoe-making, printing or mechanical engineering. The Brothers of Christian Schools succeeded the Fathers of the Catholic Mission in 1875, and managed it for the next forty-six years. In 1921, the Maryknoll Fathers took over from the Brothers and ran it for seven years before it was given to the Salesian Fathers in 1927. The School was then transformed from a training school for tradesman into a Grammar School that prides itself on academic excellence.

On my first day, I am fully clothed in the school uniform of white shirt with collar and school tie, blue trousers, socks and laced black shoes. As I walk through the entrance of the school, it's the proudest moment of my life. Here I am attending one of the most elite schools in Hong Kong!

As I look around, searching for a friendly face, the first thing I notice is that other students' school uniforms are better fitted than mine, which is grossly over-sized.

The school has a soccer field with a concrete surface, a basketball court also with a concrete surface, and a number of ping pong tables on the ground floor of one building. Before class and during lunch time, all playing spaces are packed. It is normal for a number of soccer games to be occurring at the same time. In the basketball court, apart from the two main baskets on either end of the court, there are also baskets fixed to the side of the court on the columns of the building. With so many players on the courts, no one ever knows how many games are happening simultaneously. Getting the ping pong table is a case of first in, first served. There are never enough tables to go around. Those who miss out have to play on the concrete ground with the layout of the table outlined with white chalk.

All subjects are in English except two: Chinese Literature and Chinese History. Private schools, especially the most exclusive, are very selective, due to the high fees and the high esteem in which the school is held. In order to be selected, prospective students have to sit for an entrance examination and pass at the school's required standard. Surprisingly, I passed.

St. Louis English School prides itself on impeccable academic results. It engages top-class teachers and produces the best students out of the education system. The school education system is fiercely competitive. Such competition leads to a great deal of fear and anxiety among the students. Failing is deemed a disgrace to the family and causes a severe loss of face.

Students are divided into classes based on their academic merit, with brighter students in the top classes. Some students in the top classes are classified as 'book worms', and their inevitable success will certainly deliver 'face' to their families. Most of those high achievers have private tutors, and their parents spend whatever is needed to ensure their success. This puts enormous pressure on students to be high achievers academically.

Although I have already completed six years of primary school, my entrance examination result is equivalent to a Primary Five standard at St. Louis. I drop back two classes. Just as well I am only eleven and the right age for the class. If I was older, my enrolment might not have been accepted by the school.

Before the class starts, all students except those in Primary One to Four are at assembly, listening to the principal's address. Because it is the first day of the new school year, there is very little for him to tell the students, except to welcome old students back after the long summer break and add best wishes and to welcome new students.

After the principal's address, our Primary Five teacher leads us to our classroom. He sorts the students by progressively seating them from the shortest at the front to the tallest at the back. As the second shortest in the class, I sit in the first row on the second seat.

I am not concerned about not doing well, because it is now just a matter of months before I will be off to Australia to further my education. For the past six years, at primary school, I was a poor scholar. Why should I bother now? I can learn all the English I need when I get to Australia.

"I will call the roll now," says the teacher. "When I call your name, I want you to answer 'Present, teacher', and put up your hand."

Will I suffer the same humiliation as I did back in Primary One at Hennessy Road Primary School—laughed at for having girl's name. After six years of that, I now have a thick skin and it doesn't bother me any more.

"Kwok Loo Shang," the teacher calls.

"Present, teacher." I raise my hand.

The teacher lifts his head and nods, signalling me to put my hand down. There is no comment from him regarding my name and no questions are asked. To my surprise, there is silence in the class. Maybe these exclusive school students have a better upbringing than those at the public school? Maybe they don't want to embarrass me in front of this strict teacher. Perhaps they'll wait until there is an opportunity outside the classroom?

Before I started at St. Louis, I received the school's book list. I shopped around second-hand book stores for the school textbooks. I was fairly lucky, although it took quite some time. I then went to the trouble of covering the books with brown paper, but still could not hide the fact that the textbooks had been used previously.

I find in class, that if I am using an earlier edition of a textbook, the page numbers are different. I have to check with my fellow students which sections of the book have been updated, then copy out the sections added to the earlier edition. Using the second-hand or earlier editions of the textbooks is a sure sign of being poor.

I soon learn the social hierarchies—whose families were wealthy; whose parents are in high income positions; whose fathers are high position bureaucrats; whose mothers dress in the latest fashions; and whose parents give their children money as if it poured out of a tap.

As the son of a working mother—a sales assistant in a women's clothing shop—I am no match to any of my peers, financially or socially. The majority of the students in my class are not interested in talking to me. My family background is not at the same level as theirs. I don't fit in with these affluent students, so I am isolated and a loner... again.

A couple of students invite me to go with them to see a film. Without any money, it is impossible to accept their invitation. I make up excuses. They say I live a boring life. I can't tell them that I have no money to have fun with them. I've never had pocket money given to me and I am too young to work. Other students can't understand why I am so frugal.

Occasionally, Leung-por and my aunts give me some money for the odd chores I do for them. On a few occasions, my mother gives me a dollar or two. I never ask her for money. My mother pays my school fees, and for books and uniforms, but nothing else. My main source of money is actually from Australia. Ah-por and Ah-kor send me ten Australian pounds for my birthday and Chinese New Year. Because my birthday is two weeks before the Chinese New Year, it is a combined birthday and New Year present. Ten pounds converts to one hundred and twenty Hong Kong dollars.

It is a Chinese custom for older generations to give the next generations red packets containing money for good luck and prosperity for the forthcoming year. I hope to collect between eighty and a hundred dollars out of the red packets during the New Year period, which will give me at least two hundred dollars to cover my expenditure for the whole school year. I need five dollars a week for forty weeks of schooling to cover tram fares and food. I learn to budget and be responsible. I shout myself a special treat only when Leung-por gives me something for doing household chores.

FEBRUARY 1959

One of the students from my Primary Five class invites me to go to a restaurant for lunch.

"There are three of us and, including you, four," says another student.

I am really happy being accepted into a group and invited to a restaurant for lunch during a school day, but I am concerned that the lunch might cost more than I can afford. I usually lunch at one of the open-air food vendors on the streets. Three students show off their money and say they plan to spend about five dollars each on a good lunch. Five dollars normally covers my whole week's expenditure.

"Are you coming or not? If you aren't, we need to get going."

The temptation to be accepted is too great. "Okay, I'm coming."

At the restaurant, I cast my eyes down the menu searching for the cheapest dish. I spot one that will cost me only a dollar and twenty cents.

"You don't want to eat that dish. It isn't very good."

"Let me pick something for you," says another student, who must be a regular customer because all the waiters know his name. He does, and it is delicious. I hadn't had such good food before. I wish I could have a second serve.

"Yours is four dollars and fifty cents, yours five dollars, mine five dollars and ten. Kwok Loo Shang, yours is the cheapest. Put in three dollars and eighty cents please." He put his hand out to collect everyone's payment.

Lunch had cost me nearly four days' expenses, but it was too late now to regret it.

"Let's come back tomorrow," says one of the students.

"Fine with me," says another.

"I'm in tomorrow. What about you Kwok Loo Shang? You probably have no money."

He is right. I don't have the money to dine in a restaurant for lunch. It's disheartening when some of my fellow students tell me how rich their parents are, how big their homes are and how much money their parents give them to spend. I don't want to pretend to be someone I'm not.

I normally buy my lunch for less than a dollar from one of the open-air food stalls on the streets, or from a one-man snack-seller who carries the food on his shoulder with a bamboo pole. Cooked by steaming, boiling, baking, stir-frying or deep frying, the food is generally pretty good. Different stalls serve different types of food, such as noodles and rice noodle soups, stir-fried dishes, and steamed food such as buns and dim sims. During the busiest time, people queue up for one of the few tables. Some of the food stalls don't have any tables and chairs at all and people sit on small stools placed on top of a bench seat, known as chair-on-chair. The foods are cooked on open ring gas-burners in large woks. You can see the meal cooking and you are served as soon as it is ready, in minutes. You can hear the flames roar underneath the wok.

For the next few days, having spent nearly four dollars for a single lunch, I had to fill my stomach up with congee for lunch. Congee is rice porridge combined with other ingredients such as fish slices, dried fish and peanuts, meat balls, combination seafood, lean pork, century egg (known as hundred-year old eggs) and solidified pig blood. It costs next to nothing at the open-air street stalls. Thirty cents buys a very large bowl. Congee and deep fried dough sticks are popular breakfasts.

Century eggs are made by preserving duck eggs in a contained mixture of clay, ash, lime and rich straw. The process can take from several weeks to several months. The long preserving time allows the eggs to absorb the flavours. When the process is completed, the yolk becomes a dark green with a creamy consistency and an odour of sulphur and ammonia, and the egg white becomes a dark brown. The egg is cooked by boiling it in the usual way, until it becomes a hard or soft-boiled egg.

༄

Despite moving to an elite school, I continue to perform poorly in my studies. I don't enjoy school work. I muddle through Primary Five and manage to pass, then move up to Primary Six.

As the prospect of going to study in Australia intensifies, my attitude toward study diminishes even further. I drift along with my school work in Primary Six A, telling myself that I must be doing all right because I am still in an 'A' class, the class of high achievers.

Some students envy me the opportunity to study overseas. Some are jealous, refusing to believe that the poorest student in the class could have such an opportunity. They come from rich, famous and powerful families and believe they are born to rule. They don't understand how a student like me—who wears a grossly oversized uniform, bought second-hand textbooks, and travels forty-five minutes by public transport from a low income district to go to school—could have such an opportunity.

Not learning the lessons and doing homework properly finally catches up with me. My Primary Six examination result is a disaster. I believe I am near the bottom of the class. I face the prospect of failing and being expelled from the school, or staying back and repeating the year. Although my result proves to not be as bad as I first thought, I am no longer in the 'A' class. I end up in Form One D—a deeply humiliating drop. My new classmates frown on me due to my downgrading.

There has been talk of me going to Australia for over two years now. Why is it taking so long? I can't help doubting whether I will ever go. I wish Ah-por and Ah-kor hadn't told me I'd be going. If they hadn't mentioned it, I might have put in a better effort. Maybe my former Primary Four teacher was right about me when she said I was not dumb, but needed to put more effort into my work. But none of my family seem to realise how difficult it is to make the transition to this English School. Not being academically inclined presented enough challenge, without the added burden of coming from a different socio-economic background and not fitting in.

✆✆

WINTER, 1961

It is sports day for the whole upper school. We gather at a football stadium for an athletic meet, with a teacher acting as the official for various races. I am no sportsman. I am one of the cheering spectators for our team. Half an hour before the 4 x 100 yards relay is to start, an announcement over the loud-speaker requests that participating athletes gather at the starting line. Unexpectedly, I hear someone yell, "Kwok Loo Shang, come down here. You're running in the relay."

I am not in any of the sporting teams in the school and have never had any training in running. Why do they want me to be in the relay team?

"Come on, quickly," another voice shouts. Three of my fellow students, dressed in running gear, wave their hands at me, signalling me to join them.

"One of the members of the 4 x 100 yards relay team sprained his ankle while warming-up and is unable to run. Instead of forfeiting the race, and to save 'face' for our team, you're now to run in this relay," says the leader of the relay team.

I am plunged into a race for which I am not prepared. While I busily put on the borrowed sporting uniform and running shoes, I overhear the other three discussing the race strategy.

"Don't let Kwok Loo Shang run the first leg. If he comes last in the first leg, we'll not be able to catch up the lost time," says the relay team leader.

"How about we have the second fastest runner run the first leg and the fastest runner run the final leg and let him run either the second or third leg?" says another runner.

"That's going to be risky. If he's to run either the second or third leg, he needs to take the baton during the change-over, run 100 yards, and pass it onto the next runner. He might drop it."

"I don't think we have much option except to let him run the final leg. All he needs to do is to grab the baton and run. Let's hope he can do it without dropping it. What do you think?" the leader continues.

"Yeah, I agree."

"Yeah, let's hope he can hold onto the baton when I pass it to him."

"Come on. We don't have much time left to show him what to do. Come here, Loo Shang. Let me show you how you grab the baton while on the run," the leader says urgently. "Extend your right hand towards the back with palm facing up. When you feel the baton on the top of your palm, grab it. Keep your head up and your eyes straight on the finish line, and run as fast as you can. And remember, don't come last."

There are eight relay teams in the race and one team is made up of my old class students in the 'A' class. I have been instructed not to finish last. It is my first time running in a competition, and my mind is preoccupied with all the instructions. When I hear the starting gunshot, my heart starts racing, although it is at least another thirty to forty seconds before I need to run. The spectators roar in the grandstand. As the leader of our relay team reaches me, sweat pours from my forehead and the palms of my hands. Now the race has reached the final leg, there are runners beside me and in front of me. I can't hear anything except heartbeats pounding faster and harder.

Saving 'face' for the team and our school house is the only thing in my mind, so I run as if my life depends on it. My legs feel heavier and heavier. That 100 yards seems such a long, long way. I wish I could stop, but the thought of the disgrace if I come last urges me on.

Finally, I cross the finish line. I want to vomit. I gasp for breath as if there isn't enough oxygen in the air for me to suck in. I am glad that I finished the race without dropping the baton. I don't know what place our relay team made, but I am too sick to care. It isn't until our relay team is called up to the podium that I realise we came third. Each of us is presented with a bronze medal. For a brief moment, I stand on the podium and drink in the applause.

EIGHT

||||||||||||||||||||||||||||||||||||||||||||||||||||||||||||||||||||||||||||||||||||

PERVERTS, PROSTITUTES AND PROMISES FULFILLED

Teacher Ho, my Form One Chinese Literature teacher at St. Louis, is in his fifties. Short and slim in stature, with thin grey hair, he wears glasses with very thick lenses. As I walk out of the school one afternoon, I hear him calling my name. "Wait a minute! Kwok Loo Shang, I want to talk to you."

"Good afternoon, Teacher Ho." I stare at him, eyes wide. My heart pounds. Whenever a teacher wants to talk to me, it is always about my laziness and poor performance.

"Would you like to go to a movie with me one Saturday afternoon?" I am stunned by his request and momentarily speechless. Unable to excel in anything at school, I don't gain much respect from the teachers. Teacher Ho must have noticed my predicament with the other students and decided to do something about it.

"I have to ask my grandmother's permission," I stutter.

"Of course. You do that." Through his thick glasses, his eyes are staring at mine, waiting for a further response.

"I don't see my mother often to ask her. She works twelve hours a day. She starts work mid-morning and doesn't return until very late at night. By then, I'm already asleep."

"Why don't you ask your father?"

I hate people referring to my father. For six years, in primary school, I was labelled a 'bastard'. Since I enrolled in this private boys' school, I've managed to evade these sorts of questions. But I can't lie to Teacher Ho—someone I can trust.

"I don't know where my father is," I confess.

"All right. Ask your grandmother. Don't tell anyone—not even your best friend. This is between you and me. A secret. I'll be very disappointed if you tell," Teacher Ho says, grabbing hold of my hand and squeezing it really hard. It hurts. Perhaps it is a warning that I'll be hurt if I tell?

I nod. Little does Teacher Ho know that I don't really have a close friend at school. There is a student with a hunchback in Form One D. He is not a brilliant scholar and he isn't good in any physical activities due to his hunchback. He runs like a camel because of his long legs and very short body. Both of us are rejects, so we hang around together during lunch hours and for short periods after school. I don't consider him a close friend. True friends support one another, sharing joy and sadness together. They complain about things to one another and reveal their failures and successes. I have never asked him about his family background and the cause of his hunchback, and he has never queried my family background.

Leung-por gives me permission to go out with Teacher Ho. After watching a movie and dinner, I find my own way home. I can't believe a schoolteacher has been so kind and generous to a lazy and under-achieving student. *But why did he hold my hand throughout the movie? Just as well it was dark inside the theatre and no one would have noticed.*

༄༄

EARLY JANUARY 1961

Half-yearly examinations over, Teacher Ho is standing at the school entrance saying goodbye to students. I stroll toward him, wondering if he will ask me to go a movie with him again.

"Kwok Loo Shang, how would you like to go to a movie and dinner again this Saturday?" he whispers in my ear.

"Yes," I reply without hesitation, "but I'll have to let my grandmother know."

"Of course. Instead of meeting me in front of the theatre, come to this address and I'll be there waiting for you." He shoves a note into my shirt pocket. "Do you still have the pen that you used for the Chinese Literature examination? If you do, bring it with you."

Why he would ask such a question?

"I think so, and I'll bring it with me."

To my surprise, the address Teacher Ho has given me is not his home, but a low class hotel. Inside the hotel room, there is a large bed, a wooden table with four chairs, a small wardrobe and a sideboard with a few cups and thermal flask on top. Curtains are drawn and the room is dimly lit, stuffy and airless. A pile of students' Chinese Literature examination papers rest on a table. Teacher Ho pulls my examination paper out and says, "I've already had a look at your answers, Kwok Loo Shang. You have failed to gain the 60% pass mark in the subject. I'm going to help you to get an 80% mark. Did you bring the pen that you used in the examination?"

I nod.

"Start writing, while I dictate some of the correct answers to you."

I am so grateful to him. He is not only taking me out for movie and dinner but also helping me to get a better mark for my examination. Heaven must have sent him to take care of me. After amending my examination answers, he says, "We'll go to movie now and come back here. I'll finish all the marking before we go to dinner."

I can't concentrate on the movie. My mind is racing. *Why did he have me amend the examination paper? What will other students think when I, an under-achieving student, get 80% for the Chinese Literature examination? Will I be expelled from the school if they find out? Why is he being so good to me?*

He is holding my hand. Sweat comes through my palm. My heart starts pounding. *I wish I could get out of here. Perhaps it is too late to correct? What is done is done. My teacher has helped me cheat to gain more marks in the examination. I cannot possibly tell anyone that. I wish Leung-por hadn't given me permission to go out with him in the first place.*

After the movie, I say, "Sorry, Teacher Ho, I can't go to dinner with you because my grandmother said I must come home for dinner."

He doesn't insist. He lets me leave.

☙☙

I have to let Teacher Ho know that I'll be leaving the school soon to further my education overseas. I walk towards the front gate of the school as soon as the last class finishes. I wait patiently for him. Getting 80% in my Chinese Literature examination has been bothering me. My fellow students suspect that there is something not quite right about my marks. Even my mother couldn't believe that I did so well in the subject. I have been worried sick. *If I leave the school, perhaps no one will ever find out how I achieved such high marks.*

"Good afternoon, Teacher Ho."

"Kwok Loo Shang, have you been waiting for me?" he replies with a smile.

"Yes. I'll be going to Australia soon," I say.

"How soon?" he asks, his smile disappears.

"I don't know. My grandfather already made the overseas student visa application on my behalf and I'm waiting for the Australian Government's approval."

After that, his attitude towards me changes, and he doesn't speak to me again. Knowing what I know now about adults molesting children, I'm glad I left St. Louis at that time.

෧෧

"Loo Shang," Leung-por calls, "run down to the store and get me a bottle of soya sauce so I can finish preparing the dinner. Here's the money. Don't forget the change, and don't take too long."

Any excuse to get out of the tiny apartment delights me, but I promise her that I won't wander around the neighbourhood this time, but will come straight back from the store. She needs the soya sauce for cooking.

I go happily down the stairs in my flip-flops. When I reach the first floor landing, I notice a filthy man squatting on the other side of the stair landing. Curious, I stop and watch. He holds a small piece of silver foil, no bigger than a cigarette box, with one hand. A small candle burns underneath the foil, heating some white powder. With his other hand, he is holding a drinking straw. One end of the straw points at the heated white powder and the other end is drawn close to one of his nostrils. He takes a deep breath and inhales half of the white powder.

I stare at the man, gaping. How can I get past him? He realises someone is standing on the other side of the landing, looks up and shouts, "What are you looking at?"

I tremble. I don't know what to say. My hands are sweating.

"Do you want to come through?" he bellows.

"Yes," I say, lips quivering.

He shifts his squatting position a little. He is letting me through. I run down the stairs as fast as I can, without taking a breath. Reaching the bottom of the stairs, I dash out onto the footpath without a backward look. I sigh with relief. *But how I am going to get past him again on the way back home?*

I run back from the store. A police car screeches to a halt. Three policemen get out. A woman, standing by on the footpath, directs policemen, pointing at the stairs leading to our apartment. Two policemen rush up the stairs. The third stands guard at the bottom, stopping anyone trying to get through.

I'll get into trouble with my grandmother for taking too long to go to the store and back. I wait anxiously on the footpath. Scuffling noises echo down the stairs. Two policemen escort the man towards the police car. This time, I have a good look at him. His face is heavily creased, encrusted with dirt. Black lines stand out like stripes on a zebra. Tears and mucus cover his long, drawn face. Two black rings show around his eyes. He is very thin. Although he is wearing a shabby singlet, every bump and knot in his spine is visible. His arms are skin and bone, like sticks. He is doleful. He offers no resistance, allowing himself to be bundled into the back of the police car. It takes off without the siren.

"Where have you been? What took you so long?" my grandmother asks.

"I — "

My grandmother cuts me off before I have a chance to explain. "I told you to come straight back and not to wander around the neighbourhood."

"I did, Leung-por," I reply, raising my voice slightly, "but the police blocked off the stairs and wouldn't allow anybody to come up."

"Why?"

Slowly, I explain to her what I've seen, starting from when I first saw the man on the landing. She calms down. "The man is taking heroin," she says. "Someone in the neighbourhood must have phoned the police to arrest him. Let that be a lesson to you. If you take heroin, the police will come to get you and you'll be locked up for a long time."

At fourteen, I am too naïve to understand why people take heroin, but I know that they are needlessly wrecking their lives.

∽∽

MID-JANUARY 1961

I have started to take notice of the opposite sex. This is a subject for discussion with my brother or my father. My brother is in a foreign country, but, in my imagination, my father is always accessible.

When I get off the tram on Friday afternoon, after school, a beautiful young woman is walking in my direction. From a distance, her face looks familiar. I can't help staring as she draws closer.

At about a half-head taller than me, she has deep brown eyes and a friendly smile. Her clothing is inexpensive, but nicely coordinated. It shows the curves of her well-proportioned figure. Minimum make-up allows her natural beauty to shine through, and a light fragrance of expensive perfume wafts from her. She walks slowly, stepping out in a pair of stilettos. I am not the only one who stops for a second glance. Men seem entranced by her and stop in their tracks as she passes. She has all the attributes needed to win a beauty pageant.

We walk past each other without making eye contact. I stop and turn to have another look. It is Bing, a neighbourhood girl. I hardly recognise her without her school uniform. I haven't seen her around the area at this time in the afternoon for over two months. I had wondered whether she'd left the neighbourhood.

Having lived in the area for ten years, I practically know everybody who works in the shops or lives along this stretch of Lockhart Road by sight. I only know Bing's name because I once accidentally overheard a friend of hers calling out to her. I'd worked out, by noticing the textbooks she carried, that she would be in either Form Four or Five. I am in Form One, so she is about three or four years older than me.

She moved into the neighbourhood a couple of years ago and we quite often ran into each other on the street. Our relationship has been casual — a smile, and occasionally a few words exchanged. There is never a conversation between us, because she is older and in an upper form. I thought she was just being polite by exchanging casual greetings.

Today, something tells me things are not right with her. *Why has she given up school? Why is she dressed up and walking towards the 'no-go' zone.*

The district of Wanchai is well-known locally and internationally for the wrong reasons. Wanchai became famous as the setting of *The World of Suzie Wong* (1960), starring William Holden and Nancy Kwan. The film was about a Westerner befriended by a young Chinese woman who claimed a lofty social status, but was a prostitute. William Holden played the Westerner, Robert Lomax. Nancy Kwan played the prostitute, Wong Mee-ling, also known as Suzie Wong.

For over fifty years, from 1879 to 1932, prostitution in Hong Kong was legal, requiring only a license to operate. Wanchai was a boom district for one of the world's oldest occupations. In the early 1930s, the Government dispensed with the licensing system and only permitted prostitution with strict guidelines and limitations.

Wanchai — in particular the red-light precinct along sections of Jaffe and Lockhart Road, and Leung-por's 'no-go' zone — is well known to the locals for its exotic night life, girlie bars and hostess clubs. At fourteen, I am fully aware that, in those hostess clubs, clients pay the club for the hostesses' time to entertain them. Clients enjoy the hostess's company, drinking expensive alcoholic drinks, dancing and chit-chatting. Some buy longer periods of their time and take the hostesses out. Activity that transpires outside the club is between the client and hostess.

Wanchai is legendary not only for locals, but also for Westerners. Sailors off trading ships and American servicemen on rest and recreation leave are particularly keen visitors.

To satisfy my curiosity, I follow Bing. To my amazement, she heads towards the 'no-go' zone. I have walked through the 'no-go' zone many times, during daylight hours, to post letters. Posting letters is a chore my grandparents have expected of me since I was old enough to cross over the busy local roads. Leung-por warned me not to go near that area from late afternoon onwards, but when I was twelve, I did check the area out late one afternoon. There were a number of so-called hostess clubs on both sides of the road. Coloured lights were flashing. Women with heavy make-up went in and out. Men walked in and came out with women on their arms. I was too young and naïve then, to understand what was going on.

Today, following Bing, I remember what Leung-por told me. The women working in these places are no good. Men pay them to drink and dance with them. While their good looks remain when they are young, half of the women will eventually become alcoholics, heroin addicts and prostitutes. Society frowns on them. I can't understand why a beautiful young woman like Bing is in a place like this.

"Hi Bing." I catch up with her.

"Hi," she replies. She recognises me in my St. Louis school uniform. She must have pretended not to recognise me as we walked past each other earlier. She continues on her way.

"Wait," I call.

She looks impatiently at her watch and tries to get away.

"What? I have to go."

"What are you doing in this area?" I ask.

"I work in this area. Why are you asking such a stupid question?"

"What about school?"

"I have given up school. I need the money. I really have to go."

"Please tell me."

"You are too young to understand."

"Try me."

"After I tell you, will you leave me alone?"

I nod.

"My father was killed in a road accident a few months ago. My mother was so devastated that she fell ill and was unable to work. I had to leave school and work to bring home some money to support her and my two younger brothers." She tries to control her tears. "Will you go away now?"

"Do you have to work in a place like this? It is a bad influence. Why can't you get a proper job to support your family?"

"I juggled split shifts as a waitress, kitchen hand and whatever other casual job I could find. All the money I earned each month just wasn't enough to cover my mother's medication and my brothers' education. I made a bold move to sacrifice myself for the benefit of my family. Sure, I could survive without selling myself, but what about my mother and my brothers? Where would they get the money to support themselves? If you've got a father with the right connections, then you can get a well-paid job, become a manager, or join the high ranking staff in no time. Money is the motivating factor for me to work in these clubs. Who are you to tell me what to do? You're only a school boy I met on the bus a few months ago. Just go away."

She turns and heads for the entrance of a hostess club. I manage to grab her arm and say, "It's wrong. You shouldn't be working in a place like this."

She shakes my hand off her arm. Her anger has subsided. Her lips quiver. Then her whole face turns red, and tears well. Her hands tremble like the ground before an earthquake. She tries hard to hold back the tears. She takes a deep breath and wipes her eyes gently, without smudging her eye make-up. She says, "I tried to do the right thing. For a person like me — someone without connections — getting a proper job without the necessary qualifications is very difficult. At first, I found a job working in a clothing factory. The monthly salary I received was barely enough to buy food for the four of us.

"A few weeks ago, I managed to find a secretarial job. The monthly pay was much better, but at times, I was treated like a pretty flower vase. One of my duties was to go out to business dinners with the managers, young and old, for them to show off to their prospective business clients. They used me, not only as bait to catch business deals, but also as a little plaything that can be disposed of with a snap of their fingers. I was dismissed when I refused to do certain things that you are too young to understand." Her voice started to break. Before long, she burst into tears.

I am dumbfounded. I don't know what to do or say to comfort her.

"No one made me do what I am doing. I'm a victim of circumstance. I need the money to support my mother and brothers. Other people want 'face'. You think cleaning toilets in a hotel, washing dishes in a restaurant from morning to night, or working in a clothing factory gives 'face'?"

"Hey, Bing! What are you doing talking to a school kid?" a man standing at the entrance shouts at the top of his voice. "There are men waiting for you inside. Is he your little brother? Send him away. Hurry up."

Bing touches my face gently. She turns around and walks away, still swiping at tears.

A few weeks pass. I am unable to shake off my concern for Bing's well-being. I decide to front up to the hostess club to see her. I notice that some of the good-looking bar girls are just teenagers who should be in their final year of schooling. Perhaps they all have sad stories and good reasons for ending up in places like these. Male patrons hire the girls for entertainment. Charge rates are by quarter of an hour, half an hour and an hour. I don't quite understand how the timing works. I guess someone must be keeping track of the time as a girl moves from one patron to another.

Hostesses can be hired for a whole night if patrons are willing to spend the money. I never find out, because I am absolutely forbidden to go inside places like these. Being under-age, I probably wouldn't be allowed inside anyway.

Even though it is the middle of the day, inside the joint where Bing disappears is dark. The whole front is draped with heavy, dark-velvet curtains. A little daylight comes through the single door at the shop front. Artificial lights are low wattage, violet fluorescent tubes hanging from the ceiling. The only bright area, with white tubes, is the bar area at the back. The air is thick with the smell of alcohol. Although the ceiling fans are circulating on low speed, the thick smell from within is suffocating. I don't think any outside air has penetrated inside for a very long time. There are alcoves on either side. A few small tables and chairs are placed around an open floor area. The floor is made of timber, and I guess it must be for dancing. "You are not allowed in here, kid," the bartender says. "Get out of here quick!"

"I'm looking for Bing."

"Bing doesn't work here anymore. She left because another place offered her better money. She's very beautiful and popular you know? She always talks about going back to school one day and continuing on to university to create a better future for herself... You better get out of here before I get into trouble for letting you in."

"Do you know where she's working now?"

"She told me... can't remember right now. I know it is not in this area."

I walk out, disappointed.

There are a couple of bars along Lockhart Road. Each time I walk past them I can smell the thick stink of alcohol. The air inside is stale, as if fresh air has never entered the place. Many young women work in clubs. The life of a club hostess is more financially rewarding than working in a restaurant or in a factory. The financial reward and the burden of supporting the family motivates these young women to enter this often lucrative profession.

Bing didn't like the work in the club, but the financial reward allowed her to take care of her mother's medical bills and to pay for her brothers' education. Not all these young women are greedy and looking for an easy way out in life. Some of them choose this type of occupation for the right reasons. But society takes a negative and hypocritical attitude towards these girls. It is too early yet for Bing to understand the long-term effects this life might have on her.

Who am I, Father, to judge what is right and what is wrong? What would I do if I were in Bing's situation? What if my family's livelihood depended on me? At least I'm not fighting for survival as Bing is.

I never meet up with her again before leaving for Australia, although I really hoped to. I could only hope that her life situation improved.

ᝪᝪ

END OF JANUARY/EARLY FEBRUARY 1961

The Spring Festival, for the Chinese, is like the Festive Season of Christmas and New Year in most Western countries. A joyous occasion, it is full of excitement, particularly for children. The Spring Festival takes place on the first day of the first month on the Chinese Lunar Calendar. It symbolises the arrival of the Chinese New Year and celebrates the change from old to new. It falls on a different date each year — any day from the 21st January to the 19th February on the Western calendar. In 1961, Chinese New Year's Day falls on Wednesday, 15th February, and marks the beginning of the Year of the Ox. This might be my last celebration of the Chinese New Year in Hong Kong. The granting of my student visa application to study in Australia is imminent. It is matter of months, if not weeks, before my departure.

In the weeks before the Chinese New Year of 1961, Hong Kong is buzzing with preparations for a new beginning. The markets are more crowded than usual. Everyone buys extra food for the reunion dinner and for the holiday period, when all businesses, including the market places, are closed. Clothing shops do a roaring trade, because it is customary to wear new clothes on the first day of the New Year. Shoppers buy gifts from local shops for new-year visits to relatives and friends. Street vendors at the open-air night markets sell everything that will bring wealth, health, family well-being and prosperity.

Flowers are believed to be symbolic of wealth and prosperity. Blooming flowers and plants invigorate a new year: plum and peach blossoms symbolise good luck; narcissus and chrysanthemum good health and longevity; and cumquat plants prosperity and happiness. Chinese believe that if flowers bloom at home on New Year's Day, the year ahead will be prosperous.

Oranges represent good health, whilst tangerines with twig and leaves represent lasting relationships. Candy is for sweetness and a circular tray is for togetherness.

Every household has some sort of red decoration, because, in Chinese culture, red symbolizes wealth, prosperity, fame and happiness. Messages like good fortune, good health, wealth, or longevity are commonly used. It is customary to have couplets written on red paper glued on either side of doors. Chinese calligraphers set up small tables on footpaths and in open-air markets to write red banners and couplets in gold paint. Red symbolises happiness. Gold symbolises wealth. The messages contain New Year greetings and wishes for good fortune, happiness and longevity. Also, in the open-air night markets, fortune tellers read faces or palms, predicting what the new year might hold for their client. Single people want to know about romance, love and marriage; children and teenagers about school grades; married couples about the possibility of children; young men and women about job prospects and promotion; older people about health and longevity. They ask: What should I do in the new year? Start a business, marry, have children, travel or buy property? *I wonder just how accurate the predictions are.*

Mothers and grandmothers buy red money packets from shops and queue up in banks to exchange old worn-out coins and notes for yet-to-be-circulated shiny coins and brand new notes. They put these inside the red packets in preparation to hand out to young children. It's a way of passing on best wishes for the year to come. Handing out red packets of money is similar to giving presents at Christmas in Western countries. The red packets should always be in even numbers, as odd numbers are associated with the amount of cash given during funerals. However, the amount never ends up in four, since four sounds like the word death in Chinese.

For children, getting red packets is much better than receiving presents. We can buy toys, sweets and anything we like with the money. For me, the red packet money is for the tram fare and lunch money for the school year at St. Louis.

It is customary to have the house completely cleaned from top to bottom to rid it of all the unpleasant things associated with the preceding year. Thorough cleaning sweeps away all the bad luck of the previous year and readies the home for good luck in the new year. Extra effort is expended cleaning the kitchen. The Chinese believe that, a week before New Year's Day, the Kitchen God returns to heaven to present his report to the Jade Emperor. The Jade Emperor will then hand out rewards and punishment according to their good or bad deeds throughout the past year. To ensure a good report from the Kitchen God, people make food offerings with wine and tea over his shrine, which is always located in the kitchen. They burn incense, paper gold and silver ingots, and paper money to help him on his journey with a full stomach. Paper gold, silver ingots and money are given to cover expenses along the way.

Customarily, the celebration starts on New Year's Eve with a reunion dinner of close family members. Married daughters do not attend, because they have become members of their husband's family. Although my mother married into the Kwok family, her parents and siblings treat us as part of the Leung family, so we all join in the Leung reunion dinner. Before dinner, it is necessary to make offerings and pay respect to ancestors. Chinese believe the ancestors are responsible for the well-being, good health, longevity and prosperity of future generations. I don't take part in the offerings because I am not a member of the Leung family.

The reunion dinner is sumptuous. Some of the Chinese food names are homophones for Chinese words that also mean good things. Some of the essential ingredients for the dishes are fish, chicken and duck. Vegetables include lettuce, shallot and celery. Fish is a homophone for 'yu' and means abundant. Chicken symbolises fortune and duck fidelity. Vegetables generally signify the cleansing of people's internal systems, but specific vegetables have a specific meaning. Lettuce symbolises vigour, celery diligence, and shallots wisdom. Fish and chicken are cooked whole. The chicken is cooked with its head and feet to symbolise completeness—meaning that whatever a person wishes to pursue, it should be good from start to finish.

After dinner, the older family members sit around chatting, eating snacks and playing mah jong or card games for money until late at night or early in the morning. Sometimes they play all through the night. The custom of staying up late signifies farewelling the old and welcoming the new. I am the youngest in the household, but my mother allows me to stay up until past midnight.

It is my task to ensure all the lights are switched on before the arrival of the new year. Chinese believe switching on the lights during the night scares off the spirit of misfortune that may compromise the prosperity of the new year. It is also customary to open every window at midnight, in order to let go of the old year and to usher in the good luck of the new year.

Even from a very young age, adults have drummed the dos and don'ts of New Year's Day into me. Greet people by saying, "Gung Hei Fatt Choi". 'Gung Hei' literally translates to congratulate, and 'Fatt Choi' means to be prosperous. The four words together mean: wishing you prosperity and wealth. Traditionally, Chinese people believe material riches and high social status are the greatest successes a person can attain in life.

Most of my lessons have been don'ts:

"Don't sweep the floor during the first day of the New Year because you will sweep away all the good fortune and luck." Hence, on the eve of Chinese New Year, all brooms, brushes, dusters, dust pans and other cleaning equipment are put out of sight.

"Don't cut or wash your hair on New Year's Day." Hair is a homophone for the word 'fatt', meaning prosperity. Thus, to cut or wash the hair could result in cutting or washing your prosperity away.

"Don't cry during the New Year period. If you do, you'll cry all through the year."

"Don't buy books in the first few days in the Chinese New Year. Book is a homophone for the word 'shu' meaning lose."

"Don't drop your chopsticks. If you drop them while eating, you will have bad luck, or perhaps you'll be poor."

"Don't use knives or scissors on New Year's Day, as this may cut off fortune."

"Don't greet people who are in mourning."

"Don't owe anyone money, because it constitutes a bad start to the new year, and you'll be dogged by debts for the year to come. Before the New Year, pay off the debt so that you can start the new year afresh."

"Don't lend money to anyone, because not only will you never get your money back, but also you'll be setting yourself up for other people to come knocking on your door all year long."

"Avoid talking about death and ghosts, because it's considered ill-fated."

"Avoid quarrelling with anyone. Make peace and resolve differences with family members, friends, neighbours and business associates."

"Avoid wearing white (which relates to death) during the festivities."

In ancient times, people burned bamboo — which bursts with a popping sound — to scare off evil spirits at New Year. After the invention of gunpowder, the firecracker was made by rolling gunpowder in red paper. Firecrackers come individually or strung on a long string. Once ignited, the crackers let out a loud popping sound. The deafening explosion of firecrackers is used not only to frighten away the evil spirits, but also to send out the old year and to welcome in a healthy, happy and prosperous New Year. They are also used in other celebrations. I remember the firecrackers and fireworks set off at the stroke of midnight, welcoming the new year.

In the mid-1950s, disorder flared up in China. When demonstrating on the streets during their confrontations with police, pro-communist activists used the gunpowder from crackers to build home-made bombs . After that, the Hong Kong government banned firecrackers and fireworks in the New Year. New year celebrations haven't been the same since. We miss the popping sound of firecrackers intensely.

People are very conscious of the things they do and the words they say during New Year's Day, because they believe their actions and words may impact on their lives for the rest of the year. They greet and wish others a joyful year. To ensure a prosperous and healthy year, they stimulate positive energy-flow at home. Any unkind act or negative words toward others will bring bad luck and unfortunate events to self and family.

At the reunion dinner, on the first day, people are selective as to what they eat. This day welcomes the deities of the heavens and earth, and it's a tradition to abstain from eating meat. Killing animals may jeopardise longevity. Often, the vegetarian dish, jai choi, is eaten. It comprises many ingredients, including a black, hair-like moss seaweed pronounced fatt choi, which sounds like prosperity; dried bean curd, which sounds like and symbolises wealth and happiness; and bamboo shoots, which mean 'may all go well'. Chinese New Year cake, neen gao, is eaten by children who want to grow taller, or symbolically, by working adults wanting to improve their promotion prospects. Gao makes a homophone similar to the word for tall or high. Noodles symbolise longevity and are served uncut. Jai gok is fried dumpling, which resembles the shape and size of the ancient Chinese gold ingot. Oranges and tangerines, which are golden in colour, are symbols of luck and wealth. Candies are eaten to ensure the consumer a sweet year.

Besides being a time for family reunions, part of the celebration is to visit friends and relatives, a practice known as new-year visits. Traditionally, the first day is a time when younger families visit the oldest and most senior members of their extended family, usually their parents, grandparents or great-grandparents. On the second day, married daughters visit their birth parents. Whole families can be seen going from place to place visiting. Distant relatives, and friends who haven't met for the whole year, also visit one another at this time.

This is the only time of the year that my mother and I have a couple of days out together. At New Year, we visit her friends and distant relatives. It is also the best time for me, due to the number of red packets I collect. The more visits we make, the more red packets I receive.

∽∽

7TH MARCH, 1961

For the past three weeks, I have stopped my usual wandering around the streets and have gone straight home after school. I am waiting anxiously for a letter from the Australian Government Trade Commission. It's been three weeks since my interview with Australian Government officials regarding my overseas student visa application.

Today, before I have a chance to put away my school bag, Leung-por hands me an envelope that has already been opened. I guess Leung-gong has already read it. There is an Australian coat-of-arms on the letterhead.

Look, Father! Here is the letter:

Dear Sir,

I desire to advise that your application for permission to enter Australia for educational purposes has been approved and you will be admitted for that purpose.

```
Will you please call at this office with
your travel document at your earliest
convenience?
```

```
This letter may be produced to the necessary
authorities for application of your travel
document.
```

```
                              Yours faithfully,
                              Migration Officer
```

For a few seconds, my heart stops beating. I am gasping for air. Quite a few of the words in the letter are unknown to me. Did the Australian Government approve or reject my overseas student visa application? Should I be anxious, frightened or relieved?

With shaking hands and sweating palms, I take my English-Chinese dictionary out of my school bag and look up the words: permission, educational, approved and admitted. I soon understand my luck.

My dream of going to Australia is finally a reality! After nearly three years of anticipation and uncertainty, I will soon join my grandmother and brother.

Perhaps, with luck, I will meet you there, Father?

ᏜᏜ

28TH MARCH, 1961

I am three months from finishing Form One, the first year of middle high school in Hong Kong. How astonished my fellow-students are to hear that I am finally going to Australia.

"When are you going?" they asked me often. "Never, never, never! He is lying. Where would his family find the money to send him to Australia? It's all rubbish."

"He hasn't got the brain to study," some students said, pointing at me and laughing.

The students who've been teasing and bullying me realise now, that I've been telling the truth all the time. Now they envy me. Although they don't apologise for their wrong-doings, there is definitely remorse on their faces. I wish that I hadn't told them, back in Primary Five. It would certainly have saved me a lot of humiliation. How could I know, at the time, that it would take nearly three years to come to fruition?

I don't have many friends at St. Louis. I don't have many friends at all, even outside school. After I say goodbye to a handful of fellow students, I find my way to the principal's office to pick up my Leaving Certificate. This document states the date that I started and the date I finished and states that my conduct during my time in the school was good. Today, with neither regret nor many good memories, I walk out of the school for the last time.

Leung-gong spent the following week organising the necessary travel documents for Australia. Because I was born in mainland China and lived there for three years, a Certificate of Identity, in lieu of a British passport, was issued to me by the Immigration Department of Hong Kong when I reached the age of twelve. A Student Visa for five years has been arranged with the Australia Government's Migration Office in Hong Kong. My Re-entry Permit was issued by the Immigration Office. I have all the necessary injections for travel. My grandfather purchased my plane ticket, departing at half-past-seven on Friday night, 28th April 1961.

Most people travelling to Australia go by ship, as it is much cheaper than by air and the luggage allowance is not as limited. There is a general notion that goods sold in Hong Kong are much cheaper and more readily available than in Australia, so people take the opportunity to load up. The ship journey takes about a fortnight. Because I am travelling alone, and only fourteen, Ah-por decides I should go by air instead of sea. She worries I might suffer from sea-sickness.

For the next three weeks, Leung-por takes me around to close and distant relatives to broadcast my pending departure to Australia. I am not sure whether she is ecstatic about my fate or relieved that eleven years' guardianship of me is coming to an end.

"You are lucky boy! You go and get a good education. Don't come back," says Uncle Ting, one of the distant relatives. "Make lots of money and get your mother over there so that your family can be together again. There are constant rumours that Mao Tse-tung is going to liberate Hong Kong. If this is the case, who knows what the Communists will do to the people in Hong Kong. Your family has suffered enough under the Communists back in China. Hong Kong people also worry about what is going to happen to Hong Kong when Britain's lease on it runs out and it is handed back to China in 1997."

The sentiment is echoed from every direction.

My sixth aunt buys me new clothes and essentials for my journey and packs them into a new suitcase. I can't believe that I have so many new things all at once. I am used to all hand-me-down clothing. Also going into my bag is a new transistor radio and a camera to give to my brother, and dehydrated mushrooms and scallops for Ah-por. Somehow everything fits in. My suitcase bulges.

On the night before my departure, worry and excitement stop me sleeping well. I wake very early. My mother has taken a day off work so that she can see me go. She gives me a few more words of wisdom. Such intimacy is rare between my mother and me. Is it a joyful or sad occasion? I am not sure if my tears are of joy or sadness.

One after another, my grandparents, uncles and aunts, give me the same well-intentioned advice. "Be a good boy. Don't be lazy. Work hard. Study hard. Don't get into trouble. Don't smoke. Don't drink. Don't gamble. Make lots of money. Have 'face' for your family."

For the first time in my life, I will be away from the secure but strict environment of my maternal grandparents' place. I am both relieved and afraid. I am happy to get away from the years of humiliation and intimidation at school, but to be away on my own at such a young age is frightening. And yet, fear and sadness at leaving loved ones is not enough to dampen a fourteen-year-old's excitement.

I put on a new shirt with a collar and tie, a new pair of trousers, and new socks and shoes, to get ready for my journey. This is the first time that everything I wear is brand new.

My mother says she will be too upset to see me off at the airport, so we say goodbye at the apartment, my home for the last eleven years. I am leaving a mother I don't know very well. We didn't have a close mother-son relationship. She was always busy working. I couldn't really blame her for the long work hours she worked, and apart from Chinese New Year outings, I can't recall a single outing with her.

It's an old Chinese custom that parents' love for their children is rarely shown through physical contact. There is no embracing and hugging. Cuddling and kissing on the cheek is for babies and toddlers, but even this ceases when children are about three years old. I can't remember a cuddle or hug from my mother, so it is not surprising that she doesn't touch me, except for a hand-shake.

She gives me some Australian money. I have a pound note, a ten shilling note and some silver coins: shillings, sixpences and threepences. The money is for the taxi fare to my paternal grandmother's place in Spring Hill, in case no one picks me up from Brisbane Airport.

꩜

Leung-gong, Leung-por, my uncles, aunts, cousins and I arrive at the Kai Tak Airport in Kowloon at half-past-five, two hours before departure time. An hour later, a voice from the loud-speaker invites passengers to board the plane. My relatives gather around to wish me luck. One by one, they take me aside and give me some last words of wisdom and encouragement. I can't register what they are telling me. I am crying, and suddenly I don't want to leave them all behind. My youngest aunt calms me down. My sadness gradually dissipates and excitement returns. After handshakes with all the adults, and hugs with all my little cousins, I start toward the gate and the waiting plane.

My Chinese way of life is over. I will be living in a new country, speaking a new language and learning a new culture. I don't know anything about Australia, but my paternal grandmother's belief that I will have a better chance in Australia has never wavered. One thing I am certain of: life in a Western culture is going to be very much different from mine in the East.

I have seen planes up in the air and from a distance at Hong Kong airport, but I have never seen a jet plane close up. I am in awe as I walk up the flight of stairs. Two smartly-uniformed air hostesses with smiling faces stand inside the plane entrance, greeting and welcoming the passengers.

I am fascinated by the one standing in the front. I have never seen a woman with golden hair. (Years later, I find out that golden haired women are called blondes.) Her long, straight, golden hair is neatly combed and tied back with a black velvet ribbon, like a black butterfly with its extended wings resting on a huge yellow sunflower. With her milky white skin, sparkling green eyes, straight and pointed nose and full lips, her face reminds me of a beautiful porcelain figurine I once saw.

She glances at my boarding pass and points to the middle section of the plane. I am captivated by her beauty. My legs prevent me from moving and I stare at her.

I am small in stature and only up to her shoulder height. She stands behind me, placing one hand on my shoulder and gently propelling me down the aisle toward the middle section of the plane. I am overwhelmed. My face registers the plane's cool air, which has a fresh and fragrant smell. I couldn't have imagined how big the inside of a plane is. There are five seats in a row, three on one side and two on the other, with a centre aisle. A plane must be able to carry over a hundred passengers.

The hostess stops her gentle push and glances at my boarding ticket again.

"This is your seat, the one next to the window," she says.

I don't understand what she is saying. I guess what she means is that I should take the seat that her finger is pointing at. I turn to look at her, pointing at the window seat. She nods.

She makes a gesture, meaning to let her take my hand luggage and put it in the overhead lockers. Remembering that my mother told me not to let my hand-held bag out of my sight, I shake my head. She then points underneath the seat. Again, I guess what she means, and I respond to her direction by putting my bag underneath my seat.

When I sit down, something hard presses against my back. Before I have a chance to find out what it is, she squats down and searches with both hands around the back of my waist.

"Let me undo the seat belt buckle and help you to put the seat belt on," she says.

Our heads face each other, only a few inches apart. I smell the freshness of her golden hair and the scent of her make-up. We gaze into each other's eyes. My face is reflected in her sparkling green eyes. I feel uneasy.

My penis starts to grow and become stiff, as if it might explode inside my trousers. Like a baby turtle trying to hatch, it keeps pushing and pushing with its head on a long neck. I am worried about when this stiffening phenomenon is going to end. This has never happened to me before. Unexpectedly, I feel her breasts beneath her uniform pressing against my bulging member. I hope she hasn't noticed what is happening inside my trousers.

My feet are cold, as if the blood has been pumping toward the top of my body and head. My face is hot. I am sweating. My heart races. *Is this how a normal male reacts when close to a person of the opposite sex?*

"Good boy," she says after she has managed to undo the seat belt buckle behind my back. She brings it around to the front and buckles me up. I look up. She has a big grin on her face. *Maybe she did feel me pressing against her breasts?* My face becomes even hotter.

It is close to take-off time and there is a constant flow of passengers boarding the plane. Nearly all of them are

Western foreigners. There are only a handful of Asians. They speak in English, and I can hardly understand. Western passengers are not foreigners here, on this Australian airline. We, the Asians, are the foreigners.

It is getting dark outside the plane window. The airport ground-staff are busily loading the passengers' luggage onto the plane. The engines start to roar. I wait nervously for the plane to take off. When it does, excitement and anxiety nearly suffocate me.

Through the window, I see the plane is taxiing toward the runway for take-off. Jet engines roar and gain speed. The plane rises. Clunk! The wheels retract, and we are off to Australia. My heart jumps out of my mouth. There are butterflies in my stomach and I feel dizzy. I close my eyes. My heart beats faster than normal. I take a few deep breaths and try to calm myself. At least, my erection has now subsided.

As the plane settles at the desired altitude, my mind is on the ever-present hope that, at the end of this journey, I might at last meet my father.

NINE

IIIIIIIIIIIIIIIIIIIIIIIIIIIIIIIIIIIIIIIIIIIIIIIIIIIIIIIIIIIIIIIIIIIIIIIIIIIIIIIII

A NEW LIFE BEGINS

With the plane aloft, I feel like I'm sitting in a comfortable air-conditioned bus, but without the bumpiness of the road. Because this is my first time inside a plane, I start to explore the surroundings. Above my head, lights shine downward for reading. Adjustable air-conditioning jets provide personal comfort. A life jacket is packed under the seat.

A small fold-up bench attaches to the back of the seat in front of me. Below the fold-up bench, a large pocket holds a pictorial magazine, an instruction card on how to put on and inflate the life jacket and how to use the oxygen mask, two paper bags and a clear plastic bag with ear-phones inside. The paper bags, I guess, are for passengers who succumb to air-sickness. I came prepared. I have two small plastic bags in my trouser pocket. As an added precaution, I took an air-sickness tablet before boarding the plane.

Accidentally, I figure out that the button on the side of the arm rest is for reclining the seat. I also discover how to plug my earphone into the music channel to hear four different types of music.

Just before take-off, the air hostesses serve passengers sweets. Sucking and chewing motions reduce pain in the ears caused by pressure in the plane during take-off. Not long after take-off, hostesses begin to serve passengers food. Two small sandwiches are packaged inside a clear plastic container, and an empty cup holds a small container of milk and two sachets of sugar. It's disappointing just having sandwiches for dinner. Two hours later, hostesses come around with food trolleys again. This time with a dinner of chicken, ham and roast pork with vegetables, followed by fruit salad and cream. What a treat.

I recline the seat and stretch my legs under the seat in front of me. I fold my arms in front of my chest and rest my head on the head-rest, taking deep breaths while listening to the soft music through my earphone. The music blocks the noise of the roaring engines. I am in paradise. My body feels like jelly as it settles into the shape of the comfortable seat. I have never felt so relaxed and comfortable in all my life.

Although it is nice to rest on a comfortable seat, I find it difficult to sleep in a sitting position. I doze. I feel tired when I wake to hear the Captain's announcement that we will be landing in a few minutes. It is close to eleven o'clock, and pitch black outside. As the plane starts to descend, air pressure causes pain in my eardrums. The pain eases when the plane lands and starts taxiing into the terminal.

Through the window, I see Asian workers, but not a single Westerner. Leung-gong said I would need to change flights in Darwin. If we landed in Darwin, there ought to be Westerners working at the airport. Have I caught the wrong flight?

Passengers start leaving the plane. I follow them down the mobile stairs attached to the exit door. *Perhaps I shouldn't be getting off? Something is not quite right.*

Inhaling deeply, I walk back toward the bottom of the stairs. Building courage, I ask the air hostess, "Here, Darwin?"

"No, this is not Darwin. This is Singapore," she replies. *Oh, no! Leung-gong has put me on a wrong flight. How could he make such a mistake? What am I supposed to do now?*

"Me go Darwin. Not Singapore."

My grandfather has written a note. I have it in my shirt pocket. He told me to show it to the air-hostess when the plane landed. The note says, "This boy needs to change to a TAA flight in Darwin, onto Brisbane."

"This plane stops here for re-fuelling. Afterwards, it continues on to Darwin," the hostess explains. I scratch my head to indicate I don't understand. She points at the fuel tank and then puts her index finger up and says, "One hour, to Darwin."

"One hour," I repeat. I extend my arms out and move them up and down like a pair of flying wings, saying, "Darwin?"

She nods, and so ends my first English conversation with a Westerner.

☙

It seems to be early morning when the Qantas plane lands again. I ask the air-hostess, "Here, Darwin?" She points to a dimly lit sign that reads, "Welcome to Australia—Darwin Airport."

It's still dark and I can't see much of the surroundings. But I have finally arrived in Australia!

Only a handful of passengers leave the plane and walk towards the terminal. Most of the passengers stay to continue their journey on to Sydney.

The Immigration Department officer checks my travel documents and the Hong Kong Government Certificate of Identity, and issues me with an entry permit. He stamps "Department of Immigration— Permitted to enter Australia on 29 April 1961 for stay of thirty (30) days—Darwin Airport". The Australian Government has granted me a five-year stay in Australia, on an overseas student visa. Concerned, I point at the permit and say, "Five years?"

"You will get your five years in Brisbane," he replies, handing back my travel document. I am reluctant to take it, because I don't understand why he is only giving me a thirty day stay. I only have a one-way ticket. I also worry that my suitcase might end up in Sydney. At fourteen, leaving home for the first time and arriving in a foreign country hardly able to speak English is traumatic. My heart thunders, and the perspiration dripping from my forehead is not from the Darwin heat.

Within half an hour, the other disembarked passengers have left the terminal and the Immigration Department officer is no longer at his post. I am the only person left there. I am frightened. Alone at the Darwin airport, I don't know what to do. My pulse races. My breathing is heavy and my forehead and palms sweat. I have no idea how long I will need to wait for the TAA flight to Brisbane. It seems an eternity.

I am afraid, Father. I wish you were with me. I hope I will find you soon. I think I am too young to be alone in a foreign country. Do you speak English well? Will you teach me?

Two hours later, there is human activity inside the terminal. A ground air-hostess arrives and opens up the TAA departure reception area. I hand her my travel document and the ticket. She issues me a boarding pass.

"Me bag in Qantas plane to Sydney. Me go to Brisbane. How get bag back?" I ask her.

"Don't worry! Your luggage is on this TAA flight. You will collect it when you arrive in Brisbane," she says.

"Me bag in Brisbane?"

"Yes."

Passengers bound for Brisbane finally board the TAA flight, an aeroplane with four-engine propellers on the wings. I sit in the middle of the plane, on an aisle seat. I can't see, but I can hear a coughing noise. Soon, the aeroplane begins to tremble. The noise of the four engines grows louder and louder. The plane starts taxiing, bumping up and down as it gains speed. Finally, the noise reaches a terrifying volume and the aeroplane begins to rise.

The plane has only half the capacity of the Qantas jet. The flight is not as smooth as the journey from Hong Kong to Darwin. We encounter a number of turbulent areas en route. Breakfast plays havoc in my stomach. Nausea overcomes. I close my eyes and try to take my mind off the sickness by imagining Ah-por, Ah-kor and my other relatives at the Brisbane Airport, awaiting my arrival. *Will my father be there too?*

What will my life be like in Australia, Father?

The plane finally lands in Brisbane at four in the afternoon. Brisbane Airport doesn't look like a gateway to a prosperous country. Passengers have to walk nearly a hundred yards into the terminal, which is inside a dome-shaped building. There is no comparison with the airport in Hong Kong. I learn, later, that these dome-shaped buildings, the igloos, were built by the Americans during the Second World War.

I follow other passengers to the luggage collection area, praying that my suitcase will be there. I wait patiently.

There it is!

It has arrived, together with other luggage on a conveyor. Suitcase in hand, I walk towards the customs section, remembering what the Immigration officer in Darwin told me. Sure enough, the officer stamps "Department of

Immigration permitted to remain in Australia on 29 May 1961 until 28 May 1966 — Brisbane."

Standing among a sea of people, I look for Ah-por, Ah-kor and my other relatives. There is a tap on my shoulder. "Ah-kor," I whisper. I haven't seen my older brother since he left Hong Kong four years ago, in 1957. He introduces our little aunt's husband, Jimmy Lee.

But where is my father? I am afraid to ask.

"Ah-por is working at a snack bar in Ipswich and couldn't come. She'll see you later tonight," my brother explains. Soon we are travelling from the airport to Ipswich where my uncle, aunt and their family live.

On the way, I suddenly remember my mother at home. "I need to send a telegram back to mother advising her that I have arrived safely in Brisbane."

"Is it all right to go to the General Post Office in the city to send a telegram?" Ah-kor asks our uncle.

"It's okay. Let's go and get it done. I'm sure your mother must be very anxious to know," Uncle Jim replies.

My mother now has two sons living in a foreign country and no idea when, if ever, she might see either one again. Looking back, I often ponder the pain she must have suffered and admire the courage and strength that drove her to make such sacrifices to give us a chance for a better future.

☾☽

After sending the telegram, we head towards Ipswich, where Sai-goo and Uncle Jim live and operate Golden

Dragon Products, a dim sim and spring roll manufacturing business.

Uncle Jim was living in Sydney when Sai-goo arrived to join him in 1951. Not long after Ah-por arrived in Sydney in 1954, they all moved together to live and to start the business at Ipswich. When Ah-kor arrived in 1957, he stayed with Uncle Jim, Sai-goo and their family, and worked in their business.

Over an hour after leaving the post office, we stop in front of a hot food shop at Ipswich.

"This is the snack bar where Ah-por works," Ah-kor says. When I am about to step inside the shop, he adds, "Don't go through the front. We have to go around to the back door to the kitchen, because Ah-por is working in there."

Ah-kor leads the way. He knocks on a screen door and calls, "Ah-por."

A woman shows her face and says, "Lu Kee."

"Ah-por, Loo Shang is here."

"Come on in," she says, quickly washing her hands and drying them on her apron.

"Ah-por," I greet her.

"Loo Shang, you're here," she says, extending a hand.

I take her hand, feeling the dampness.

Facing me is my fifty-five-year-old grandmother, whom I haven't seen for seven years. I only recognise her from the occasional photographs she sent to us throughout those years.

She was taller than me when she left for Australia, but now I am taller. Her hair is short and straight, with no obvious sign of grey. Although she is well-built, there are signs of shallow wrinkles on her round face. I notice that her lips are trembling and her eyes are beginning to well. She lets go of my hand and quickly grabs the lower section of her apron to wipe her face. She is wiping away tears of joy.

"Come and meet the uncles, Cheong, Bill and Wah. They are brothers, the owners of this snack bar, and I work for them every Friday night and all day Saturday."

They are not really our relatives. It is Chinese custom to refer to older family friends as uncles and aunts, as a mark of respect. I greet them from a distance because they are so busy cooking that they don't have time to stop, even to shake hands.

Ah-por says, "You people better go now. We're very busy here. Loo Shang, have a good night's rest and I'll see you in the morning, before I go to work." With a soft smile, she resumes work. Her dream has become reality. Both her grandsons are now in Australia with her.

Ah-por had come to Australia on a tourist visa. Her youngest daughter paid for her trip and she was permitted to stay for only three to six months at a time. In 1959, after five years of constant extensions, her daughter made application to sponsor her as a permanent resident. She was then able to fulfil the promise she made to me when I was seven, that she would find a way to bring me to Australia to join her.

TEN

FAMILY HISTORY

It was my great-grandfather, Ah-por's father-in-law, who built up our family's wealth. Born in 1862, he lived to age seventy-two and died in 1934. He was born in the village of Jyuk-Sou-Yuen, meaning Bamboo Garden. The village had a population of about two thousand. Most, if not all the families in the village, had the surname Kwok, from the same ancestor, dating back many generations. People with different surnames were considered intruders and were discriminated against.

Village people were mainly farmers who lived on the land growing rice, and members of our family were also farmers.

In the mid to late 1800's, many Chinese were attracted by the promise of finding gold in places like 'gao gum san' (old gold mountain) in San Francisco, California or in gold-mining areas of Australia. In his wisdom, my great-grandfather decided to leave his family behind to seek his fortune in 'sun gum san' (new gold mountain), Bendigo in

Victoria, Australia. In the late 1890s, he boarded a three-masted Chinese junk to set sail for Australia.

The junk was supposed to be heading for Melbourne, Victoria, but no one could be sure it would land at the intended destination. Depending on the strength and direction of the prevailing winds, the vessel could end up in Darwin, Townsville, Cairns, Sydney or even on one of the Pacific islands. After thirty days at sea, the junk landed in Sydney. The passengers probably did not know any different, and they were all happy to land in Australia, with an opportunity to make money to send home.

Passengers on these junks were mostly male, possibly because Chinese males left their wives and families behind in China, determined to return home after striking it rich. By leaving their dependants behind, their ancestral village would forever remain their home.

From the time of the gold rushes in the 1850s, there was opposition in Australia to the immigration of Chinese. During that period, the white settlers believed that there was a fundamental clash of cultures between Chinese and Australians. By 1888, all the British colonies in Australia had passed laws that excluded Chinese.

In 1901, the first Federal Parliament introduced its Immigration Restriction Act, commonly known as the White Australia Policy. Its prime objective was to exclude non-Europeans from putting down roots on Australian soil. The policy also restricted the access of Chinese residents to Australian citizenship. Thus, wives and children were prevented from joining their husbands and fathers permanently. Travel between China and Australia became essential, as Chinese tried to run businesses or work in Australia as well as raising a family back in China. So the Chinese immigrants came to Australia to work for a number of years, then returned home for marriage. After a year or two in their villages, they left their young brides behind and returned to Australia to continue to make their living. It was not unusual for the colonial generation to make a number of trips to and from Australia, until such time as they were prosperous enough to either retire or purchase rice paddies in their ancestral homes.

My great-grandfather journeyed to Australia, hoping to make money and then return home to raise the family without too much hardship. Like other Chinese of his generation, he came to a foreign land not knowing the language. He had to work as cheap labour, with the hope that one day he would make enough money to go home and never return to Australia again.

After he arrived in Sydney accidentally, he decided to stay and not to continue on to Melbourne. He worked and saved hard and managed to open up his own fruit and vegetable store in Sydney. He imported bananas and tropical fruit from Far North Queensland and the Pacific Islands, and shipped processed foods and manufactured products, largely sourced from Hong Kong.

In 1897, a distant relative, Kwok Lock, opened his own store, Wing On Fruit Store, in Sydney. Within two years, Kwok Lock was joined by four of his brothers. Together, they built up the Wing On Empire in Sydney. My great-grandfather met up with Kwok Lock and his four brothers, all of whom were from the same village back in China. With the same surname, we all came from the same ancestor.

In 1907, the brothers established a department store in Hong Kong. The Chinese name for a department store is Bak Fo Gung Si. Literally translated, it means "one hundred products company". The brothers named their one-hundred-products company, Wing On Department Store. By then, my great-grandfather was already back in China, enjoying the fruits of his labour. He bought many acres of good, fertile rice paddies and became a land owner.

Kwok Lock and his brothers decided to expand Wing On into China. In 1918, the Wing On branch opened in Shanghai. In 1921, Wing On Textile also opened in Shanghai. At its peak, Wing On Textile consisted of nine factories. The one in Shanghai employed twenty-thousand workers, and my great-grandfather held the position of treasurer/financial controller of this operation. Through my great-grandfather's ownership of rice paddies in the village, and shares in the Wing On Company, our family became very wealthy.

Wing On expanded further and established companies in the hotel industry, life insurance and banking. In accordance with Chinese tradition, my great-grandfather's position passed on to his son, my grandfather. Unfortunately, my grandfather died in 1933, at age thirty, leaving Ah-por pregnant and with three children to care for. My father was aged nine and my uncle was five at the time. They were far too young to be his successors. Without a successor to take over his position in Wing On Textile, our family involvement in Wing On Company virtually ceased. Nevertheless, our family was still considered well-off, because we owned a large number of rice paddies in our village.

Our family still owned rice paddies when I was born. World War II had recently ended and, in China, fruitless negotiations were in progress between Communists and Nationalists. In 1947, Civil War broke out again.

By 1949, the Kuomintang forces were defeated and Chiang Kai-shek fled to Formosa to set up yet another centre of National Government. Standing on the Gate of Heavenly Peace and facing millions of people in Tiananmen Square, Mao Tse-tung declared the birth of the People's Republic of China on 1st October 1949. The Communists had brought the entire mainland under their control.

New challenges now presented. The Communist Party was determined to make the country's people equal. To this end, it planned to take the land from the owners and redistribute it among the peasants, and to nationalise industry so that the profits would benefit everyone, not just the owners.

Once in power, the Communists carried out land reform, confiscating land from landlords and redistributing it among the peasants. This started in 1950. Landlords were brought before people's courts and tried for crimes against the peasants. In most cases, they were found guilty and subject to execution. They were paraded through the villages with dunce caps on their heads and subjected to verbal abuse and humiliation. Heavy placards hanging from their necks denounced them as criminals. Every few steps, they were forced to go down on their knees and kowtow to the watching crowds by knocking their heads on the ground. At the end of such parades, they were placed in front of the people's court and forced to kneel down on rough surfaces while the court denounced the crimes they had committed against the peasants as landlords. In some instances, they were forced to kneel on broken glass.

We were landlords, which made us politically incorrect under the Communist regime. Ah-por, as head of the household, was in trouble. She expected she might face trial and end up being imprisoned or sent to a reform farm.

My grandmother had experienced a lot of heartache and hardship during the Japanese invasion, and now she knew the Communists would soon take away our rice paddies. Although she was kind and well respected in Bamboo Garden, she realised that she could not possibly stop disgruntled or jealous villagers from instigating a trial.

Up until this time, our family was very well off and financially secure. How quickly life can change! The Communists took control of the mainland and robbed us of our livelihood, family wealth, dignity, and self-respect. Our lives were shattered, our existence turned upside down. Suddenly, we had nothing.

To avoid public humiliation—fronting-up to the so-called 'people's courts' for an unjust trial—Ah-por decided to flee. Early in 1950, she took me and left our village with very few personal possessions. She fled to Hong Kong.

At just three years old, I was too young to comprehend the political happenings around me, but I certainly lived through the effects. Under my grandmother's instruction, my mother and brother had already fled earlier — soon after the Communists took control of the country.

Ah-por's eldest daughter, Kwok Yun Ying, married Leung Shek Chor in China in the early 1940s. My brother and I call our big aunt Goo-mah — in Cantonese it means father's older sister. Although Uncle Shek Chor shared the same surname, Leung, with my mother's maiden surname, the two families are not related.

After the Second World War ended, Uncle Shek Chor managed to find his way to Australia on a tourist visa. A Chinese restaurateur in Brisbane sponsored him as a cook. He already had three children before he left for Australia. Goo-mah and her three children lived in China until the Communists took over the mainland. They, too, had to flee China and live in a rural district, New Territory, in Hong Kong. She hoped one day the family would re-unite in Australia.

Soon after the Second World War, Ah-por's younger son, our little uncle, Kwok Jen Hong, left China and migrated to America on a refugee visa. I have no recollection of him. I was only about two years old when he left China for America.

Jimmy Lee, a naturalised Australian Chinese, was back in China in search of a bride in 1949 and in 1950. After a few months of searching, he married our sixteen-year-old aunt, Kwok Yuen Ping. Not long after the marriage, Uncle

Jim returned to Australia and left his new bride behind. In 1951, she, together with their three month old son, joined him in Sydney. Ah-kor and I call her Sai-goo, which means father's younger sister.

Lu Kee, my mother and I lived with my mother's parents, the Leungs, in Hong Kong. Ah-por lived by herself in a small rented room. It was supposed to be used as a single servant's quarters. It was so tiny that a single bed would only just fit in and there was barely enough room to get on and off the bed. All her personal effects and clothing were packed into two worn-out suitcases placed underneath the bed.

After so much hardship, it is little wonder that my grandmother sought to ensure my brother and I escaped the poverty and hopelessness of life in a cramped apartment in Hong Kong. Her father-in-law had made his fortune in Australia. For her, it was a land of opportunity—a place of promise. I suspect that even before she fled China, she planned to find a way to migrate, and to bring her two grandsons to join her in building a new life.

ELEVEN

‖‖

LIFE IN THE WEST

We stayed overnight at Sai-goo's place in Brisbane Street, Ipswich. Next morning, she suggests that I visit her older sister—my big aunt Goo-mah—and her family, before leaving for Brisbane. The last time I saw them was in 1957, when Ah-kor travelled with them, bound for Australia. To my surprise, they live only fifteen minutes' walk from my little aunt's place. We exchange greetings and I meet Goo-mah's husband, Uncle Shek Chor, for the first time. They have extended their family with two girls. It would be years before I would meet up with them again.

Ah-por and I are to catch the six-thirty train to Brisbane. We walk along Brisbane Street, which, she tells me, is the main street of Ipswich. Shops line both sides of the street, but even though it is about six o'clock Sunday evening, the only shop open for business is a bar. A few patrons are drinking inside. There is hardly anyone walking on the main street. Wanchai would be busy at this time on a Sunday evening. People there come out to enjoy the various night life entertainments.

My brother told me earlier, that Ipswich was not a district of Brisbane, but was a country town that used to be a coal mining centre. Still, I am surprised at its emptiness.

After crossing a few streets, we turn left onto Bell Street and walk towards Ipswich Railway Station. Although I have off-loaded some presents, my suitcase still weighs about twenty pounds. I am glad when we finally reach the station. It is dimly lit, and we can hardly see where we are going. We have to be careful not to trip on anything. My grandmother walks toward an office with a small window opening on one side, and I follow her.

"One, boy, Valley," she says to the man behind the window.

"One adult and one child to Brunswick Street?" The railway man replies.

I don't think my grandmother knows what the man said. She smiles and repeats, "One, boy, Valley," and she hands him some money. He hands her back the change and the two tickets. I hope that we are going to the correct station, because all she has said is Valley, but the railway man said something else. I guess Ah-por knows what she is doing. It is not the first time she has caught the train from Ipswich to Brisbane.

She tells me the trip between Ipswich and Brisbane should take about an hour and fifteen minutes. My brother had told me, earlier, that the Ipswich to Brisbane train should be at the station, because Ipswich is the last station on the line. There are quite a number of carriages and there are a number of doors in each carriage. The doors open outward. For every door opening, there are two wide leather bench seats facing each other. Each bench seat could probably seat about six to seven passengers. There appear to be very few people travelling to Brisbane.

We choose a door near the back of a carriage, and we have the whole carriage to ourselves. I put my suitcase on the bench seat and get ready to take a seat. Ah-por stops me. She pulls out a hand towel to start wiping where we will sit. She shows me the towel to point out how dirty the seats are. "You need to clean the seats before sitting down, because they are covered with burned coal dust. It is a steam train and the engine uses coal in its boiler," she says.

At East Ipswich, the next station, three youths aged about seventeen or eighteen enter our carriage. They occupy the seats near the front end of the carriage, about six seats in front of ours. They are making loud noises. Their lack of consideration for others shocks me. I hope that, as we are sitting far away, they won't cause us any trouble. As soon as the train leaves the station, one of the youths pulls one of the timber louvres up. It is probably used as shade to block out the sunlight during the day. Another youth takes off his T-shirt and uses it to wrap up his right hand to form the shape of a boxing glove. He starts punching the timber louvres. Obviously, his intention is to smash the louvres, but to no avail. They take turns, but none are able to break any of timber slats with their punches. One youth jumps on the seats and side-kicks with his right foot, and gradually the timber slats start to give. One slat finally breaks. They cheer, as if they had won a boxing competition. They stop once the train pulls up at the next station, and they start again when the train is on the move again. They seem to be proud of their destructive achievements.

Ah-por is concerned for our safety. She says, "Don't look at them. We'll move to another carriage at the next station." To our relief, after destroying three louvres, they get off at Dinmore Station, before we have time to make a move to another carriage.

After the commotion, I have a chance to glance outside the window. It is pitch black outside, with just an occasional flicker of lights from distant houses. For about fifteen minutes of the journey, there isn't a single light in sight. The train stops at every station, but there are not many passengers getting on or off. A man joins us in our carriage at Sherwood Station. The train has travelled about forty-five minutes. There is only half an hour to go. As the train travels through Taringa, Toowong, Auchenflower and Milton Stations, I can see houses on either side of the railway line lit by the street lights. They seem to be of timber construction with corrugated iron roofs. They look more like sheds than houses.

The train finally pulls up at Brunswick Street Station. Ah-por decides to show me around Chinatown. I am not too happy about the idea, because I have to lug my suitcase. I am more anxious to find out where I will live than to have a night tour of Chinatown. We walk out of the station onto

Brunswick Street. I realise the railway station was named after the street.

Tram tracks run down the middle of the road. They are like those in Hong Kong. Motor vehicles have to stop behind the tram so that passengers can get on and off the tram to cross the road onto the footpath. There is a tram with a sign 'Valley' above the tram driver's window. I figure that the name of the railway station is Brunswick Street, and the district we are in is Valley. Brunswick Street is far too difficult for Ah-por to pronounce.

As we walk along Wickham Street, my grandmother points out four Chinese restaurants and names the owners and the cooks who work in each establishment. I guess in such a small Chinese community, it hasn't taken her long to get to know everybody. It seems hard to believe this area is called Chinatown when there are only five Chinese restaurants.

Our route winds along dimly lit streets. I follow Ah-por, stopping occasionally to rest my arm carrying the luggage. I write down the names of streets along the route so that I will remember them in future. I try to absorb the scenery along the way. There isn't much to see because all the shops are closed like the ones in Ipswich. There are hardly any people walking on the streets. It is like a ghost town.

We finally reach the place in Gloucester Street, Spring Hill, that my grandmother calls home. I had imagined large open spaces and wide roads where you could ride a bicycle without the worry of heavy traffic. I had also imagined a

IRON RICE BOWL

large house and a bedroom of my own, and a big yard to play in with plenty of large trees to climb.

Nothing could have prepared me for the disappointment I now feel.

☙☙

Five weeks ago, my grandmother began renting a room in a shared house in Gloucester Street in anticipation of my arrival from Hong Kong.

"Be careful," she says as we walk through the timber gate. "There's a step down here."

There is a very strong aroma in the air.

"Is something burning? What's that smell?" I ask.

"Opium. There's a very old Chinese man living next door. He lost all sense of time and does nothing except smoke opium. Occasionally, other old men join him at night for the smoking ritual."

"Where does he buy the opium?"

"Don't ask a question like that. It is illegal to smoke opium in Australia. If a neighbour should ask you what that smell is, just say it's burnt coffee beans. Understand?"

I nod.

Because it is dark, my grandmother struggles to find the keyhole. After a few attempts, she manages to open the door. It is pitch black inside. She runs a finger of her right hand up and down the door frame until she locates the light switch. In the dim light, I can barely see a narrow corridor leading from the front door to a door at the back. I follow her down the hall. There are two small empty rooms

140

on my left and a wall with two windows on my right. The dim corridor light is enough to enable her to find the switch to turn on the light in the very small kitchen at the end of the corridor.

The kitchen is basic. The timber floor is lined with worn-out, torn linoleum. Paint on the walls and ceilings is peeling. There is a cast-iron gas stove with three gas rings and an oven. There is no refrigerator. A small cabinet is used as a pantry. There is a small, rectangular timber table butting against the wall beneath a window and a chair next to it. A wooden box, placed underneath the table, doubles as a sitting stool. There is no hot water supply to the kitchen.

Diagonally opposite the back door is a flight of timber stairs leading to the two bedrooms upstairs. Our room is on the left hand side of the landing. According to my grandmother, the other upstairs room is occupied by a man who works at one of the local Chinese restaurants.

Our room is no bigger than ten feet by ten feet. Behind our bedroom door is a wooden wardrobe. There is another, smaller wooden wardrobe behind my grandmother's bed. Opposite her bed, my bed butts against the corner of the back bedroom wall and an external wall with a window. Between the two beds stands a worn-out three drawer dresser.

I am to sleep in a spring bed with a mattress instead of a bed made of wooden planks. What a luxury! I have a wardrobe in which to keep my clothing and personal things. Next to my bed head, there is an old vanity cabinet with a marble top that I can use as my study desk. For all my fourteen years of life, I have had very few luxurious things. Humble though this room is, I feel I have come up in the world. This is far better than the crowded room I shared with my mother in our apartment in Hong Kong.

Through the back door, on the left, is the bathroom. It features a claw-footed cast-iron bathtub with an overhead shower and an old shower curtain. It has an unrestricted supply of water, unlike in Hong Kong with its daily water restrictions. There is also unlimited hot water, thanks to a gas hot water system.

The toilet presents significant discomfort, especially during inclement weather. It is annexed to the house and accessed by going past the bathroom, down three steps and along a concrete pathway around the back. There is neither a light along the pathway nor a light inside the toilet. To use it at night, one needs a torch, both to find the way to the little room and to find the box of matches kept for lighting a candle placed on a shelf.

After a quick inspection of our home, Ah-por suggests that I wash and go to bed. I'd had my first shower in Australia at my aunt's place the previous night. Because I was so excited to see my brother and wanted to spend as much time with him as possible, I had foregone the opportunity to enjoy the unlimited supply of hot water and had a quick shower. This time, I plan to enjoy the luxury.

Back in Hong Kong, I took a bath in a metal tub just big enough for me to sit in, and with about three inches of warm water heated up in a kettle on the kitchen stove.

In winter, I needed to bathe quickly because the hot water turned cold quickly.

Lighting the gas pilot light presents a challenge, but soon the hot water starts to flow. I remember seeing a picture of a man having a shower in a magazine advertising hair shampoo, back in Hong Kong. I pop my head under the jets of water. The feeling is amazing! Hot water, at the perfect temperature, cascades down my hair and over every part of my body. I open my mouth to breathe and let the hot water fill my mouth. It feels so good that I keep my mouth open and let the water glide over my face and down my whole body.

I shampoo my hair under the shower for the first time, letting hot water run over my face. Every muscle in my body loosens up. Blood circulates rapidly through every vein. I imagine what it might be like to submerge my whole body in a bathtub filled with hot water. That is something I want to experience next.

♋

MONDAY 1ST MAY, 1961

Labour Day holiday means no school. That enables me to have a good look around my new home. Ah-por is already up and busy doing something downstairs in the kitchen.

"Good, you're up. You can help me to clean this place up," she says as soon as I reach the bottom of the stairs.

"We don't know who has been living in this house, but it is quite obvious that it hasn't been cleaned for a long time."

Cockroaches run amok in the small, head-high pantry cupboard. The cupboard contains a few bowls of various sizes and a few plates. A Chinese wok hangs on a hook fixed on the wall, and other cooking utensils are placed inside the cupboard under the enamel kitchen sink. Four pairs of chopsticks and some knives, forks and spoons are in a wooden box inside the kitchen sink cupboard. Although there isn't much crockery, we have enough to get by for just the two of us. The extra two pairs of chopsticks are for visitors, in case grandmother invites guests for dinner. I don't think there will ever be any visitors.

Past the bathroom, and down a small flight of stairs to the backyard, is the laundry. An old washing machine has a pair of rollers attached at the top that squeeze the water out as wet clothes are pushed through. My grandmother prefers to hand-wash the clothes. She thinks the twisting and turning in a washing machine can damage the clothes. I have to hand wash my own clothes and school uniform.

There is an old copper boiler for boiling up clothes. Judging by the number of cobwebs inside the boiler, it hasn't been used for a long time.

The whole building seems to have been purpose-built, with a dividing wall separating two small houses. It is a timber house with a corrugated iron roof and front veranda. Windows are opened by sliding them up and down on guides, but there are no fly screens. The only internal decoration is a coat of paint that is peeling off.

It was obviously applied many years before. The house is really run-down, due to years of neglect, and it appears, in daylight, even more wretched than it had seemed when I arrived last night.

Weeds in the garden grow to shoulder height. The boundary fences are falling apart. Most of the external paint work has already peeled off, showing bare timber beneath. A number of the timber stumps have already subsided and are not holding up the bearers. This explains the squeaking of the floorboards and the incline on the internal stairs.

Having explored inside and outside the house, I understand the reason why the rental—according to Ah-por—is so cheap. It is five pounds a month including power and gas.

I am not ashamed or embarrassed by the place we live. We have all the essentials, including unlimited hot water supply, which I didn't have when I was living in Hong Kong. I am content to call this shared house 'home'. I am grateful that Ah-por has thoughtfully chosen it because it is only a two minute walk from the back entrance of the St. James's Christian Brothers' School, where I am to continue my education.

∾∾∾

Lunch on this Labour Day holiday is very simple: cooked rice mixed with home-made lard, soya sauce and vegetables. After lunch, we set to cleaning the cockroach-infested cupboard. My grandmother has already fired up the three gas rings. As she lights a tiny hole in a burner, I watch the circle of flame flare up through the rest of the holes. It is like magic. She boils water in a kettle and two aluminium pots. I am puzzled as to why she is boiling so much water.

The kitchen cupboard is made of timber. It is about eighteen inches wide, a couple of feet deep, and about five feet in height, and there are five shelves inside. It has two doors — a solid one at the bottom and one with insect screens at the top. It is heavy. It takes two people to move it around. It is a cockroach haven.

Ah-por intends to use the cupboard to store groceries, vegetables and leftover food. To prevent the cockroaches crawling all over our leftovers, she is keeping leftover food inside empty coffee bottles. There are half a dozen bottles of various sizes in the cupboard. The two large ones are Bushells instant coffee bottles, about five inches in diameter and eight inches high, with metal screw-on lids. She has been buying fresh food practically every day to make sure there won't be too many leftovers to keep overnight. To keep food for the whole weekend without a refrigerator is a problem.

We half-lift, half-drag the cupboard down a few steps onto the concrete path outside the house. We rest it on its side with the doors facing upward. Ah-por instructs me to pour boiling water slowly into the cupboard, making sure the water covers all surfaces, especially reaching the gaps where cockroaches can lay their eggs. It seems to be working. Cockroaches, facing attack, run away in all directions. Lucky ones escape, but many are killed by either a ladle of boiling water or by me stepping on them if I happen to see any escaping on the concrete path. There is no shortage of ammunition. Grandmother keeps the boiling water coming. After our killing frenzy, it seems there are no more live cockroaches.

"Scrub the surfaces clean both inside and out," grandmother instructs me, handing me a bucket of hot water mixed with dish-washing liquid and a ball of steel wool. The water is so boiling hot I can hardly dip the steel wool into it without it burning my fingers. "Make sure you scrub it clean," she says.

I start scrubbing, and white foam turns black. The water in the bucket gradually turns black. Ah-por keeps changing the water for me. My fingers grow red, soft and crinkled. I wish I had a pair of rubber gloves for the task.

After I've spent a couple of hours scrubbing, Ah-por insists it should be rinsed off. This time, she hands me a bucket of clear hot water and a dish-washing sponge. She doesn't seem to have any faith in me doing it properly, so checks on me constantly. I don't understand why we are spending so much time and effort cleaning this cupboard. Sooner or later, won't the cockroaches return? After the rinsing is complete, we stand the cupboard upright and open the doors to let the sun's heat and the breeze dry it out.

Our last task is to move it back. This time, it is to be placed against the corner of the walls, but we leave a gap between the wall and the cupboard. Afterwards, Ah-por hands me four saucers and tells me to put one under each of two legs while she tilts it up on two legs. I lay flat on my belly and place the saucers underneath the two legs. We repeat the procedure for the other two legs. Then, she tells me to fill the saucers with water. She has used this technique before. Whenever she has leftovers after dinner, she fills the kitchen sink with about half an inch of water, submerges an upside down saucer and places the bowl of leftover food on top. Cockroaches can't crawl over water.

From now on, it will be my task to check on the water levels regularly and refill the saucers when necessary.

೮೦೦

It is time for me to explore the neighbourhood. Because I have been living in a densely populated place in Hong Kong, I will come to appreciate the open spaces in this country. But here, in Spring Hill, the houses are in very close proximity to each other. Some are so close that I'm sure people can hear their neighbour's conversations.

My first casual walk, under the trees on the footpath, is quite an experience. There are plenty of established trees filled with native birds chirping away. Bird noises can only be heard in parks in Hong Kong.

One of my favourite observations is the way Thornbury Street becomes a playground for young and old late in the afternoon. Children play ball games, hitting a small ball with a wooden board which has a handle. Children push and pull home-made carts made of old wooden boxes with wheels on them, steered with a rope attached to the front wheels. They roll them down the sloping street, screaming with delight.

There are trees for children to climb as well. Children don't seem to be concerned about getting hurt climbing trees or falling off the carts. There seems to be no fear of danger. Children play in the street, but there are plenty of fathers keeping a lookout for traffic. In the backyard of one house, men gather around an open flat stove watching meat cook, talking and drinking, while the women sit and chat around the tables. They seem to be enjoying themselves immensely.

༄༅

A question has been bothering me for nearly ten years. I want to know where my father is.

In Hong Kong, I asked my mother, twice. She didn't answer but told me not to bring up the question ever again. I am afraid if I ask Ah-por, I'll end up with the same response, yet I resolve to wait for an appropriate moment to pop that question to her.

"Loo Shang, set the table for dinner."

She never says please or a thank you. Perhaps it is traditional for the older generation of Chinese to show authority in the household in this way. Setting the table for dinner is a simple chore. I place two rice bowls and two pairs of chopsticks on the table. I pull the chair out for her and take out the wooden box underneath the table for myself. The dinner itself is very simple—cooked rice, steamed salt fish and stir-fried beef and beans.

Since Ah-por's arrival in a new country in 1954, not knowing a single word of the English language, life has been difficult for her. She has been a live-in helper for her younger daughter, my little aunt Sai-goo, looking after her young children and helping out in her dim sim business. For the last twelve months, before my arrival, she also worked on Fridays and Saturdays at a snack bar in Ipswich. This is how she earned and saved for my plane ticket here. But now she has an extra mouth to feed and also the cost of my education to consider.

"Loo Shang, I brought you here because I believe that you'll have a better opportunity to succeed in life in Australia than back home in Hong Kong. I understand that you had to leave your mother, her relatives and also your friends behind. But now, you are with me and you'll soon make new friends."

"Yes, Ah-por. I know it's a real privilege to study overseas and be the envy of all my Hong Kong classmates. I'll study hard to get a good job and earn lots of money to repay you, and one day, I'll bring my mother out here."

"Good. You do that."

Having started this conversation during dinner, I see the opportunity to ask her the question for which I have craved an answer for so long. I had hoped to meet my father here. I had convinced myself this was where he was, and that we would be together. I struggled with deep disappointment. My heart ached for news of him — for a chance to know him and to turn to him for comfort and guidance.

I take a deep breath, now, and ask, "Ah-por, where is my father?"

She looks up. "Don't you know?"

"Know what?"

"Your father died ten weeks before you were born. Didn't your mother tell you?"

"No. I've asked her twice. She told me not to bring the subject up ever again. She has never talked about him. I don't even know what he looks like. We have never had a photograph of him. I assumed that he was living and working in Australia. All these years, I've been telling my friends that my father is working in Australia."

Suddenly, I don't feel hungry and don't want to eat. My heart aches, and I struggle to hold back my tears.

"How did he die?"

"He died of tuberculosis."

She was silent for a time, and then she related the story of my father's passing and my birth — an event that must have brought great joy, mixed with terrible sadness and fear for my mother, facing the task of raising two young sons without the aid of her husband.

ॐॐ

MID-1946, IN CHINA

No family member knew how long my father had been ill. Even he didn't know how he contracted tuberculosis.

He suspected that he could have caught it while he was studying in Shanghai in the early 1940s.

The first symptoms were similar to those of a common cold. My father began to lose his appetite, get tired easily, feel feverish, and cough frequently. He treated the illness as if it were a common cold, hoping that Chinese herbal medicine and plenty of rest would eventually cure it. It was not until he was coughing blood that the family realised his illness was more serious than originally thought. Then they started treating him with western medical know-how. It was too late. He was in the advanced stages of the disease.

The family must have been in constant fear that tiny droplets of saliva or mucus from his coughs, sneezes and speaking would also infect them. I imagine he must have realised that he had become a burden to them, lying helplessly in bed without a hope of recovery. He must have wished death would arrive gently to end his suffering. Perhaps he remembered when he was a nine-year-old, witnessing the death of his own father, who took his last breath at the age of thirty. His pregnant mother, Ah-por, was left to care for my father and his two siblings — an older sister and a younger brother. Like me, his younger sister was born without knowing her father.

We all eventually die, hopefully in peace and after a long and satisfying life rather than in young adulthood with so much yet to be achieved. My father would not have wanted to die at twenty-two, leaving behind a young wife of three years and a two-year-old son, Lu Kee, without knowing whether his yet-to-be born child would be healthy. He surely would have wished to live a few months longer — at least until after the birth of his second child. It would have been impossible for him to die in peace, leaving a widow, just twenty-one, with a son and another child in her belly. He would have gone to his grave bearing the sorrow of knowing he would never have a chance to see his children growing up; never get to play with them, help and guide them, discipline them, or take them out to share life with them.

My father had decided to marry when he was eighteen. It was a match-maker's task to find available young women. The two young people needed to be compatible in terms of family background, wealth, education, personality and temperament. More importantly, the match-maker needed to know the prospective couple's date and time of birth, so that she could check their compatibility.

The male's family hoped the new bride would bring fortune and happiness to the family and that she would give birth to many sons. According to an old Chinese custom, young women should marry between the ages of fifteen and twenty. Men considered a twenty-year-old woman to be too old. She could have something wrong with her.

My mother, Leung Miu Hung, married my father when she was seventeen. It was an arranged marriage. They had seen each other only a few times beforehand. Chinese people believe that love develops after marriage.

No one, not even my mother, ever told me anything about my father. I did not know that he had even existed. Maybe my mother thought that I was too young to handle the trauma of hearing about his death. At the time, perhaps it might have been better for me not to know. I have always wondered whether I would have been better off knowing, so that I could have fended for myself a bit more easily instead of making up stories about an imagined father figure.

I never mentioned to anyone the humiliation I suffered when I was at school in Hong Kong. I assumed that my father was working somewhere overseas. I sensed he could have passed away, but I refused to believe that unless my mother told me so. Perhaps Chinese culture frowns on talking about the tragic happenings in one's household, or perhaps she was upset and didn't want to discuss the subject. So I lived a life of make-believe, presuming that he was still alive somewhere. Nevertheless, I realised something was not quite right, because I never received anything from him — no letters or cards, nor even a single photograph. I didn't even know what he looked like.

I had noticed, on my application for a student visa to Australia, that my father's name was Kin Chiu. I saw the word 'deceased' in brackets next to his name. I had to look up an English-Chinese dictionary to find out the meaning of 'deceased'. But I still refused to believe that my father had died, because no one in my family had ever told me.

Now, hearing Ah-por relate what had occurred ten weeks before my birth, my dreams of playing with my father, going fishing, riding bikes and all the things that fathers and sons do are gone. Reality hit. I realise that my life is going to be different from now on. The hope of someday meeting my father is gone forever.

TWELVE

‖‖‖

MY JOURNEY INTO MANHOOD

"I can't afford to pay for your education," Ah-por says, after shattering my hope of ever meeting my father. "You'll have to find a job to earn some money to pay for your own school fees, uniform and books."

Yet another challenge! I have neither mother nor father. I live in a place where the language and customs are strange. I have no friends. And now, I must find a way to pay for my own education.

"But I'm only fourteen," I protest. "What sort of job will I be able to do? Who would employ me?"

"Your little aunt might give you a weekend job in their dim sim factory. If she doesn't need you, you can get a job in a restaurant kitchen washing dishes. I can take you around to all the Chinese restaurants in the Valley and the city to see whether one of them is prepared to give you a job after school and during the weekends."

It's clear that I have no option but to find a job to ease her financial burdens.

"Next weekend, when we'll travel to Ipswich, I'll ask your little aunt for a job. It will work out well for us if you work for Golden Dragon Products and I work at the snack bar. I'm glad you have enough sense to understand. You're not a boy any more. You're going to work as a man."

Since I arrived in Australia, she has been telling me that she has no money to support me with school expenses. Whatever education I am to receive, it is my responsibility to make it happen. I need to work hard to make a life of my own. There was nothing left for us back in China after the Communist takeover of the mainland. Now, I have to make a life in Australia.

Ah-por drummed into me that I should be forever thankful for what I have and never forget anyone who has done a good deed for me. The important things in my young life were hard work, integrity and self-sufficiency. When working, I was not to be lazy. I must never answer back the elders, and I must do the work properly and always be well behaved.

That night over a simple meal of rice, fish and beef, I began my journey from boyhood into manhood.

∞∞∞

I lie in bed wondering if my life in Hong Kong would have been different if my mother had told me about my father's fate?

My mother and I seldom communicated with each other. She never read me a bed-time story. She never taught me anything. Other parents spent time with their children and played with them, but I was deprived of that kind of childhood. Perhaps she never had the time? Perhaps, after losing her husband at such a young age, she was too overcome with grief, so she put the responsibilities onto her parents to take care of me?

Even when I grew older, we never laughed or shared fun time together. We didn't tell each other things. My poor grades always got me into trouble. She seemed not to want to know what I was going through at school — the intimidations and humiliations from other students. She never had time to listen to me; never asked how I was doing at school.

I could not recall my mother ever asking me, "How can I help you?" or "What do you need?" Support from her was a rare treat. The odd times we managed to get together, she was full of criticism, nagging and lecturing.

After a while, I just couldn't be bothered anymore. I left her alone to live her life as if nothing ever happened to me.

I didn't know what my mother expected of me. I wasn't cut out to be a scholar. I was not interested in schoolwork. I was not really interested in anything. I merely drifted along. But sometimes, I wished that she could say something encouraging. I would have loved to hear, "I feel really lucky to have you for a son," or "I feel really proud of you," or "I love you."

Because I didn't know my father's whereabouts, I was a laughing stock among other students — labelled 'bastard', and a curse to my family. I was even accused of somehow causing my father's disappearance!

I was often depressed, but I suffered in silence. Despite all the name-calling and humiliation, I was never aggressive. I just hoped that one day they would tire of teasing me and would leave me alone. That day never came.

Perhaps it was part of the culture she was brought up in to not show any affection or emotion. Maybe she felt that there was something wrong with praising me for what I was supposed to do in the first place. Maybe I had just never done anything that my mother could be proud of?

❦

2ND MAY 1961

It is my first day attending an Australian school. It has been just three days since I arrived in Brisbane.

I am up two hours early, before school starts, filled with excitement and apprehension. I eat no breakfast, as there is no food left over from last night's dinner. After getting ready, I pick up my school port—which is like a small brown suitcase—and walk down Gloucester Street, along the bitumen footpath, across Hartley Street, and towards the back entrance of St. James's Christian Brothers' School.

It takes about two minutes. I don't take much notice of the school surroundings, because I am too anxious to find my way to the School's front entrance. Ah-por told me to meet up with a Chinese man named Mr. Low. I have never met him, but he was a former student of the school and helped me to gain acceptance into St. James's. He is to introduce me to the School Principal.

It is about eight o'clock when I see a Chinese man walking towards the school's front entrance. I guess he must be Mr. Low. He is a young man in his early twenties. We shake hands and briefly greet each other. He asks me, "Are you Mrs. Kwok's grandson?"

I nod.

He tells me to follow him. As we walk, he mumbles, "Where is Brother Baillie? Where is he?" While we wander around the school grounds looking for the School Principal, I seize the opportunity to ask Mr. Low a burning question.

"Who gave me the name, Tommy, that shows on the School's acceptance letter?"

"When I first approached Brother Baillie for the letter, he asked for your first name. I knew your surname was Kwok, but I didn't know your first name. He said he couldn't just write 'Kwok'. You needed to have a Christian name — Tom, Dick or Harry. In the end, he put Tommy Kwok on the letter. Is there a problem?"

"No problem. I'm just curious, because Ah-por didn't know. My mother and maternal grandparents in Hong Kong assumed that she had given me the name 'Tommy'. I never used the name Tommy in Hong Kong."

Nobody would ever believe that my Christian name was given to me by a Christian Brother! Now, as well as adjusting to a foreign country and to having to be self-sufficient, I have also to adjust to being known by a new name.

"There he is," Mr. Low says, pointing to a bald-headed man wearing a black gown. He is chatting to students. From a distance, he looks like Friar Tuck, a character I'd seen in a Robin Hood movie.

"Good morning Brother Baillie," Mr. Low says. "Say good morning to Brother Baillie, Tommy."

"Good morning Brother Baillie." I nearly addressed him as Father Baillie, because in Hong Kong we address Catholic priests who dress in black gowns as 'Father'. In Australia, we say 'Brother'. To distinguish between a Father and a Brother, Brother Baillie wears a long four-inch wide black band around his waist, with both ends of the band hanging down on one side of his body.

"Good morning, Norman. You must be Tommy Kwok, so good morning to you. Welcome to St. James's. I've been expecting you." Brother Baillie shakes hands with Mr. Low, then with me.

"Yes, I'm Tommy Kwok." It feels rather odd hearing my English name roll off my tongue.

"When did you arrive?" Brother Baillie asks.

I hesitate to answer, not quite understanding. Mr. Low translates the question, "Saturday," I reply.

"Oh, last Saturday. Three days ago. How did you get here?"

This time, I understand the question. "Qantas plane," I reply without hesitation.

"So, you flew over. That's good. Did you have a pleasant flight?"

I am again a little lost, and again Mr. Low comes to the rescue and translates the question.

"Good."

I wonder if Brother Baillie is using this opportunity to test my English language competency.

"You have a gift for Brother Baillie," Mr. Low reminds me. He had told my grandmother to organise a small gift, such as a watch, as thanks to the School Principal for accepting me into the School.

"Yes." I pull out a small packet from my pants pocket. Brother Baillie refuses to take it from me at first.

"This is just a token of appreciation from Tommy's grandmother for accepting her grandson as a pupil. It is just a watch," Mr. Low explains.

"She shouldn't have done that. It is really unnecessary. I am happy to accept Tommy here as a pupil, and I hope he'll do well."

Mr. Low takes the watch from my hand and pushes it into Brother Baillie's hand. "Please take it, and she'll be happy."

"Thank you then." He accepts the watch reluctantly. "Tommy, thank your grandmother for me."

"I'd better go and leave you two. Thank you, Brother Baillie," Mr. Low says.

"Okay, Norman. I'll look after this young fellow, and I'll see you later." They shake hands again, and Brother Baillie signals me to follow him. As we walk, other students stare at me, as if I am an alien from another planet. Some pull faces and point at me and laugh. Brother Baillie doesn't seem to notice their rude behaviour.

We walk along the side of the building until we reach the bottom of a flight of wooden stairs. He climbs the stairs and I follow. He leads me to one of the classrooms and says, "sit and wait," pointing to one of the twin desks near the door. All the desks have bench seats attached.

Soon after Brother Baillie leaves, a bell rings. Within minutes, silence falls. The clock on the front wall of the classroom shows eight-thirty. Above the clock is a cross.

All the noise has subsided. There is no more yelling. A few minutes later, footsteps approach. Boys make ooh and aah sounds as they enter the room. They seem surprised to see me sitting alone. They enter the room in an orderly manner, standing behind their respective twin desks. The colour of the boys' hair fascinates me — golden, reddish, light and dark brown. Chinese hair is always black.

"We have another ching in the school," one student says.

"Hope he is not a commo," says another.

"Could be a Jap?"

Other students laugh.

"What is so funny?" asks a man from the back. He must be the class teacher. The laughter subsides.

They must be laughing at me. Although I don't know the meaning of 'ching' and 'commo', I know these words can't be complimentary.

The room fills, but the students remain standing as if they are waiting for something to happen. I decide to stand, emulating what the others are doing.

"Let us pray," the teacher says.

I know, from my three years' studying at a Catholic Boys' School, that they are going to say prayers. Because I'm a Buddhist, I only went into the school chapel a few times, out of curiosity. I know one should make the sign of the cross before prayers. I watch the student next to me and emulate his actions. He places his left palm on his chest and moves the fingertips of his right hand to his forehead, the centre of his chest, his left shoulder, his right shoulder. Then he presses both palms together. While making the sign of the cross, the students say in unison, "In the name of the Father, and of the Son, and of the Holy Ghost." After that, they say a prayer to Father and to Mary, the Mother of God.

The teacher is an aging man, probably in his sixties. "May I have your attention please?" he says loudly. "I would like to introduce Tommy Kwok, a new student."

Thirty-nine pairs of eyes stare at me. How will I cope mixing with all these white kids? They chat and whisper among themselves while the teacher goes around to each student checking and making comments on their work. He must be checking last night's homework. After completing his round of checking, he starts spelling, times table and general knowledge tests.

I don't know which primary class I am in. I was in Form One Algebra and Geometry back in Hong Kong.

Students are doing arithmetic in an exercise book full of little squares made by faint vertical and horizontal lines.

The teacher starts to teach the students the nine times table.

I soon learn that students are to remain silent and not talk in class unless they are requested to do so by the teacher. If a student wants to ask or answer a question, he has to raise his hand to ask for permission to speak. Our teacher takes exception to a student who clicks his fingers.

When I was at St. Louis English School, every subject, except Chinese Literature and Chinese History, was taught in English. Although I had nearly three years of English schooling in Hong Kong, I can hardly speak the language. I only half-understand what our teacher is saying and what other students are trying to tell me. It is as if I am deaf and mute, so I emulate whatever the student sitting next to me does. His name is Peter. He writes JMJ and puts an addition sign on top of the M, in the middle and at the top of every page of the exercise book. He explains to me that JMJ are the initials for Jesus, Mary and Joseph.

The school bell rings at half-past-nine. Without a word from our teacher, the students leave their work on their desks and walk down the stairs to the front entrance. I follow Peter and ask him, "Go where?"

"You mean, 'where are we going?'"

"Yes. Where are we going?"

"To drink a bottle of milk."

"No money!" Fresh milk was expensive in Hong Kong.

"No need to pay. It's free."

Crates and crates of small bottles of milk are stacked just inside the school entrance. Students queue up, pushing and shuffling. Our teacher is trying to control their behaviour.

The milk comes in a small bottle, about a third of a pint, with a foil lid. Milk is a food, but I am unable to drink it because it is too rich for me. Once, I drank a small glass of cold fresh milk and it made me vomit. After that, I never again drank fresh milk. Perhaps the cream in the milk is too rich for my system.

I queue up without taking a bottle. Our teacher notices. "Tommy," he says, "it is all right to take a bottle." I move my head from left to right a few times, meaning I don't want one. He takes one out of the crate and hands it to me. I refuse it. I put my tongue out, bow my head, bend my body and imitate vomiting.

"Does milk make you sick?" he asks. I understand the word 'sick' and nod. He doesn't insist any more.

While drinking the milk, a few students try to make conversation.

"Are you a Ching or a Jap?"

"Where do you come from?"

"Are you a commo?"

"How did you get here?"

I can't understand the questions, because they speak so quickly. I don't answer. Some students greet me by putting their palms together as in prayer, while bowing their heads and saying, "Aaaah-soooh!"

One student says, "You Chinese eat anything with four legs except tables." There is laughter all around. I flare with anger. Perhaps it was meant to be a joke, but it was insulting—not just to me, but to all Chinese people.

After the milk-drinking session, the students file back to our classroom, but at a slower pace. The teacher yells from the back, "Hurry up at the front. We're taking too long." Students speed up a little after hearing the instruction, but still take their time. It might be better if our teacher led the way, but then he wouldn't be able to see those fooling around at the back of the line.

English is next. We learn new vocabulary, grammar, sentence construction, reading and writing. Students use pencils to write English words in running writing.

The bell rings at ten-twenty-five. As soon as our teacher signals that we can leave, students rush out of the classroom. Students at the back push those at the front. I have to hang on to the handrail to avoid being pushed over and rolling down the stairs.

"Don't push from the back. Walk slowly," our teacher calls.

At the bottom of the stairs, I look for Peter. "Go where?" I ask, forgetting his earlier correction of my grammar.

"Little lunch," I don't understand, until he brings the fingers of his right hand close to his mouth and starts to open and close it rapidly. I realise we're having a break for something to eat.

Ah-por told me to keep a look out at school for a Chinese student whose name is Dennis Fung. He has been in Australia for a year. According to her, all the Chinese living in Brisbane came from the same Province in China.

She knows Dennis's father. Obviously, they'd been talking with each other. Dennis knew that I was coming to this school, although he didn't know when I was due to arrive.

During the morning break, I run around the schoolyard looking for a Chinese boy. Finally, I spot Dennis and we greet each other in Cantonese, a Chinese dialect. He is a Grade Six student. I learn from him that the class I am in is Grade Four. I am fourteen years old, and mixing with ten-year-olds in Grade Four. I am devastated. This is the second time I have been down-graded into a lower class.

The morning break lasts twenty minutes. Dennis and I agree to talk more during the lunch break. I'm glad that I am not the only Chinese in the school, and I'm sure Dennis is equally pleased to have me as a companion.

Because it is my first day at school, Ah-por told me to buy some lunch here instead of coming home. Dennis shows me the place called the tuck shop, where food is sold.

The period after the morning break is devoted to Social Studies. I partly understand the lesson. After that comes Religion. Students learn the Catholic religion from Catechism. I am not the only one struggling to understand the religious teachings but, being non-Catholic, I am not interested in the lesson. I struggle to stay awake. All periods are about forty-five minutes long, but Religion seems longer. It is so boring. I am relieved when the bell rings for the lunch break.

Students rush out of the classrooms in all directions. They take their time going to class, but rush when leaving. Every minute of free time is precious.

I walk toward the tuck shop and notice that students queue up in lines, one section for food and the other for drinks. Both sections have two lines each. Any student who needs both a drink and food has to queue up twice.

Several women serve behind the counter. I note how these women address the students:

"What would you like, love?"

"Sixpence for the cream bun, darling."

"Here's your meat pie, sweetie."

"Honey, give us another threepence."

I understand that they couldn't possibly remember all the students' names, but I don't understand why they call them names like love, darling, sweetie and honey. Later, I learn from Dennis that these women are mothers of students, and they sometimes address their own children like that instead of using their proper name. But the students queuing up are not their own children, so I find it an interesting and unexpected Australian custom.

At big lunch, students sit at designated areas according to their grades. I am in the Grade Four area. No student is allowed to go out of the designated class area while they are eating lunch. Teachers on duty ensure that no one does.

Some students unwrap their sandwiches and, seeing what lies between the two slices of bread, shake their heads with disappointment and toss their lunch into a nearby bin. The waste shocks me.

While I am eating—two cream buns—one of my classmates asks me, "How come you are a Chinese and have the English name, Tommy?"

I shrug my shoulders. I know why, but I lack the language skills to explain. "Brother Baillie give me name," is the best I can do.

"How could Brother Baillie give you the name? Dopey bastard," he says and continues to eat his lunch. I sense that what he is saying isn't nice.

After fifteen minutes, students move out of their designated areas to play. Soon, the schoolyard fills with boys running, shouting and playing ball games with oval shaped balls on the compacted sandy ground. Some students pair up to play games similar to ping-pong, but with a tennis ball on the concrete pavement. There are a dozen or so students learning to play tennis on the tennis court. Since I don't know the games, and I have a communication problem, I have no hope of participating.

I meet up with Dennis again. Now, with two students with black hair, olive skin and slant eyes, the school's Chinese student population has doubled. We find a bench seat and start talking. He explains to me that the days are divided into periods. Because I'm in Grade Four, only one teacher teaches all the subjects except religion, which is taught by a Brother. In high school, there are various teachers.

While we are talking, a few students walk towards us yelling, "Ching chong Chinaman, ching chong Chinaman!" They laugh and point their fingers at us. I don't know what their words mean, but the tone of their voices and their facial expressions suggests they are insulting us. Dennis confirms this. It is difficult for us to defend ourselves from such insults. As retaliation, we call them names in Chinese and we laugh and point at them. Although they don't understand, I'm sure they know what we are saying is not nice.

There are school bullies everywhere. One can never tell whether such behaviour is just a bit of fun or genuinely insulting. Although I never suffered any physical abuse in Hong Kong, I suffered verbal abuse, intimidation and humiliation. I became immune to verbal onslaughts and developed a very thick skin. I've been called far worse names than 'ching chong Chinaman' and 'commo'. I have been conditioned not to be upset. As overseas students in this school, we understand that we will always be outsiders.

The few teasing students have their fun, then walk away. A student asks whether I am a Ching or a Jap.

"What is Ching and what is Jap?" I ask Dennis.

"Ching means Chinese people and Jap means Japanese. The Australians hate the Japanese due to the Second World War. Don't ever say you're Japanese, even if you're joking."

"Why would I say I am Japanese when I am not? I am Chinese. Now please tell me, what does 'commo' mean?"

"Commo is short for Communist. Don't admit that you are a communist either. People are worried about the communists infiltrating Australia," Dennis replies. He goes on to explain that there is tension between him and a few of the students in Grade Six because of their ignorance and fear. He assures me that Grade Four students might not be so bad, because they are still young. "Still, they will call you names," he warns.

"Why would I admit to being Communist?" I ask angrily. "It was the Communists who caused us to flee China. Communists confiscated our family's rice paddies. They caused us to lose everything our family had worked for, for so many years... Dennis, what does that phrase, ching chong Chinaman mean?"

"The Australians say ching chong Chinaman to ridicule the Chinese. There is also a story of how the ching chong Chinaman came about, but I don't know how true it is. Back in the old days, the currencies were in gold coins. The Chinese used to carry those gold coins in a small cloth bag of pocket size. They constantly shook the bag of gold coins and, over time, gold dust deposited at the bottom of the bag. They sold the gold dust for money. The shaking of the gold coins made the 'ching chong ching chong' sound, so the Australians started calling the Chinese ching chong Chinamen."

At one-fifteen, the bell rings and we rush off to line up in the playground in our respective classes. After a short address by Brother Baillie, we march off in different directions, heading towards our classrooms.

The period after lunch is Drawing, followed by the last period of the day, Nature Study. Around three o'clock, our teacher begins setting homework. We start to pack up when the bell rings, at twenty-past-three, then sit still and

TOM KWOK

and wait for the three-thirty bell, marking the end of the school day

℀℀

Ah-por and I eat dinner that night in silence. She senses something is not quite right with me. My first day at school in this new country was disappointing, not because of the insults, but because I am only in Grade Four. With a five year student visa, I'll only be in Grade Eight when my visa expires.

Finally, Ah-por breaks her silence and asks me, "How was your first day at school?"

"All right," I reply, determined not to reveal my disappointment. I know she can't help me, so why worry her?

"Is there a problem at school?" she asks.

"No."

"Is the school work too hard for you?" she persists.

"Ah-por, I can't understand why I'm in Grade Four. Although I can't speak the language, I half-understand the work. I believe my standard of education is higher than Grade Four."

"Why don't you talk to the teacher tomorrow and see whether you can go to a higher Grade?"

"I don't think it's going to help. I understand the subjects, although not all the time. But I have a problem with actually speaking English. Maybe that's the reason I'm in Grade Four."

If I'd continued to study in Hong Kong's Chinese curriculum after Hennessy Road Primary School, I would have finished my three years of middle high school. Having chosen to study an English curriculum at St. Louis, I was in the first year of middle high school. Naturally, I assumed I'd be admitted to Grade Eight here at St. James's. Who would have thought that the school would put me in Grade Four? In Mathematics for example, I was already learning Algebra and Geometry. Here, in this class, they are learning only simple fractions and multiplications.

There are six subjects, including Christian Doctrine, in Grade Four at St James's. The other five subjects are English, Nature Study, Social Studies, Arithmetic and Drawing. Every day we have a forty-five minute period for each of the subjects. English, Arithmetic, Religion and Social Studies are taught every day; and Drawing and Nature Study every day except Wednesday. Wednesday afternoon is for physical exercises and ball games in the playground.

I have little in common with the other students. The age difference compounds the challenges presented by language difficulties and cultural differences. I feel alienated, confused and intimidated. Dennis feels the same way in his Grade Six class. Eventually, we would form a close friendship. Despite the fact that he is two grades ahead of me, we are always together during lunch breaks.

It is cold comfort to notice that there are other students whose mother tongue is not English. These students' schoolwork solely depends on the teachers. Their parents can't help them — either with speaking or writing.

Every evening, I spend hours and hours looking in my English-Chinese dictionary for the meaning of unfamiliar English words. What I don't understand, I spend time and effort to memorise, hoping that my memory will help me pass the morning tests.

I am no scholar, and I wasted time at school back in Hong Kong. Now, I struggle to keep up. Despite the fact that I attended one of the best private English schools in Hong Kong for nearly three years, I didn't make good use of the opportunity to build up a solid foundation. Now, I regret it.

෨෬

"Don't forget to bring in your money tomorrow for our Lamington Drive," our Grade Four teacher reminds the class just before the bell rings. "It's today week. Put the money inside a small envelope and write your name and the amount on it. Make sure you seal the envelope so that the money doesn't fall out."

I push a writing pad toward Peter and indicate to him, by moving my right hand over the top of the pad, to write the instruction down for me. He seems to understand my hand gesture. "You want me to write it down for you?" he asks.

I nod. He whispers as he writes, "Lamington Drive, a shilling and sixpence." He hands the pad to me.

I look in the dictionary, but there is no meaning for 'Lamington'. 'Drive' means moving a motor vehicle.

"I need a shilling and sixpence to take to school tomorrow," I tell Ah-por.

"What for?"

"Going to a place call Lammton or something."

"When are you going?"

"Today week."

"How're you going to get there?"

"Parent driving."

"We don't have a car. Who's going to drive you there?"

"All my fellow Grade Four students seem to be going. I can go with one of them."

"You have only been here for two weeks. I'm not comfortable with that. I'll be worried sick. You'd better not go. Wait until next time."

I know, now, that my father is dead, yet I continue my habit of talking to him whenever I'm upset or confused. Somehow, it is comforting.

෨෨

Today is the 'Lamington Drive' day, Father. Because I'm not going, I'm not sure whether or not I need to attend school. I can't see the point of going to the class if nobody else is around. My grandmother insists that I need to go and report to the school principal, who might find some schoolwork for me to do. I'm disappointed that I'm going to miss out on my first school outing.

Walking into the school grounds, I notice that students are still in school uniform. I wander to the area where the Grade Four students are gathering. They are playing the usual ball games, chasing one another, talking and finishing up the last bit of homework. They don't seem to be excited about the impending drive to Lamington. It is no different to any other school day. Nor do I see any of the students' parents around. Perhaps the drive is to be in the afternoon?

I find Peter and ask, "Lammton, when?"

"What?"

"Drive to Lammton, when?"

"Oh, you mean the Lamington Drive. Later, about lunch time," Peter answers.

During the little lunch break, more mothers than usual are working in the tuck shop area. The usual six mothers sell food. At least another half a dozen busily cut up large slabs of cake into cubes. They dip the cubes into chocolate coloured sauce, drain off the excess and toss them in coconut to coat them all over. Then they pack them into small cardboard containers. These cakes must be delicious, because they keep licking their fingers. I hope to try one at lunch time. I wonder how much they might cost.

Half an hour before lunch, the class teacher points to the six students sitting in the front and says, "Go down to the tuck shop to pick up the lamingtons for this class."

They are excited and rush out the door. They race down the stairs. On their return, each carries a large carton that they place on top of the front row of desks. Our teacher opens the carton and starts calling out student's names, as labelled on the small cardboard containers. Most students have only one container. A few have two, and a couple have three.

"What this?" I ask Peter.

"Lamingtons," Peter replies.

"When drive to Lammton?"

"No, no, not Lammton! It is lam....ming....tons. A Lamington is a chocolate and coconut-coated small cake. This is a Lamington Drive... fund-raising for the school. You know, making money for the school."

"Lam...ming...ton. Make money for school. Not car drive to Lam...ming...ton?"

During lunch, Peter gives me one of the lamingtons from his carton. It is my first taste and it sure is delicious.

৩৩

"The Grade Four class is going tenpin bowling next week," I tell Ah-por that night.

"Where is tenpin bowling? How are you going to get there?"

"I don't know where tenpin bowling is. We'll be going by tram, and I need sixpence for the tram fare. My class made the most money on the chocolate and coconut-coated cakes. Peter, my school friend, told me that the prize for the class making the most money is to go tenpin bowling in the morning, and have classes only in the afternoon."

Tenpin bowling is as much a surprise as the Lamington Drive. I am starting to like Australia. It is certainly proving an exciting place.

๛

I've been in Australia for four weeks. Settling in was difficult, due to language problems. After three years at St. Louis in Hong Kong, I know enough English to be able to comprehend some of the things people say. I seize a few key words here and there, combine them with hand and sign language, then guess the rest. I can't talk back, due to lack of confidence, but also because I can't pronounce some of the words. I struggle to express myself.

Written English is even more challenging than spoken English, due to my lack of understanding of the fundamentals of grammar and punctuation. Learning grammar is a progressive process. Because I don't have a reservoir of words, writing a hundred word composition is a mammoth task which takes hours to complete. Words never seem to come out when I need them most. Not understanding the schoolwork means I might not pass examinations. That might result in cancellation of my overseas student visa. The thought of returning to Hong Kong without an overseas education haunts me as guilt might haunt a criminal. A student who fails causes his family to lose 'face' and brings disgrace to the family name.

I curse all those years spent lazing around, not interested in school. I need to do well in order to gain a university degree before returning to Hong Kong. It will be a disgrace and a huge opportunity lost if I return home without a degree.

"Tommy, will you please stay back for a minute?" my Grade Four teacher asks.

Am I in trouble? Unlikely, because I don't talk in class, and I don't get into trouble with my fellow students because I don't mix with them during lunch.

"Tommy, you are able to do arithmetic without any problem. You seem to be able to cope with the other subjects except English. You'll need to do more work to catch up."

Is he going to offer me extra tuition?

"You can learn more English at night," he says. "The Government runs English classes for newcomers to Australia. These classes are free and held every Tuesday evening between six and eight o'clock at the Fortitude Valley State Primary School. There is no examination and no grading of pass or fail. You can keep turning up to the lessons and repeating them until you become competent. These extra lessons will be helpful to you. The class might already have started for this term, but there is no problem. You can join in at any time."

Although I didn't understand all the words he said, I get the idea and am happy with the prospect of having extra English tuition. "Thank you let me know. I go," I reply.

"Here is the address of the Fortitude Valley State Primary School. It's in Brookes Street. Let me know how you get on."

⚏

On the evening of my first class, Ah-por and I have dinner at four-thirty, instead of our normal six o'clock. I had been to the newspaper shop the day before, after school, to check the distance from Brookes Street in a street directory. It will take about twenty minutes to walk from home to Brunswick Railway Station and probably another twenty minutes to walk to the Fortitude Valley State Primary School. I leave home at five-fifteen and allow forty-five minutes for my journey.

Brookes Street is off Wickham Street. I can't miss it as long as I walk along Wickham Street. All the shops along the street are closed for business. The only business still open, and doing a roaring trade, is the hotel close to Brunswick Street on Wickham Street. Its customers are all men.

The trams running along both Wickham and Brunswick Streets are packed with workers heading home. Wickham Street becomes quieter as it runs towards Brookes Street, and even the street lights are not as bright. It is dark along Brookes Street, but the school grounds are even darker because there is no lighting. I can see from a distance that one room is lit up. I head toward the light.

As I draw closer to the door of the classroom, I see a man inside. He must be the teacher because he greets me as I walk in.

"What's your name?"

"Tommy Kwok." He writes my name in a book.

"You take a seat... anywhere... and I'll talk to you again later."

The room is just like any other classroom, filled with double desks with attached bench seats. Eleven other students are scattered in groups all over the room. They are all middle-aged women. There are two groups of two, a group of three and a group of four. They all dress in dark clothes. Some of them struggle to fit into the bench seats attached to the desks. They chat away in their own language, and they sound so different. Two of the women also knit, while chatting and waiting for the class to start.

At the stroke of six o'clock, the teacher starts the class. He speaks slowly. "My name is Bill." He points to one of the women in the class. "What is your name?"

"My name is Sophia," the woman replies.

Bill then asks the same question around the class. The women look surprised to see me here. I guess they think a young boy should be studying at school, not in a class like this.

"How are you today?" Bill asks the class.

"I am very well, thank you, Bill," the class responds in unison.

"How are you today, Sophia?" Bill asks.

"I am very well thank you, Bill," Sophia replies.

Bill continues to ask a simple question, and then explain what the question means and answer the question. He then asks that question to the whole class. Everyone in the class responds in unison. Next, he asks the same question to each person individually. Each responds with the well-rehearsed answer. At times, there are questions that some women don't understand. Their friends translate into their mother language so that they can understand and answer back in English. It goes on like this the whole evening — conversational questions and answers.

Why am I here. I need extra lessons to help me to understand English grammar better, not everyday conversation.

After two hours, the session ends. "Thank you every one. I will see you all next week. Good night," Bill says. The women say good night as they walk out of the classroom.

"Tommy, will you please stay back for a minute?" Bill says as I walk toward the door.

"Do you go to school?" Bill asks.

"Yes."

"What class are you in now?"

"Four," I reply, feeling embarrassed, as I am fourteen years old.

"How long have you been in Australia?"

"Four weeks."

"Do you understand what we are trying to do in this class?"

I nod.

"I think the lesson was too easy for you. You seem to understand the English language, so why are you coming here?"

"To learn more English."

"I don't think these classes will help you to improve your school work. They are for European migrants, the new Australians, who are trying to learn everyday conversational English. These women are from Italy, Greece, Poland and Yugoslavia. You probably noticed that they sat in groups of their own nationalities."

I gather Bill thinks that the class won't help me a great deal, but I can see that at least it might help me learn how to pronounce words properly. Besides, I feel comfortable in class because they all speak with accents, like I do.

"Okay I come?" I ask Bill.

"Yes, you can come back. But I think you'll be wasting your time. There is a correspondence course for newcomers to Australia conducted by the Department of Education, Queensland, for the Department of Immigration. It teaches English grammar, punctuation, constructing sentences and other aspects of the English language. I believe it will be more beneficial for you." Bill writes down the contact address of the Education Department of Queensland. He hands me the address.

"Thank you," I say.

"Well, good luck, Tom. Try to do the correspondence course."

I retrace my steps along Wickham Street. It is dark and quiet. Even the hotel has now closed, and the only shops still open are the Chinese restaurants. It seems to me that my future is just as dark. Three hours ago, I was excited about the chance of getting extra tuition. Now, I am back where I started, searching for a way to improve my English. I have doubts about whether the correspondence course will do me any good.

After two weeks of procrastination, I decide to take up Bill's suggestion. I receive my first books for the course by mail, a lesson book and an exercise booklet. There will be more lesson books and exercise booklets as soon as I have completed and returned the first few. It is recommended that I complete and return one of the exercise booklets to my allocated tutor every two weeks. It is also suggested that I study one lesson at a time and wait for the return of the corrected exercise, with comments from the tutor, before submitting the next. At this rate, it probably will take about a year to complete the course. I will have to be patient and trust the process.

THIRTEEN

‖‖‖

MY FIRST YEAR IN THE WEST

After six weeks in Grade Four, I am elevated to Grade Five. The class teacher is Brother Murphy. He puts me right at the back of the classroom, with another student sitting next to me at the twin desk. I can barely hear what he is saying. Reading what he has written on the blackboard is also a problem, because I am in the very last row.

Some of the students in my class think me stupid, due to my lack of understanding of the English language and my inability to communicate with them. Sometimes, I manage to mutter a few words. My heavy Chinese accent and the improper sentence structure and grammar makes it hard for them to understand what I am trying to say. I feel blind, deaf, mute and stupid.

Brother Murphy carries a leather strap about twelve inches long, an inch-wide and half-an-inch thick. It is stitched and stained. Anyone who hasn't done his homework receives 'the cuts'—hits with this strap—on their hands. Students offer excuses like, "I forgot to bring my homework from home;" "I forgot to take the textbook home to do the work;" "I lost it in the train, bus or tram;" "my younger brother or sister ruined it;" or "the dog chewed it up." It's rare for any student to come up with an excuse that saves him or reduces the punishment.

The cuts are given on the palm of an outstretched hand. Six cuts seem to be the maximum number — three on each hand. Students receive six cuts for not doing homework. Anyone talking and not paying attention during class or misbehaving in the classroom or in the school grounds receives two or four cuts, depending on the seriousness of the offence. Before getting the cuts, students rub their hands and blow hot air onto them. The action of rubbing the hands and blowing hot air onto them makes the blood circulate, hopefully reducing the pain. As soon as students have received their cuts, they place their hands under their arm pits and press hard. One student rubbed some sort of cream on his hands. Brother Murphy smelt the cream and made him wash his hands clean before giving him the cuts.

Sometimes, students get the strap across the backside. To soften the blow, they push an exercise book down the back of their shorts. But Brother Murphy isn't fooled. As soon as he hears the sound of the hit, he asks the student to remove the exercise book, and he gives him an extra strap across the backside for trying to be smart.

There appears to be no grudges between the students and Brother Murphy. Students accept their punishment without protest. Once the punishment is over, everything seems to be forgotten. There is no malice or ill-feeling. They seem to accept that the punishment was deserved.

ಬಬಬ

Wednesday afternoon is a period for physical activities. The Grade Five class walks to the playground at Spring Hill to do exercises and play a game of football. It is about a fifteen-minute walk to the grass playground. Back in Hong Kong, we played soccer. Here, the ball is not round but oval shaped. How one can kick a ball in that shape, on the ground, is beyond me. I have never played with an oval-shaped ball. I don't understand the game.

The class is divided into four teams. The first two teams are to play against each other. While our team and the fourth team are waiting for our turn, one of my team mates demonstrates how to handle the ball. "You hold onto the ball under your arm," he says, "and run forward. If you want to pass the ball to your team mate behind you, you need to pass the ball backwards to him. Likewise, if a team mate passes the ball to you, make sure you're behind, not in front of him. Understand?"

I nod, even though I haven't a clue what he is talking about.

The ball is so unpredictable when it hits the ground, it can bounce off in any direction. We are to carry the ball and run forward, but have to pass backwards to a team mate before we are tackled by an opposite team member. To stop the opposition from moving forward, we need to tackle and pull them down and not allow them to get up and run again. The idea is to get the ball to the opponent's side of the field in order to make a score. After tackling our opponents a few times, the rule is for them to kick the ball toward us. Then we are to catch the ball and start to move forward. What a stupid game it is! It is so easy for players to hurt themselves, or even break their bones.

☙❧

The Grade Five class was the second highest fund-raising class for the Lamington Drive. The students are rewarded for their effort by going to see a movie at one of the cinemas in the city. One afternoon after lunch, the whole class walks to the city. It only takes about fifteen minutes before we reach our destination in Albert Street. To my surprise, the cinema bears the same name as our school. I can't understand why the school seems to run a cinema. Do St. James's students get a discounted rate for movies?

Last month, when I was in Grade Four, the whole class went tenpin bowling. Now, in Grade Five, the whole class is seeing a movie. I can't believe my luck. St. James's is my kind of fun school.

☙❧

"Empty your desk please Tommy, and go to see Mr. Elford," Brother Murphy says as I enter the classroom one morning. Mr. Elford is the Grade Six teacher. I have been in Grade Five just four weeks, and at St James's a total of ten weeks. Now, I am in Grade Six.

Mr. Elford obviously knows that I'm going to be in his class, as he has reserved a desk for me. I am now in the same class as Dennis Fung. He greets me with quiet enthusiasm.

We study English — composition, grammar, spelling and dictation — plus reading, writing, nature study, social studies, mathematics and drawing. The subject, social studies, is a combination of history and geography. Every morning we are tested in social studies, spelling and mental arithmetic.

Mr. Elford, like Brother Murphy, has a twelve inch leather strap. It seems every teacher has one. Students receive the strap if they misbehave, haven't done their homework or if they don't know their lessons from the previous day. One student, of migrant descent, never does his homework or learns his lessons, so every day he receives six of the best from Mr. Elford. It puzzles me why he thinks it worthwhile to suffer pain instead of working.

Grade Six school work is harder. I have little trouble handling written and mental arithmetic, as I studied algebra and geometry back in Hong Kong. I understand and can do mensuration — the rules for finding lengths, areas, and volume under the imperial system of measures. I struggle with English, nature and social studies, but at least I am not coming last. I continue to spend many hours in the evening looking up my English-Chinese dictionary for the meaning of English words and trying to make sense of the day's lessons.

I dread Mr. Elford asking me any questions. When he asks a question, sometimes, I raise my hand as if I know the answer, though actually I don't. I avoid eye-contact with him, hoping he won't pick on me. Occasionally, I do know and am able to give him the correct answer. On other occasions, my memory serves me well on the day, and I do well.

I don't know how to develop study skills. No one has ever taught me goal setting, time management or the technique of taking study notes. I have to work hard on my own. There is no one to give me any guidance. The difficulties I face are my problems to resolve myself, or simply muddle through by memory, without understanding.

By Grade Six, my understanding of the English language is improving. I can understand half of what Mr. Elford says. The other half, I ask the student who sits next to me. Most of the time this isn't successful, because we are not allowed to talk during class. I continue to regret that I wasted the opportunity to build up a solid foundation in Hong Kong.

After a month in Grade Six, I sit for the term examinations. Although my overall results are not bad, Mr. Elford's recommendation is that I should remain in Sixth grade for the rest of the school year.

☙❧

Ah-por and I walk around the various food shops in Fortitude Valley searching for bargains. With no refrigerator, she has to be careful of the quantity of food she buys, as she doesn't want to have too much left over. Since she can speak only a few words of English, I have to translate. There have been many incidents that have caused me embarrassment. Sometimes, she spends a long time choosing items and bartering with shopkeepers. I dislike shopping with her intensely. It also makes me realise just how poor we are.

The fish shop is very cool inside. Different types of fish of assorted sizes and various types of shellfish lie neatly covered with ice inside the display refrigeration unit, their price tags clearly visible. Ah-por paces up and down in front of the display, shaking her head and mumbling, "Too mudgee! Too mudgee!"

As far as she is concerned, everything inside the display unit costs too much. She is searching for a cheap buy. The man standing behind the display unit waits patiently for her order, but it never comes. When she is about to walk out, with me not far behind, something in a large stainless steel bowl catches her eye. She tells me to ask the man what he is going to do with those large skeletons inside the bowl. She has noticed that after the fish is filleted, there is still quite a bit of flesh attached to the main bone.

"Throw them away," the man replies.

Following her further instruction, I ask, "Can we have? Okay?"

The man stares at us, probably realising that we can't afford to buy any of his fish. Waiting for a reply, blood rushes to my face and my eyes are fixed on the floor. I try to avoid contact. We are begging for fish heads and bones.

"All right. All right," he says in an unfriendly tone, "You can have the bloody lot." He wraps them up in newspapers.

Ah-por still isn't satisfied with his discards. I have to ask the man, "I come next week to take fish heads and bones. Okay?"

He ignores my question.

Ah-por steams the fish heads and bones with garlic, ginger and her home-made black bean paste. We don't have a refrigerator, so what we were unable to consume in one meal, she saturates with salt to preserve it for a day or two. We will have steamed salty fish the following day.

♋

We walk into the butcher shop. After receiving her instructions, I place our order, "Two pounds of pork bones." The butcher disappears from behind the display refrigerator and comes back with a parcel wrapped in white paper.

"Is this for your dog?" he asks, collecting the money from her. I don't expect him to ask me such a question. I can't possibly tell him that the bones are for our consumption. My face turns red. He asks me again, "What sort of dog is it?"

I raise my hands to chest height, with palms facing each other a foot apart.

"Oh," he says, "It's only a little puppy."

I nod silently.

Ah-por cuts off most of the fat from the bones and cooks them to extract the lard for future use. She steams the few pieces with meat still attached to the bones, the same way she steamed the fish heads and bones—with garlic, ginger and her home-made black bean paste. She boils some of the pork bones in water, as stock for cooking and soup. Pork bones are rich in calcium, but I am not sure whether that is part of her reasoning. It is survival on her mind, just as it has been for decades.

಄಄

Ah-por has gone out on her own. She returns, a few hours later, with her haul of snake bean and bitter melon seeds. We are to plant the seeds somewhere in the yard, which is presently overgrown with weeds. It is like a jungle, and has never been mown even once since I first arrived at the place. She has already warned me not to go into the yard because it could be infested with snakes and other vermin. She decides to plant her precious seeds at the side of the house. I have to clear a patch next to the dividing fence. Snake beans and bitter melons grow on vines. My task will be to water them and to pull the vines back from the neighbour's side of the fence.

There are no complaints from the neighbour about the vines extending into their property, because I regularly pull them back onto our side of the fence. I need to pull the vines back gently, without breaking them. After a few weeks, we see the fruits of our labour. The snake beans and bitter melons become our main source of vegetables. I quite like snake beans. Although at first I dislike the taste of bitter melon, I gradually grow accustomed to it.

Ah-por knows the medicinal values of different foods—something every young woman during the old days in China learned from older generations. Chinese food balances starchy foods such as rice and noodles for carbohydrate, vegetables for fibre and meats for protein. This diet ensures the balance of yin and yang inside our body. She is also aware that what a person eats determines his state of health. Yin foods represent cool foods, while yang foods represent hot. Deep-fried food is never good for the body because it creates too much heat inside the system. She makes Chinese herbal teas to balance heat and coolness in our bodies.

In the Chinese tradition, soup is generally taken after the meal. The soup not only tastes good but also has health benefits by balancing the ying and yang. She also makes what she calls 'Chinese jelly' from agar, which is a type of seaweed. She boils the seaweed in water, drains it, then lets the liquid set without any refrigeration. She sweetens it with syrup which she makes by boiling sugar with water. She believes this Chinese jelly will cool our internal body system and rid it of excessive heat.

⁊⁊

I never have breakfast in the morning. Because it is only a two minute walk from school, I come home for lunch. We have two meals a day, one in the afternoon and one in the evening. No matter what, Ah-por makes sure there is plenty of cooked rice. Rice is our staple diet. Many times, she has to extend the rice by cooking rice congee with pork bones, peanuts and anything else she can find to make a meal. We might not have quality food, but we never go hungry. Having lived in Hong Kong for ten years, I know there are people much worse off than us. I am thankful for the blessings that I have — a roof above my head, a warm bed and a full stomach.

∽∾

Private overseas students have to pay their own way while studying in Australia. They need funds to cover both educational fees and living expenses. Most have a wealthy family paying for their overseas education. When they return home with their university degrees, they will become highly paid professionals: medical doctors, lawyers, accountants and engineers. While studying, they make their parents proud by achieving impressive results and by taking care of themselves. They bring honour to their families. Parents gain 'face' when they tell others of their children's overseas achievements.

Parents typically send their children money to travel back home at the end of each academic year, for an almost three-month-long break. They arrive back in Australia just before the new academic year commences.

Students from poorer families have a much harder time. Without family financial support, it is extremely difficult for them to earn enough to cover all their expenses. Anyone on a student visa is not legally allowed to work. Students have to work illegally, on low pay, to survive.

My paternal grandmother brought me to Australia hoping to give me a better future. She worked hard to save for my trip, but I realized soon after I arrived that I could not rely on any financial help from anyone. I have to rely on my own efforts to get through school and university. Working doesn't bother me. In Hong Kong, I helped my maternal grandmother with household chores, shopping, and making plastic flowers and bead necklaces. But nothing could prepare me for the hard work I would have to do in Australia.

For four-and-a half-months, from the time of my arrival in Brisbane, Ah-por and I have been travelling to Ipswich every Friday after school and returning on Sunday evening. From Ipswich station, we head off in opposite directions. She works at the snack bar and I work at Golden Dragon Products.

My job in the dim sim factory is enjoyable. While we sit around making dim sims and spring rolls, we talk about life back in Hong Kong. The factory pays me a pound for a weekend's work, which is more than enough to cover all my schooling expenses, with some left over to save for the future. My first payment is an invaluable boost to my self-confidence. It gives me a taste of financial independence.

ᏮᏮ

SATURDAY EVENING, 20TH MAY, 1961

My brother and I finish work early at the dim sim factory. After dinner, we decide to take a walk to the Ipswich show ground. It is show time, but unfortunately it's a miserable night. It's drizzling rain and the ground is wet and muddy.

"Watch where you put your feet, Loo Shang," Ah-kor warns. We have to side-step the mushy ground where animals have left their marks.

There aren't many people attending the show, perhaps because the weather is bad, or because they prefer to attend the much bigger show in Brisbane in August.

One of the main objectives of the show is for country folk to exhibit their pastoral and agricultural produce to city people. It is also a good opportunity for city people to learn about life on the land.

There isn't much going on in the main arena. Perhaps we have missed a lot of events because we arrived late and had only an hour to look around before the show closed for the day.

In one section of the arena, both young and middle-aged men swing axes, competing to chop a log in half. They compete to see who is the fastest.

The undercover animal section houses beef cattle, dairy cattle, sheep, pigs, horses and dogs. It must be terrible for the animals, caged in such cramped conditions instead of in open paddocks where they usually roam freely. Adults and children pat them. They make lots of noise. The animals aren't accustomed to noise, and it must upset them.

Dairy farmers invite show-goers to participate in the milking of their cows when their udders are full of milk. A sheep-shearing demonstration attracts a lot of onlookers. Everyone is fascinated by how quickly a shearer can shear the fleece off a sheep's body.

Animal droppings are everywhere, and the bewildering smells are unbearable. I can't wait to get out of the animal pavilion. It is much better at the fruit and vegetable pavilion, because it is cleaner and there is no revolting smell. There are fruit and vegetable displays, but being a city boy, I don't know which grower's produce is better. All the displays look the same to me. How can anyone select the 1st, 2nd and 3rd prize winners?

In the cake section, the cakes all look delicious. They all appear 1st prize winners!

Sideshow alley draws most of our attention. There are rides, like the ferris wheel and the merry-go-round, and games like horse racing and sending monkeys climbing up poles. There is a laughing clown into which you feed five ping pong balls, one at a time. The balls go into the clown's mouth and land on a tray with slots containing numbers. The host adds up the numbers under each ball and compares the total amount with the winning numbers posted on a board. The prize is a cheap toy.

The amount some people spend on the game would have bought the toy outright. One has to be extremely lucky to win a prize that is worth more than the amount outlaid for the game.

I stop and watch how to turn sugar into fairy floss. I like to see the sugar become a powder puff. I learn that a dagwood-dog is a sausage coated in batter, pierced with a small bamboo stick and then deep-fried in cooking oil. After cooking, it is dipped in tomato sauce. I also discover that potato chips are deep-fried cut-up strips of potato.

Strawberry ice-cream sundaes are a must-have for show-goers. A sundae is an ice-cream cone filled with ice-cream, whipped cream and strawberries. All these foods are new to me.

There are quite a number of stores selling sample bags. I thought samples should be free, but although these bags contain companies' products—like chocolate and sweets and cheap plastic toys—the show-goers seem happy to pay for them. They don't seem to last long. I learn from my brother, that at Ipswich's first Exhibition, in 1876, visitors were given a sample of coal to take home.

The show caters for all ages. Adults might be interested in the produce, while young adults are more attracted to sideshow alley, and children are excited about the sample bags, dagwood-dogs and ice-cream.

⚉

After the Ipswich Show, I am eager to go to the Brisbane show, which is given the grand name of 'Exhibition'. My classmate Peter, tells me there is a holiday for everyone to go to the Royal Queensland Show. It seems unusual to have a holiday on a Wednesday in the middle of August. This show is also called 'The Ekka', a slang word for Exhibition. It runs for ten days. It must be much bigger than the Ipswich Show, which only ran for three days.

Since it is a holiday, I guess show day must count as a school day. I wonder how Mr. Elford would know who had attended and who hadn't. I plan to go there on foot, so I check the route on a Brisbane road map at a newspaper shop during the week.

To my surprise, when Ekka Day arrives, Ah-por wants to come along too. Initially, I am unaware that she has a completely different idea about how I am to spend the day. We walk toward the Valley, and she stops in front of the Oriental Restaurant on Wickham Street.

"When the cooks ask you to do something, do it promptly," she instructs. "Make sure you keep yourself busy. When you have finished one job, ask if anything else needs to be done. Don't stand around and talk. There are lots of things to do in a kitchen. Understand?"

"No, I don't understand," I reply. "Today is a holiday. It's a day for going to the Ekka and I ought to be there. It is like a school day."

"It's a holiday, and people can do whatever they like," Ah-por counters quickly. "You've been to the Ipswich show with Lu Kee, and the Ekka is more or less the same thing."

"What am I supposed to tell my teacher if he asks me if I've been? Not going might mean I will be marked as absent from school."

"I don't believe the school can mark you as absent on a holiday day," she replies. "All right then, you can go if there is nothing to do in the kitchen."

I don't want to argue with her. I hope I might get to the Show in the afternoon. Without another word, I follow her into the kitchen.

"Good morning Mr. Lee." She greets a middle-aged man, then turns to me. "Mr. Lee is the owner of this restaurant, and you greet him."

"Hello, Mr. Lee. How are you?"

"I am fine. Thank you. Why are you two out this morning? Are you going to the Ekka?" Mr. Lee asks.

"No, we are not going there," Ah-por says. "I know that your restaurant is going to be very busy today, so we're here to give a helping hand in exchange for a free lunch and dinner. Besides, I want to show my grandson what it is like to work in a Chinese restaurant kitchen."

I can't believe what I just heard my grandmother say.

"Oh, thank you, Mrs. Kwok. It's very kind of you and your grandson to offer to come and help. It is going to be extremely busy with all these country people in town. They love to have Chinese dinners while they're here. Your offer is really appreciated. Lunch and dinner are on me," Mr. Lee replies, smiling widely.

Ah-por hands me an apron she had brought along, made of calico flour bags. We have these aprons in plentiful supply, because Golden Dragon Products uses a lot of flour for making the dim sim pastries.

There is no shortage of work. There are many vegetables to be chopped up, potatoes and onions to be peeled, meat to be sliced, and pots and pans to be washed and cleaned.

By one-thirty — already an hour past my lunch time — we have been working for three hours. The cooks are still busy cooking lunches. They have been going nonstop since the restaurant opened at eleven o'clock, and there are a string of orders. My stomach starts to rumble and I need to have some food if I am to keep going. I wonder when all this work is going to cease so I can go to the Ekka.

Three o'clock is the normal lunch time for the restaurant workers. I fill my stomach with nearly twice the amount of rice I would normally consume. After about fifteen minutes of so-called lunch break, everyone is back at work. There is no time to digest the food.

Knowing if I walk to the Ekka by four o'clock, I can still enjoy five hours of looking around before it closes for the day, I ask, "Ah-por, can I go to the Ekka now?"

"Yes. You can go, but be back by five."

"It'll take me half an hour to get there and half an hour to get back, leaving only about half an hour at the Show," I protest. "It is hardly worthwhile to go. Why do I have to be back by five o'clock?"

"Some people might start to come in for early dinner at five, so that they can go to the Ekka after. Your task is to keep an eye on all the ingredients in containers and fill them up as the cooks use them up. We'll go next year."

I am more concerned about how I am going to face the teacher tomorrow, having not attended the Ekka. I give up on going this year.

It promises to be a very busy night. One of the cooks has indicated that, in the past, on the night of the public Ekka holiday, the kitchen had to produce three times more meals than normal. For three hours, I fetch this and that, fill more of this and that, chop more of this and that, and finally, at about half-past-eight, it seems to have quietened down a bit. All the bench spaces around the large kitchen sink are filled with dirty dishes, cups, saucers and cutlery. No one seems to have time to do any of the dish washing. Ah-por says, "Loo Shang, You start doing the dish washing."

We have dinner at ten o'clock, and I am so tired I hardly have the energy to eat. Mr. Lee and the three cooks can't thank us enough for our help, and they all commend me as a very good worker.

I hope Mr. Elford won't set an English exercise called 'My Day at the Exhibition'.

☙❧

Ah-por and I survive on our Ipswich earnings until October 1961. I am paid on Sunday after dinner, then we catch the train back to Brisbane. My one pound earnings for a weekend's work more than covers my school expenses. I never know how much Ah-por earns for her Friday night and Saturday at the snack bar, but she pays for food, rent and household necessities.

In October, 1961, Ah-por loses her job. I don't know why, and I don't dare ask, but we don't travel to Ipswich any more for the weekend. I lose my one pound per week income. We are now forced to live on Ah-por's meagre savings.

The rent is five pounds a month for the room, including the electricity and gas. We are very conscientious about using the gas and electricity. We don't want the landlord to use our consumption as an excuse to increase the rent.

I don't know if Ah-por might be eligible for a social welfare payment from the Government for unemployed people, but she is a proud and determined person. She won't want to rely on welfare. She has been brought up in a tradition of hard work, and she believes it is a disgrace for a person to depend on welfare.

Life is a constant struggle. On a few occasions, we go to her closest friend's place to do some household chores in exchange for a meal. I remember the very first time we went there. She instructed me, "If my friend invites us to stay for the evening meal, be polite and well-mannered at the table. Don't embarrass yourself. Don't gorge yourself, even if you are hungry."

After spending the entire afternoon mowing the lawn and cleaning up the yard, I was very hungry at mealtime. I didn't feel fully satisfied after having my restrained meal, but I remembered Ah-por's instruction. At least there was some food in my stomach.

☙❧

A Chinese restaurant in the city, owned by three partners, is looking for an extra business partner. My grandmother presents, with me in tow, in the hope they might accept her as the fourth partner. "If you accept me as partner, the kitchen will have an extra pair of hands," she says. "My fourteen-year-old grandson will work in the kitchen after school, and there is no need to pay him."

Silence!

I remember the Ekka Public holiday, when I worked at the Oriental Restaurant, and what was required of me that day.

The three partners aren't convinced that a schoolboy would do very much. Perhaps they worry that I might actually be a nuisance around the kitchen. Ah-por senses their reluctance and adds, "How about let's try for a fortnight with no pay. We can talk about the partnership at the end of the two weeks?"

The partners glance at one other and remain silent. Eventually, one says, "Let's give it a go, starting next Monday. There is no guarantee of a partnership after the two week trial, even if you have worked well."

I work there after school and all day Saturday and Sunday. Through the week, I spend about an hour doing my homework after school before going to help. At least the sixth grade school work isn't too demanding. I do just enough to get by.

It is a fifteen-minute walk from school to the restaurant. When I arrive, at about five o'clock, Ah-por always has something ready for me to eat. After that, she always makes sure I have plenty to do to keep me busy.

We all have our evening meal together at around nine-thirty. Because it is a Chinese restaurant, there is always plenty of rice. I have a full stomach, without restricting my consumption. I don't have to worry about being chided for being a big eater. The partners encourage me to eat. "You're a growing boy and you need to eat in order to grow big and strong," they say.

After dinner, we clean up, seldom arriving home before eleven o'clock.

The partners praise me as a 'good little worker', but after two weeks, Ah-por announces that we won't be going back there. I am sure our work was up to the partners' expectations, but I suspect they disliked the idea of having a fifty-five-year-old woman and a fourteen-year-old boy as business partners.

∽∾

After losing her job, Ah-por—in desperation I suppose—turns to gambling. She buys casket tickets, hoping for a big win to get us out of poverty. I don't know the legal age for buying casket tickets, but she has me purchase them on her behalf. It is necessary to put her name on the ticket to endorse ownership, and she needs me to write it.

A full ticket is ten shillings, and a one-fifth share is two shillings. She has won some money before, but never enough to cover the cost of the tickets. One day, though, I find myself holding a £20 win. It is her biggest win to date, and I am thinking it will cover four months' rental. Ah-por has another idea. She believes her luck had turned and she is going to have a big win. She tells me to spend the whole £20 on full casket tickets. Not shares. She wins nothing, but it doesn't deter her. Although fourteen, I look about twelve. I wish the shopkeeper would say I am too young to gamble and refuse to sell me the tickets. Ah-por is going through her savings fast.

∽∾

5TH NOVEMBER, 1961

Sunday is Cracker Night, Father. Since the middle of October, shops have been selling all sorts of fireworks in preparation. For a whole week, my class mates have been talking about this upcoming Cracker Night — how much they had spent on buying bungers, strings of tom-thumbs, sky rockets, roman candles, semi-exploding fountains, Catherine wheels and sparklers. They boast that they are going to have the biggest bonfire in the neighbourhood.

The celebration commemorates an event in English history that occurred on 5th November 1605. Together with two others, Englishman Guy Fawkes staged a failed attempt to blow up King James I. Bonfires were lit at night to celebrate the King's survival and as a sign of thanksgiving that the plot failed

In Spring Hill, Ah-por and I watch to see how the evening will unfold. A neighbourhood teenager can't wait until dark. He fires a rocket up into the air, which sets off a chain-reaction. Firecrackers go off all around the neighbourhood. During early evening, excited children run around waving sparklers and throwing small bungers.

To make an effigy of Guy Fawkes, a group of small children stuff a potato sack dummy with scrap paper and newspaper, and then haul it around. A teenager lights a larger bunger under a jam tin, while younger children watch and wait for the bunger to explode. It shoots up into the air, accompanied by a big cheer.

Letter boxes are blown up. In one big backyard, a huge bonfire is built with tree loppings, hedge trimmings, cardboard and newspaper soaked with kerosene. An adult holds a hose in case the fire burns out of control. Perhaps this bonfire is also a good way to get rid of household rubbish.

Explosions sound constantly, and there's a smell of burning gunpowder in the air. Dogs locked up inside houses bark uncontrollably, fearful of the sounds of the explosions. Their hearing is sensitive, so this is traumatic for them.

People here seem unconcerned that bonfires can cause house fires, and children can end up in hospital with nasty burns or part of their hands missing.

❧

7TH NOVEMBER, 1961

Walking through the back entrance of the school on Tuesday morning after 'Cracker Night', there is a buzz among students. Students from various classes have pieces of paper in their hands and are asking their fellow students, "Do you want to be in a Melbourne Cup Sweep?"

One of my classmates says, "Tommy, if you want to be in the Melbourne Cup Sweep, you need to see Michael."

What is he talking about? Why should I see Michael?

"Tommy, do you want to be in the Melbourne Cup Sweep?" Michael asks. "You can be in a sixpence or a shilling sweep, or both. The sixpence sweep pays nine shillings for the winner, three shillings for the second and one shilling for the third. You can have as many horses as you like."

I stare at him and scratch my head. "It's a horse race," he explains.

"A horse race?" It seems that horse racing is a form of gambling.

Why would the school allow such activity during school hours? Gambling is only for adults.

"Yes, a horse race. Do you want to be in it or not?"

"Race in Brisbane?"

"No, at Flemington Racecourse, in Melbourne, at two o'clock this afternoon."

"I pick horse?"

"No, you can't pick your horse. Draw your name from one hat and your horse from another...Never mind!" He gives up and moves on to ask other students.

Canvassing for the sweep goes on during both little lunch and big lunch. At one o'clock, Michael runs around telling everyone that the sweep with students' names and their horses has been posted on the outside wall, next to the door to our Grade Six classroom.

By about quarter-to-two, students lose concentration on the lesson and keep staring at the clock. Ten minutes later, Mr. Elford says, "We can stop work now." One student takes out a transistor radio, tunes into one of the radio stations and turns it to full volume. Students are holding the names of their respective horses, chatting and bragging to each other that their horse is going to win. They cheer when their horse's name is announced on the radio. I don't have a horse, so I don't share in the excitement.

A trumpet sounds, and the race caller announces, "Racing..." Students jump up and down in their seats, yelling and cheering. They drown out the caller's voice, until someone says, "Shut-up... Can't hear what's going on." They quieten, but they still jump up and down.

The race broadcaster is calling the race so fast that I can't understand a word he says, but the class seem to follow without difficulty. Some students act as if they are riding — hitting their backsides and pretending to gallop.

Within three minutes, the race is all over. The caller announces, "The winner of the 1961 Melbourne Cup is Lord Fury, Grand Print second and Dhaulagari third." Michael hands out money to the three winners. The losers tear up their horse's name and curse their luck.

∽∽∽

My final examination result for Grade Six is far better than expected. Perhaps the correspondence course helped, and the positive remarks from my tutor on every exercise submitted gave me confidence to express myself better? Perhaps my fear of deportation if I don't perform well at school drove me to work hard? I Perhaps it was a combination of all my extra efforts that enabled me to gain an Honours Pass with an overall average of over 80%?

In the comments section of my school report, Mr. Elford wrote just one word: "Congratulations".

☙☙

My first year of school in Australia has ended. For weeks, Ah-por has been searching the Brisbane Chinese business community for any sort of employment, but to no avail. Being an older woman, without any understanding of the English language, it is impossible for her to gain any sort of employment outside the Chinese business community, which is centred on the restaurant trade. Finally, she finds a kitchen job at a small café at Shorncliffe. It is only temporary. It means she has work for a few weeks during the Christmas and New Year holiday period.

Since my arrival in Brisbane, I have been her translator. Now, I'm not only translating the food orders for her to cook at the café, but also helping her to do the preparation, washing-up and cleaning in the kitchen.

The remoteness of this café and the lack of public transport make it difficult for the owner to find anyone to employ without providing live-in accommodation. A residence is attached to the back of the shop. I am not sure how many rooms are inside the residence, because the owner will not allow us to go inside the house except into our room and the bathroom. The area where we sleep is right next to the kitchen. I guess it was once a small storeroom, turned into worker's quarters. It is just big enough to hold two single beds, a wardrobe, a small table and a chair. There would have been only one single bed before we arrived.

The owner of the café is a New Australian who enjoys a drink and a bet on the races. On our second Saturday working there, he has apparently had a bad day at the races and lost a substantial amount of money. He has been drinking excessively. I can smell his strong alcoholic breath. He is in a bad mood, and his face is splotched red from anger, or alcohol, or a combination of both. His eyes seem to spill out of their sockets. He can't control his saliva. When he speaks, it is like a water spray.

For some reason I can't fathom, he starts abusing me and threatening me with physical violence. This behaviour has happened once before, but not with such aggression. This time he has gone too far. My grandmother fears that something terrible could happen to me. She tells me to get out of the kitchen. The blood is rushing to my head, and my eyes well up with tears. My throat feels as though someone is choking me. Outside the kitchen, I gaze at the starry sky above. A gentle breeze stirs the air. I take a few deep breaths. My anger subsides. I focus on keeping my thoughts positive, reminding myself how lucky I am not to be among the people living on the rooftops or begging in the market place back in Hong Kong.

Ah-por comes out. "Let's get out of here," she says. The veins in her neck bulge and blood pumps hard into her face. We pack all our belongings into two suitcases and carry them back into the kitchen. Ah-por opens the suitcases and says to the owner, "Look, look." She wants to show him that we haven't taken anything that is not ours. He ignores her. "Look!" she yells, and this time, he glances over and nods his head.

Hearing the commotion in the kitchen, the owner's wife appears. She knows her husband has been drinking heavily. "Stay, stay!" she says to my grandmother, while trying to calm her husband.

"No." My grandmother shakes her head vigorously. We pick up our suitcases and walk towards the Shorncliffe Railway Station and along dimly lit streets. We are without a job again, but we are safe. My main concern now is whether there is still a train heading to Brunswick Street Station. On the journey home from Shorncliffe, not a single word is spoken. We don't know what to say to each other. I wish Ah-por didn't have to struggle so hard to make a living. For me to get out of the poverty cycle, I need an education. I begin to think about the reasons students like me come to Australia, the options available to them, and the challenges we all face.

Not all students from Hong Kong are here to study. Some, from wealthy family backgrounds, come for a good time. Their parents support them, because their children are studying abroad. It doesn't matter to some parents what their children study. As long as children attend universities, parents continue to send them money.

Some students come for the money. Using a student visa as a passage to Australia, they start looking for a job as soon as they arrive, mostly working illegally in the local Chinese community for low wages. They work hard, hoping that, in a few years, they can save a small fortune to take back home.

Government regulations require overseas students to return home after they have completed their degree studies. Some students try to linger on, believing life is better in Australia than in Hong Kong. Many are concerned how conditions might change in 1997, when control of Hong Kong returns to China. Not wanting to risk living under Communist rule, they try to extend their visas for as long as possible, hoping that one day they might be granted permanent residency.

The non-academic overseas students in Australia have a sense of loss, because they can't cope with school work. Generally, they are not from wealthy family backgrounds, so they have to work to support themselves. Some question whether it was right for them to come here. When their student visas expire, some become illegal immigrants and disappear, hoping the Immigration Department will never find them.

I see no future in staying in the country illegally, hoping to avoid detection. Despite not being a scholar, I need to do well at school. Ah-por has given me an amazing opportunity, and I must work hard to take maximum advantage of it.

ᔕᔕ

We are glad to leave the Shorncliffe café. We have worked there two weeks. It is now two days before Christmas Day. Every business is closed for the Festive Season. Even Chinese restaurants close on Christmas

Day. Back in Hong Kong, Chinese people don't celebrate Christmas unless they are Christian. This will be my first Christmas in Australia, but I doubt I will receive any Christmas gifts from anyone — not even my grandmother. I won't be disappointed. I neither celebrated Christmas, nor received presents, when I lived in Hong Kong. On Boxing Day, Ah-por sets out to find me a job. There are only four Chinese restaurants in Wickham Street, one in Brunswick Street and one in Ann Street. The Chinese people working in the restaurants all come from neighbouring villages in Chungshan Province, China. They speak the same Chinese dialect, and all seem to know each other. Only perhaps a thousand or so Chinese live in Brisbane.

As we walk past the first restaurant in Brunswick Street, Ah-por mumbles, "This one is the Leong's family business. They have enough children helping already. They don't need any outsider."

We walk along Wickham Street to a restaurant owned by Mr. Young.

"Good morning, Mr. Young. This is my grandson. Do you need an extra pair of hands in the kitchen?" Ah-por asks.

"No. We already have enough people."

Deep down, I am pleased with the outcome so far. If no one wants me, I will enjoy a good holiday break with neither school nor work.

We receive similar negative responses from two more restaurants along Wickham Street before arriving at the last restaurant in Wickham Street, the Cathay Café. It is owned by three partners. One, Mr. Woo, is busy at the front counter.

"Good morning, Mr. Woo. Do you need an extra pair of hands during the Christmas and New Year period? This is my grandson, Loo Shang. I am keen to find him a job. He hasn't worked much in a kitchen before and he has a lot to learn. Would you be able to use him?"

"No, we don't need anybody. There are three of us and a kitchen-hand already. Anyway, I'll go and ask the other two," Mr. Woo replies.

We wait patiently for about five minutes. There is no sign of Mr. Woo coming back. I am happily anticipating another 'No'. Ah-por can't wait much longer and decides to walk toward the kitchen. I follow. After exchanging greetings with the other two partners, Mr. Seeto and Mr. Low, she asks them if they would consider giving me a job. There is silence. She can't help herself. She is determined to find me a job.

"No need to pay my grandson," she says. "He has worked in a kitchen only for a few days and he is here to work and to learn. His payment is three meals a day."

I can't believe what I am hearing. Why would anyone work without pay?

Mr. Woo turns to his partners for an answer. I notice that both Mr. Seeto and Mr. Low nod simultaneously, quite happy for me to work there as a volunteer. Ah-por grins, perhaps thinking that she won't have to worry about food for me during the holiday period.

"Then, it is agreed. My grandson can start now," she says. She pulls me aside and hands me an apron made of calico flour bags. I tie it around me while she offers advice. "I know you're unhappy about not getting any payment for your work, but don't forget that you ought to be thankful that someone has given you a chance to learn something that will help you in the future. Do you think for one minute that they would employ you with pay when they already have enough people in the kitchen? They don't really need you. You could be a hindrance more than a help. You better smarten up. Work hard and keep your mouth shut. Observe and learn."

The meals served in the restaurant are mainly sweet and sour pork or fish, chicken or prawn chop suey, chow mein and fried rice. None of the partners are qualified chefs, but have learned from one another and from working in other restaurants before they formed this business partnership.

My duties are mainly washing kitchen utensils, dishes and cutlery, cleaning, and getting goods from the basement storeroom and freezer. My work doesn't require much intelligence. I just have to keep working and fetching whatever the partners want to keep them cooking. I become their legs. I lose count of how many times I travel up and down to the basement and back each day.

Although the restaurant doesn't open until twelve-midday, we start work at half-past-ten in the morning. The business stays open until eleven-thirty at night, when we finish for the day. We work a thirteen hour day. Everyone in the kitchen works those hours, taking breaks for lunch at three o'clock and dinner at ten o'clock. By the end of the working day, I am exhausted, and can't wait to get back home to wash and go straight to bed.

It doesn't take long for me to get into a routine and learn what work is required, without anyone telling me what to do. The partners compliment me. I am a quick learner and a hard worker. My body seems to cope with the long hours. A good night's sleep always freshens me, ready to tackle another day.

I started work there on Tuesday. On Sunday night, as I'm cleaning and mopping the kitchen floor before finishing for the day, Mr. Woo says, "You don't need to come tomorrow."

For a minute, I worry that my voluntary service is no longer required.

"You have been working really hard and you deserve to have a day off. Come back on Tuesday. From now on, Monday is your day off."

I am relieved that they still want me, but delighted to have a regular day of rest.

Because it is a festive season, there are still customers dining in the restaurant after closing time that Sunday. It is after midnight before I walk back home. Ah-por is still awake.

"You've been working there for a week," she says. "You might think that I am hard on you by getting you a job without pay. Back in China, if a person wants to be an apprentice, he needs to pay his master for the teaching. You have to be grateful to them for giving you that opportunity.

One might think that it is exploitation. Instead of doing nothing during the five weeks holiday, you are working and learning a skill which no one can take away from you. A skill will help you in the future, to get a job in any Chinese restaurant kitchen."

In bed, I reflect. Her words make good sense. Although we have neither a Christmas lunch, nor dinner, and I did not receive any Christmas presents, she has given me a valuable lesson by getting me that unpaid job. I am learning the meaning of self-discipline, self-worth, integrity, and the capacity to respect and learn from others.

These attributes will become the foundation of my future life.

FOURTEEN

THE YEAR OF THE TIGER

Two days before the start of the 1962 school year, I work my last day at the Cathay Café. I have been working in the restaurant six days a week—nearly thirteen hours a day—for the past five weeks. It is ten o'clock Saturday night, and the partners have let me finish work an hour earlier than usual. Just before I walk out of the kitchen, Mr. Woo hands me fifteen pounds.

"Loo Shang," he says, "You've been a great help. We have decided to pay you fifteen pounds for your five weeks' work."

"Thank you Mr. Woo. Thank you Mr. Seeto. Thank you Mr. Low."

I am excited to be holding the bank notes in my hand. I can't wait to get home and tell my grandmother of my good fortune. Fifteen pounds is a lot of money for a fifteen-year-old. I believe I thoroughly deserve the payment, though it is completely unexpected.

"Ah-por, see what Mr. Woo has given me? Fifteen pounds. Can you imagine what we can do with it? Rental payments for the next three months, better quality food on the table, and my school fees paid."

"Take the money back to Mr. Woo... now!" she orders. The expression on her wrinkled face is stony.

My excitement turns to anger. "Why? I've been working really hard. The partners have paid me only for what I have done—working six days a week, thirteen hours a day for five weeks."

"I'll tell you why," she replies, her finger pointing straight at my face. Despite her small stature, this fifty-seven-year-old woman speaks with authority. "Remember the day, five weeks ago, I took you to see Mr. Woo and asked him whether he needed a junior to work in the restaurant kitchen? I told him the job was for your benefit, and I told him there was no need to pay you. Your payment was to be three meals a day. I'm sure you remember all that?"

"Yes but—"

"Then what are you waiting for? Take the money back now. It is only ten-fifteeen. Mr. Woo should still be at the restaurant. You shouldn't have taken it in the first place."

My return journey takes much longer than it had taken to walk home. My excitement and anger has subsided. It is time for reflection. I realise grandmother is right. I shouldn't have taken the money in the first place.

When I return home, I call out, "I'm back."

"Good. Now have a shower and go to bed."

"Here. Fifteen pounds."

"What? Didn't you give the money back to Mr. Woo?"

"I did, and I reminded him about the arrangement we made five weeks ago. I also told him that I shouldn't have taken the money in the first place. But he insisted I take it and kept stuffing these notes back into my shirt pocket."

"Take the money back right now. You could have left it on the table." Her face is red and her lips tremble as she speaks.

"Why can't we just keep it?"

"No! It is only a quarter-to-eleven. Take the money back. Whatever you do, don't bring the money back."

This time, I have to hurry to catch Mr. Woo before he leaves for the night. I can't believe how much stress this fifteen pounds has caused. Back home with my grandmother, I bravely tell her, "Here's the fifteen pounds. Mr. Woo said the money is for you. It is not for me."

"Why is Mr. Woo giving me the money? I haven't done anything. Take it back tomorrow morning."

"No. I'm not going to take it back for the third time tomorrow morning. I'm not going to have anything to do with it any more. Mr. Woo has given it to you. It is your money now."

ဆၷၦ

It is a beautiful Sunday summer morning. We walk silently toward the Cathay Café.

"You take the money and give it back to Mr. Woo."

"No. You give it back to him. It is your money not mine."

She comes out of the café and, without a word, we start walking home. I am wise enough not to ask her about the fifteen pounds. I try not to smile. Somehow I suspect Mr. Woo won that epic battle of wills.

⊙⊙

1962 is the Year of the Tiger.

Chinese New Year in Brisbane is a nonevent. I don't think many Australians are even aware that Chinese New Year, 1962, is coming up. It begins on Monday, 5th February. There is no community-wide celebration in Brisbane. It is up to each family to celebrate in their own way.

The White Australia Policy (Australia's immigration policy, from Federation in 1901) favoured white European migrants, especially those from Britain, over nonwhite races. Most families of Chinese working men are still back home in Hong Kong or China, and the men can celebrate with their families only in spirit. Because Chinese New Year's Day falls on a Monday—a normal working and school day, not a holiday—men still go to work and I go to school. My grandmother will do the best she can to welcome this New Year — my first in Australia.

The Kwok family ancestors, including my father and grandfather, were buried in China. After fleeing Communist China, our family had no place to call our own. Our rented place in Brisbane's inner city isn't exactly conducive to making New Year offerings. We rent only one room in a shared house, but have exclusive use of the kitchen. The other two men here only come home to clean themselves and to sleep.

Ten days before New Year, I have finished working in the restaurant. Ah-por has me busy cleaning: scrubbing the narrow corridor, kitchen, bathroom, toilet floor and walls, and dusting and sweeping our room. We are unable to make any offerings to the Kitchen God. I hope he will take our poor circumstances into consideration. We don't have anything to offer that might lead him to give a good report to the Jade Emperor, who would bless us with a better year to come.

As tradition demands, Ah-por has settled the rent to ensure that there is no money owing to the landlord before the New Year. She fills a container with rice, together with a red packet containing eight shillings, a full bottle of peanut cooking oil, a full jar of salt and a full jar of sugar. These essentials ensure that we will not be hungry for the rest of the year. The eight shillings inside the red packet ensures good fortune. According to the Chinese, the number eight is lucky because it makes a homophone similar to the word prosper, and means 'have a prosperous New Year'.

On Chinese New Year's Eve, I pick up a chicken and a fish from Cathay Café. Ah-por must have already ordered and paid for them. My brother, Ah-kor, is celebrating this New Year with the Lee family at their place in Ipswich. He has been living with them all these years, and it is a long way between Ipswich and Spring Hill. It would take him hours for the return trip by train and on foot. The Kwok family reunion dinner is, therefore, just for Ah-por and me.

We have a chicken dish, a fish dish and lettuce with shallots. It is a sumptuous meal compared with what we have been eating. The chicken symbolises fortune. The fish means abundance. Lettuce and shallots imply vigour and wisdom. 'Abundant fortune' means we will find a job with an income, and 'vigorous wisdom' means I will do well at school.

After dinner, there is a final clean and sweep of the floor areas before Ah-por puts away the brooms. Despite having school in the morning, I am allowed to stay up until midnight to open up all the windows and turn on all the lights. This marks a farewell to the old and welcome to the new.

Ah-por is up early on New Year's Day. We greet each other with 'Gung Hei Fatt Choi' and best wishes for health and prosperity.

Ah-por is busy making Chinese deep-fried doughnuts, which symbolise plentiful gold in the year ahead. She cooks noodles for lunch and a vegetarian dish for dinner. She gives me a red packet containing a ten shilling note and two oranges. This symbolises that I will have money and gold for the New Year. I can only hope that this will, indeed, be true.

❀❀❀

Seventy students in Grade Seven are divided into seven rows. Brother Rieck, who is due to retire and is currently awaiting his replacement, arranges the bright boys at the back of the classroom and the not-so-bright, the lazy and the troublemakers at the front. He makes sure the boys at the front pay attention and do their class work, and punishes any who misbehave or disturb the class.

I sit about three-quarters of the way from the front. Because he speaks softly, and in a monotone, it is difficult for me to stay attentive. He is actually easy going, and doesn't want much stress, so we manage to get away with a lot, escaping punishment often.

In Grade Seven, there are only three required school subjects—English, Mathematics and Social Studies—but, since this is a Catholic School, there is a period devoted to Religious Studies every day. Brother Rieck takes us for Mathematics, Social Studies and Religious Studies. He nearly puts everyone to sleep. Our former Grade Six teacher, Mr. Elford, continues to take us for English. With his loud voice, he certainly keeps us awake.

Every day, the forty-five minute session before lunch is allocated to studies about the Catholic Church, the Bible and the Saints. Students learn Catholic Catechism. Being a non-Catholic, and struggling with the English language, I have little interest in listening to the doctrines.

⊚⊚

One morning, Brother Rieck's attire is different. Instead of wearing his black gown and black cummerbund, he wears a black suit. Underneath his coat is a white vest, and he has a circular collar around his neck. As soon as we have finished little lunch and gone back to our classroom, he tells the class to get ready to go.

"Where go?" I ask Paul, who sits adjacent to me in the next row.

"You mean where are we going?" he replies.

I nod.

"Going to Mass," he answers.

"Where is the place called Mass?" I ask. I must have missed what Brother Rieck has told us. I am concerned at how we would get there and how much it might cost.

"We're going to Mass at the church."

"Going to Mass at church! By tram? How much?"

"We walk. It won't cost anything."

"All day?" I ask him.

"We'll walk there. Mass starts at eleven and finishes around noon. We'll be back here before lunch."

I breathe a sigh of relief. Normally I go home for lunch. Ah-por expects me a few minutes after twelve-thirty every day.

With Brother Rieck leading the way, the whole Grade Seven class walks double-file down Boundary Street toward Wickham Street and Fortitude Valley. After living in Spring Hill for nearly a year, I am familiar with the Valley, but I can't recall seeing any church in the vicinity. We turn right onto Gotha Street at the intersection of Wickham, then left onto Ann Street. Soon, we come to a stone wall opening which doesn't resemble an entrance to a church, because there is no church. We walk through a pair of black wrought-iron gates and a pair of solid timber doors. It is cold and dimly lit, with little natural light. It looks and feels like an air-raid bombing shelter.

Directly opposite the entrance is an altar. It is about fifty feet away. There is a walking passageway leading to the altar, with a crucifix above. On either side of the passageway are rows and rows of long wooden pews. We take our seats in an orderly fashion, filling up each pew starting from the front. The pews are uncomfortable, but I like the quietness inside the church.

We settle down and wait patiently. A priest appears from the side door and strides to the altar, accompanied by two students who wear three-quarter-length short-sleeved white cotton gowns over their school uniforms. I have never been to a Mass, despite attending a Roman Catholic school in Hong Kong. Students don't have to be Catholic to attend St. Louis. They can be of any religion, or none. This is the first time I've attended Mass. I haven't a clue what I am supposed to be doing. I emulate the other students when they stand and give the sign of the cross, kneel, sit or sing. I can't understand what the priest is saying, so it is rather boring. I can hardly keep myself awake. I am unsure whether my fellow students are listening or sleeping.

The climax comes. The students line up in single file to walk toward the altar. The priest puts something white, the size of a shilling coin, in their mouths. The students make a sign of the cross and return to their seats. There is more kneeling, sitting and singing. An hour later, it is finally over.

On the way out, I realise the so-called church's main entrance is situated on Ann Street, opposite the Catholic Girls' School, All Hallows. Why is there no church building?

"This is no church?" I ask Paul on our way back to school.

"No. It is just the crypt of the church," Paul replies.

"A clip?"

"No, not a clip. A crypt! C...r...y...p...t! A crypt. You know — a basement."

"A c...r...y...p...t. Basement! Where church building?"

"No money to build the church."

"Oh, I see. No money build church. The priest speak not English. What country words?" I ask.

"Latin," Paul replies.

I have no idea what Latin is, so I just nod. That night, I look up the English-Chinese dictionary for the meaning of the word crypt. It says, "the bottom level of a church used for burials". I wonder how many coffins are buried there.

It has been an interesting day. I sleep soundly.

☾☾

Brother Rieck is wearing his suit again. What is the point of my going to Mass? Perhaps I could ask him whether I could stay back. Most likely, the answer would be no.

Perhaps I can hide in the toilet block and wait until they have all left, then sneak out to one of the cinemas on Queen Street that my brother and I have been to a couple of times. There is no starting or finishing time, so patrons can come and go whenever they like. The newsreel and short films show continuously. One can drop in to the cinema at any time to watch something and stay until that something repeats.

I will need to go home during little lunch and explain to Ah-por why I won't be home for lunch. I put forth my intention to Dennis. He also likes the idea of going to the cinema instead of Mass. Our plan is to sneak out at half-past-ten. It should take only about twenty minutes to walk from school to Queen Street. We will stay in the cinema for two hours, from eleven to one, then walk back to school before the bell rings for the afternoon periods. With seventy students, we don't think Brother Rieck will notice us missing.

"We go to Mass today after little lunch?" I ask Paul.

"To Confession, not Mass," Paul clarifies.

"How long go for?"

"Don't know. Could be back sooner depending on how many priests are there to hear confessions."

Our plan to sneak out to watch the newsreel and short films has just vanished. Although I was half asleep during yesterday's religion period, I remember Brother Rieck talked about Confession. I must have missed the bit about going to Confession today.

I gather that students are to confess the sins they have committed since their last confession. I know Catholics believe that when they die, their spirits go either to Heaven or Hell. In order to end up in Heaven, they must confess their sins before death. So they have to confess regularly. Brother Rieck also says that some spirits might not be good enough to go to Heaven, but yet not bad enough to go to Hell. These spirits could end up in Purgatory, where they could stay for months or even years, suffering for their sins until they are good enough to ascend to Heaven.

Brother Rieck has also mentioned a prayer of forgiveness. He starts writing the prayer on the blackboard for us to copy.

"I confess to Almighty God, to the blessed Mary ever Virgin, to blessed Michael the Archangel, to blessed John the Baptist, to the holy Apostles Peter and Paul, to all the Saints, that I have sinned exceedingly in thought, word, and deed."

One must strike the chest three times while continuing, "Through my fault, through my fault, through my most grievous fault. Therefore, I beseech blessed Mary ever Virgin, blessed Michael the Archangel, blessed John the Baptist, the holy Apostles Peter and Paul, all the Saints, to pray for me to the Lord our God. Amen".

Brother Rieck explains that it is traditional to strike the chest while reciting, as a sign of humility.

At Confession, students sit on the wooden pews adjacent to a small cubicle with two single door openings. They wait patiently for their turn to go inside one of the cubicles. The cubicle is slightly bigger than two side-by-side public phone booths. I guess the priest sits behind one door, listening to confession. The other door is for the confessor to enter.

After a student leaves the cubicle, he goes around the Church and stops in front of the holy pictures and makes the sign of the cross. He mumbles something, which I guess is the prayer for forgiveness, and again makes the sign of the cross. Then he moves on to the next holy picture.

The benefit of Confession is extraordinary. After confessing, the confessor is absolved of all guilt for the thoughts, words and deeds that the confessor has described. The confessor is washed clean.

I am a non-Catholic and I don't go to Confession. I wonder where Catholics suppose my spirit will go after my death, and would it matter that I have lived the life of a good person?

ᏋᏋ

During summer, there is an afternoon swimming session every week. Brother Rieck is in his suit again. This time I know where we're going. We are going to Spring Hill Baths at Torrington Street, up on the top of Spring Hill. The location of St. James's is so handy that it takes us only about fifteen minutes to walk to all the places we need to go—Brunswick Street Railway Station, the city cinemas, the church, the playground in Love Street, and the Spring Hill Baths.

We walk along Boundary Street, carrying our swimming togs and towels. I am concerned, because this is my first time at a swimming pool. I was never taught how to swim. Actually, I was discouraged from going near the water, even at public swimming pools in Hong Kong. Leung-por kept telling me not to go near water because I might get cramps, drown or die.

Before long, we reach the Spring Hill Baths. On the front wall, two storeys up, there is an inscription, '1886 — Municipal Public Baths — James Hipwood Mayor'. This was eighteen years after our school was established, in 1868. Many former students of St. James's would have enjoyed cooling themselves off here during hot summer days.

Students queue up in single file and pay the threepence entry fee. The pool is about twenty-five yards long and about half as wide. There are six swimming lanes. I am surprised that the pool is undercover. It can't be affected by inclement weather. The pool itself is surrounded by rows of little, painted-timber changing-cubicles. They remind me of a magazine photo I've seen, showing many colourful seaside huts. Directly above, on the second floor, are spectator stands.

Unable to swim, I stay in the shallow end of the pool. Students jump into the pool, making big splashes, and then climb out and repeat the process of jumping in and out of the pool. Other students are trying to swim, and become annoyed and scream at the splashers to stop fooling around. With so many students in the pool, it isn't ideal for serious swimmers trying to do laps, but it is a great place for a relaxing splash and for fooling around, as the majority of the students do. The water is warm, because the pool is heated by direct sunlight.

While Brother Rieck keeps a watchful eye on the students from the second floor, a man at the shallow end of the pool says, "Those students who can't swim, please

gather down here and I'll teach you how to do freestyle."
He demonstrates the swimming style. I am glad that I am
not the only student who can't swim. I try to float, but my
body sinks as soon as I turn sideways to lift one of my
arms into the air. I fear I must be drowning because I keep
swallowing water. My fingers and toes are wrinkled. When
I put my head underwater, with my eyes open, the chlorine
stings my eyes and my nose fills with water.

"Move your arms and keep kicking with your feet," the
man keeps yelling. I keep sinking and swallowing chlorine
water. I stand up on the floor of the pool and look around.
Other students are swimming and diving like dolphins. I
wish I could enjoy the water like them, and I wonder if I'll
ever learn to swim.

On the way back to school, we have popsicles. The
Australian kids called them ice-blocks. Our bodies are cool,
inside and out.

෨෨

On the day of the school Swimming Carnival, students
are to find their own way to the pool on Wickham Street
for the competition that starts at nine o'clock. I didn't know
there was a pool on Wickham Street until I arrived to see
a group of St. James's boys, wearing the school uniform,
gathering on the footpath in front of a brick building with
a brickwork façade. There was an inscription, 'Municipal
Swimming Bath', in the middle and on the top of the façade.

This pool is twice the size of the Spring Hill Baths
in both length and width, but is without a cover. The

grandstand for spectators is on the top level, overlooking the pool. Because I am not a competitor in any of the swimming events, all I can do is cheer for my house team.

ᏕᏕ

Grade Seven has a new teacher, Brother Kempster, for the next two school terms. All the good times in first term, with the easy going Brother Rieck, are over. Brother Kempster is much younger than Brother Rieck—in his thirties, perhaps? He soon finds that the standard of our work is not as good as he expected. Work Brother Reich let us get away with is not acceptable to Brother Kempster. To show that he means business, he lines up twelve of the worst performing students and gives them four cuts each, two on each palm.

"Lift the standard of your work or the punishment will be even harsher next time," he warns the class.

Walking into our classroom to take the next period, Mr. Elford senses something amiss and asks, "What's the commotion about?"

"Brother Kempster is on the war path," says one student.

"Yeah! Yeah!" a number of students echo simultaneously.

"What makes you think so?"

"Because Brother Kempster just gave twelve students four cuts each for not doing the work properly."

"Serves you people right for not doing your work properly. Well I hope that teaches you a lesson," Mr. Elford says unsympathetically. "You had better take notice or I might do the same."

⊙⊙

I complete the correspondence course in English language for newcomers to Australia. Although quite proud of my achievement, finishing all the exercises, I can't be sure my English has improved. Based on my oral presentations at school, I have a long way to go.

Each student has to write something on a topic of his own choosing and give a talk in front of the class for two minutes. It proves to be a nerve-racking experience. Even having written the piece myself, I am unable to pronounce some of the words properly. I stammer and tremble, feeling the blood rushing to my face. My lips and mouth are dry.

I am supposed to talk, not read like a newsreader. Although Brother Kempster tries hard to control the class, there is plenty of laughter among students. Unable to write or pronounce, and able only to read a little, at times I feel nothing but despair.

⊙⊙

"Tom, are your parents coming along this evening?" Brother Kempster asks one day. "It's the parent-teacher night, remember?"

I am uneasy when people ask about my family. Why would Brother Kempster want to talk to them? I've passed all my subjects in the second term examinations, placing 18th out of a class of 75. My grade is 'excellent', in general conduct, attendance and home exercise, and a 'very good' grade in home lessons. Brother's remarks on my report card read, "Thomas is most satisfactory".

Maybe he has found out that I forged my grandmother's signature on my report card? Because Ah-por doesn't know any English, she refuses to sign anything she doesn't understand, even my report card.

"Well, are they coming or not?"

"No. My father died. Mother in Hong Kong. Grandmother don't talk English."

"Oh, I see. Not to worry."

What a relief to know he hasn't discovered the forgery.

☙ೲ❧

After living in Spring Hill for eighteen months, we move into a two bedroom house in James Street, New Farm, sharing with a sixty-year-old Chinese woman.

The Chinese woman and Ah-por each have a bedroom in the house. My room is a closed-in veranda at the front. It is small—about eight feet by five feet—but it provides privacy for a sixteen-year-old. The area is just big enough to position a single bed with space beside for dressing.

The room has a timber back wall. Timber railing and balustrades at the front and side have long since been replaced with a waist-high fibro wall. Louvre window panes are of various patterns and colours: some clear, some opaque, some merely odd pieces of masonite. From a distance, they resemble a patchwork quilt. The timber floor shows signs of dry rot and decay, and the peeling paint on the curved corrugated-iron ceiling exposes patches of rust.

My bed butts against the timber back wall and the fibro side wall. A small wardrobe is placed at the end of my bed, with the wardrobe doors opening outwards. For privacy, a worn-out single bed sheet is hung across the opening between the wardrobe and the front wall.

We move into this house in November, 1962. Summer extends well into autumn and the heat, even in the following March, is still unbearable. It seems the temperature inside my room is higher than outside. The corrugated iron ceiling absorbs the heat and transmits it downwards, like an eatery hot-box keeping the food warm. At times, there are isolated showers in the middle of a hot summer's day. Rain hisses off the iron roof, and rain water evaporates into steam.

I can smell the heat, like pouring cold water onto a red-hot grilling plate. After the rain has stopped, the heat returns. High temperatures and moisture in the air after rain remind me of walking through a humid forest during an outdoor school excursion on a very hot day. The perspiration pours from my body — more heavily from my forehead, dripping down my face like a waterfall.

With the coming of winter, I would discover that the westerly winds blew through the floor gaps as if there were tens of small wind tunnels clustered into a very confined space. Despite three blankets covering me, the wind still blows underneath and penetrates through the mattress into my half-warm body. I learn to keep myself warm by wrapping the blanket around me.

After living there for a year, I realise that my room was, depending on the seasons, a hot-box, a humid forest, a mosquito feeding ground, a wind tunnel or a percussion chamber. There were no insect screens mounted on the louvre windows. During the night, the mosquitoes were out in force, searching for food. The incessant buzzing sounds they made drove me insane. I was always so tired that, despite being an easy target for these blood-suckers, I pulled the bed sheet over my head and tried to go back to sleep. I often woke covered in bites.

Electrical storms and winds heralded the arrival of summer that year. It sounded like side drums rolling on the iron roof. The wind hit the glass louvres and made rattling sounds, like castanets playing. The occasional heavy rain blowing onto the external fibro wall sounded like a kettledrum. And then there was the thunder. The combination of these noises created a non-rhythmic piece that sounded as if it was being played by a group of preschool children. I constantly feared that the wind might cause heavy rain to penetrate my room and wet my bed.

Despite the improved privacy, my room in the New Farm house was decidedly uncomfortable. Thankfully, Ah-por and I move out after a year, to half a house in Greenslopes, a suburb on Brisbane's south side. This new dwelling has only one bedroom, and again my room is at the front on an enclosed veranda, but it is more comfortable.

☙☙

Because Ah-por doesn't speak English, she has no chance of finding a job working for Western people. Chinese businesses aren't keen to employ a fifty-seven-year-old woman either. After the unpleasant experience at the café at Shorncliffe in December 1961, Ah-por has been without a job for fifteen months.

Having finished my five weeks' work at the Cathay Café during the 1961-62 Christmas-New Year period, I am also without an income for seven months, until September. Eventually, Sai-goo offers me a job back at the Golden Dragon Products factory, working weekends and during the eight-week school holidays. Ah-por is happy for me to keep all the money I earn working at the dim sim factory, provided that I spend it on my school expenses. I offer to give her money to cover the rent and household expenses, but she refuses.

One afternoon, in the middle of April, almost two years after my arrival in Australia, Ah-por announces, "I've found us a job, starting next Monday. Let Sai-goo know that you won't be coming to work for them after this weekend. Do you hear me?"

I am dumbfounded. Part of my surprise is realising that she has managed to land a job.

"We'll be working in the kitchen at the Greenslopes Tenpin Bowling Alley. Catch the Mt Gravatt tram and get off at the stop outside the Bowling Alley. You can keep a lookout for the Greenslopes Tenpin Bowling sign. It's fixed onto the external wall of the building."

"Do I just work on the weekends?" I ask.

"No. You'll be working every day after school and all day Saturday and Sunday. I need you there to translate the meal orders in the evenings."

I am unhappy with the prospect of working every day of the week. I will miss working with Ah-kor on weekends. *When will I have time to do my homework?* I know Ah-por desperately needs a steady income, though, and I know she needs my help to hold the job, because she can't speak a word of English beyond 'How are you?', 'good', 'thank you', and a few other simple conversational phrases.

Perhaps she has made a deal with the people who run the kitchen to ensure my employment as well. She is the cook and I am the kitchen-hand and translator. I don't know what the business arrangement is between the Bowling Alley and the two partners — Mr. Young and Mr. Mee Lee — who rent or lease the snack bar and dining section of the Bowling Alley. I didn't meet the partners until my first day working for them. It seems Ah-por has met Mr. Young before, but not Mr. Mee Lee.

The hours are long, because the Bowling Alley opens for business at nine o'clock in the morning and closes at twelve midnight. It operates seven days a week, except Good Friday and Christmas Day. My grandmother works about twelve hours a day, every day, from nine in the morning. I work four hours Tuesday to Friday — from five in the afternoon until nine at night—and twelve hours on Saturday and Sunday. Because Monday night is the quietest night of the week, it is agreed that I can have Monday nights off, and Mr. Mee Lee would help out instead. That gives me one evening to do my washing, ironing and other household chores.

My days are extremely long. I wake at seven-thirty, dress, skip breakfast, and walk down Terrace Street towards Brunswick Street, where I catch the tram to school. After school, I catch the Mt. Gravatt tram to Greenslopes and work until nine, and then we catch the tram back to the Valley, where we change trams back to New Farm. We seldom arrive home before eleven o'clock. I have a quick shower and go straight to bed. By then, I am dog-tired. I never have any trouble falling asleep. Although I have approximately eight hours sleep every night, I never feel fresh or energised when I wake in the mornings.

This pattern lasts only four months. When we move into the timber duplex in Orphan Street, Greenslopes, life is easier. Although I need to get up earlier to catch the tram to school, the distance to work is shorter. With less hours spent travelling, I can go to bed an hour earlier and I have an extra hour to sleep in the mornings on weekends.

The time I spent working in Chinese restaurants 'just for the experience' was as beneficial as Ah-por predicted. Perhaps she was right that money can't buy experience. Now, I consider myself to be reasonably competent working in a kitchen. More importantly, I have experienced long hours and hard work. I have met many Chinese cooks who are good, hard-working people. They send their hard-earned money back home to either China or Hong Kong, and they hope, one day, to reunite with their families in Australia.

Although I don't mind washing mountains of dirty dishes, pots and pans, emptying rubbish bins, and doing endless cleaning of benches, sweeping and mopping floors, this isn't the type of work that I want to do for the rest of my life. Nor do I want to own a restaurant. I don't find the work mentally stimulating.

With this steady job at Greenslopes, I can now plan my immediate future and set goals. My goal is to earn enough to pay for my own schooling and tertiary education. I hope for an education adequate to enable me to find a good job back in Hong Kong.

I calculate that by the time I finish Senior Year, I will have worked and saved enough to cover about three years of university fees, textbooks and public transportation. I believe the one thing that no one can take away from me is knowledge. In the past, I doubted my abilities, but not now. The negative things I witnessed when I was growing up in Hong Kong motivated me. Those images are etched in my mind. I will never allow myself to live in poverty, nor to do things that are morally wrong. Constantly reminding myself of our well-respected family name, I pledge never to disgrace it.

Some business owners employ overseas students on student visas and pay them at minimal rates. Overseas students are not supposed to have paid employment here. Both the business owner-employers and working students are breaking the law. To avoid trouble with the Immigration Department, business owners pay cash in hand. Payments are not recorded in a payroll. Mr. Mee Lee is a good man who puts me on the proper payroll and pays me weekly for every hour I work during the week.

I was paid a pound for a weekend's work at the dim sim factory. Now, I receive seven pounds for working forty hours a week. How much should I spend, and how much should I save? I learned, during my school days at St. Louis, how to budget. I must be very careful not to squander my earnings, because I don't know how long this job might last.

Having extra money in my pocket eases the fear of a life without prospects. It boosts my self-esteem and gives me a sense of self-reliance and independence.

I can handle the Chinese cleaver—for chopping up vegetables and slicing meat and chicken—without too much trouble. I now have to learn to make hamburgers, deep-fry fish and chips, and grill steak on a hot plate. I cook Western-style meals like steak and deep-fried chicken, and Ah-por cooks simple Chinese-style meals like chow mein, chop suey, sweet-and-sour dishes and fried rice. I also deep-fry cubes of fish, pork and chicken in batter for the sweet-and-sour dishes. For dessert, we offer banana and pineapple fritters—fruit rings deep-fried in batter and eaten with ice-cream.

The kitchen is hectic on Friday and Saturday nights. There are written meal orders that I translate for Ah-por to cook. I also organise table delivery, passing instructions to waitresses who serve at the tables. Hamburgers and chips are verbal orders only, so I have to remember the orders as waitresses call them out.

Working with Ah-por in the kitchen is no easy task. It seems that nothing is good enough. I am never patted on the back for a job well done, but she ear-bashes if my work isn't to her satisfaction. It is an old Chinese cultural thing not to praise youngsters because they might get big-headed.

Although this is supposedly a part-time job, I work forty hours a week. On top of my normal schooling, it is tiring, and, at times, depressing. Work, study and sleep are the only things I know. Lacking time to study is my main concern. It is difficult for me to perform well at school. I need the money to pay for education expenses, but to do well at school, I need time to study. My work schedule leaves none.

The generation gap, combined with my exhaustion, creates friction between grandmother and I. Being confined with one person day and night, except during school hours, is difficult to bear. Every weekend, long weekends, public holidays, and on Christmas and New Year holidays, I work in the kitchen. I look forward to those holidays ending so that I can go back to school for a rest.

There is no release. I have no friends or social life. Quite often, I ask myself if I might have been better off staying in Hong Kong. In Hong Kong, there would be no expectations from anyone. In Australia, I have this sense that I need to succeed, otherwise I will lose 'face' and be a disgrace to my family name.

♋♋

At the Greenslopes Spare Room Restaurant kitchen, there are four entrances in and out of the kitchen — the swing doors in and out of the dining room, a door to the front snack bar counter, a back door leading to the staff toilet and the car park; and another back door leading to the back lane-way connecting to the street. At about seven-thirty one very busy Thursday night, without a word of warning, two men burst into the kitchen through the lane-way back door. The shorter one is about five-feet-seven inches tall, of medium build, and neatly dressed in a dark suit and light-coloured shirt with collar and tie and shiny brown shoes. The other is nearly six feet, weighing easily three-hundred pounds, and a bit rough looking. I see the shadow of another man standing outside the back door to the car park. He seems to be guarding the door, making sure that nobody can get in or out of the kitchen without passing him.

"Who's in charge here?" asks the short, neatly dressed man. His voice is tough, but his look is not.

Eve, who does all the dishes and cutlery washing in the kitchen, points to the door leading to the front counter. Without a word, the short man walks toward the door, leaving the bigger man behind him, guarding the lane-way back door. With only thirty seconds of observation, I can tell this man is just trying to act and look tough. I suspect that, deep down, he might be a gentle person. He looks to be in his late thirties or early forties. He has dark brown hair with a few grey hairs. He wears glasses with a thick black frame that contrasts with his fair complexion. He has full lips, large ears, straight nose and a jutting chin. His voice and mannerisms are like those of a high school principal trying to prove something to his students. He leaves the kitchen and returns five minutes later. He then looks up to the big man and says, "Let's go." Both of them walk out of the kitchen and through the car park door where the other man is on guard. They signal to the third man to go with them. The three disappear into the darkness.

"Who are those people?" Ah-por asks Mr. Mee Lee.

"The short man in the suit is John Murphy, an officer from the Commonwealth Department of Immigration. The other two big fellows, the one inside the kitchen and the other outside, are from the Commonwealth Police. They were here to arrest any overseas tourists who either have overstayed their visas or are working illegally in the country. As you can see, they are not here to catch overseas students this time."

I breathe a sigh of relief.

I lived in constant fear of being caught working illegally on my overseas student visa. There are many stories—mostly from Sydney and Melbourne with their much bigger Chinese communities—of Chinese students being caught and deported back to Hong Kong. They come here to work and to earn money to send home, or to save enough to return home after a few years, with a small fortune. They probably hardly ever attended school, and they failed to meet the Department of Immigration requirements to receive a satisfactory school report from the school principal.

If I was caught, I hoped the Department would go easy on me due to my personal circumstances, and take into consideration that I do go to school every day and sit for the examinations every term.

That raid was my first meeting with John Murphy, the government enforcer. Although we weren't properly introduced, John was to have a major beneficial role in my future life.

FIFTEEN

GRADE EIGHT: WORK CHALLENGES

Until 1962, all primary school children in Queensland had to pass the State Scholarship Examination before gaining free secondary education. The State Scholarship Examination consisted of tests in English, Arithmetic, History and Geography. Provided students passed, they could move up to Sub-Junior and Junior, then Sub-Senior and Senior, and then matriculate. The State Government eliminated the Scholarship Examination after 1962. The Queensland Education Department also changed the system, and Grade Eight became the first year of high school education. The Junior and Senior Public Examinations were to be maintained.

My Grade Seven class divided into two Grade Eight classes. I am glad that Dennis and I are in same class — Grade Eight Gold. Our home room teacher for Grade Eight is Mr. Rogers, who is new both to our class and to St. James's. He is a slim, tall man in his twenties. He has the ability to capture students' interest and make learning fun. He takes us for English, Latin, Mathematics A and B, Geometric Drawing and Social Studies. A Brother takes us for Physics, Chemistry, and Christian Doctrine.

After twenty months in Australia, I have a reasonable grasp of the subjects. What I don't understand, I try to memorize, hoping I might be able to regurgitate the answers when necessary.

English studies are my biggest challenge. My problems with expressing myself continue. An English weekend homework task to write a three-hundred-word composition can take me at least three hours, and even then it is often still full of grammatical and spelling mistakes. I am unable to spell words without referring my English-Chinese dictionary. With a limited vocabulary, constructing good grammatical sentences is extremely difficult. After Mr. Rogers has corrected my composition, I re-write the work, incorporating his corrections, with sentences properly structured and without grammatical and spelling mistakes.

There are also novels to be read and poetry to be interpreted. I spend hours every night looking in my dictionary for the meaning of words. It is hard enough for me to master the English language, but when it comes to Latin, I have absolutely no idea. I learn everything off by heart, and I use my memory to get through Latin tests. For oral work, I use the homophone of Chinese words into Latin. My spoken Latin sounds more like Chinese.

In order to improve students' enunciation, a young woman comes in once a week to teach us phonics and to ensure that we pronounce words correctly. We go through tongue-twisting, breathing and sounding exercises with her. She demonstrates breathing exercises, like putting hands on hips and breathing in and out slowly. She takes us through the sounding exercises, which always give us a good laugh. We fool around as she struggles to control a class of teenage boys. We are more interested in how she looks and the way she moves her body than in what she is trying to teach us. It is a fun session, but unfortunately, it only lasts for one term.

With my work commitments at the Greenslopes Spare Room Restaurant, I can't set aside a minimum time for doing homework. There is no well-lit desk in a quiet spot. I do my homework whenever and wherever I can: during lunch times, or after school, or when riding on the tram. What I am unable to finish during the tram ride, I finish on the bench seat at the tram stop.

Students use brown school ports to carry books and stationery to school. The port is carried by a handle, like an enlarged brief case. It is strongly built, and many students sit on their port, with one leg on either side, like riding on a horse's back. I spread my books on the bench seat and use my brown school port as a desk to do my homework. Every school day, I hope the weather will be fine. If there is wind or rain; I have to set my alarm clock an hour early in order to finish the work indoors, before school.

After we move from New Farm to Greenslopes, I have to catch the tram to St. James's. On boarding the tram one morning, I move to the back of the carriage and peek through the small circular window on the door and see there is no one inside the driver's compartment. This compartment is an ideal place for me to do my study during my forty-five minute journey to school. I pull the door open and step inside. I think it must be all right for me to be inside there, because the tram conductor doesn't kick me out. He probably realises that I'm a hard-working school student making good use of my travelling time to do extra study.

I sit on a swivel seat, careful not to touch anything, especially the brass steering handle. I study my lessons sitting in the vacant driver's cabin, with an occasional peek out the windows to see what is going on along the journey. The constant ringing of the bell irritates. When a passenger wants the tram to stop, he pulls a leather cord to ring the bell once. One ding signals the driver to stop. When it is time to go again, the conductor checks that all passengers have disembarked and gives the cord two quick pulls. Ding, ding signals the driver to go.

Concentration at school is difficult without enough sleep. "Tom, why do you always look so tired? Don't you get enough sleep at night?" Mr. Rogers asks.

How am I supposed to reply? Should I lie to him, or tell the truth about working, knowing I am not supposed to work on an overseas student visa? I stare at him with my mouth open, but no words come out.

"Why?" he asks again.

"I work."

He seems surprised at my answer. "What sort of work do you do?" he asks.

My heart pumps faster. "In the kitchen at the Greenslopes Spare Room Restaurant, inside the Greenslopes Tenpin Bowling Alley."

"How often do you work there?"

"Every night except Monday, and all day Saturday and Sunday." I am concerned at letting him know too much. *Will he report this to the school principal?* "You tell Brother Harding?".

"No, I won't tell Brother Harding. Why do you have to work every night and weekends?"

"Grandmother works there and can't talk English. I translate meal orders and cook hamburgers, chips and steak."

"When do you do your homework?"

"On tram and tram stop seat."

"How do you cope with your school work?"

I can't understand why he asks me that question. It has never crossed my mind to think about it. I just do whatever I have to do.

"I don't know," I reply, shrugging my shoulders.

"No wonder you always look tired."

"You no tell Brother Harding." I plead.

"No, no. I won't tell him."

Mr. Rogers was the only person at school who knew about my after-school work.

♋♋

The name-calling, insulting and face pulling seems less frequent than last year, but I still get the occasional 'ching chong Chinaman'. One of the students in my Grade Eight class, Cliff, keeps asking me whether I have learned Chinese martial arts. I've told him many times that I never had, but he doesn't believe me. Perhaps he doesn't want to believe me. He wants to pick fights with me, to show his superiority. He teases me and insists that we fight to find out who is the better fighter.

Dennis and I have been in the same class since Grade Six. We have formed a close friendship, and we look to each other for protection. Cliff is aware of our close relationship and the protective arrangement between us. He seizes his opportunity one day when, for whatever reason, Dennis is away from school.

"Why don't you go back to the country where you belong, you Chinaman?" he says.

"Where you from?" I ask him calmly.

"What do you mean, 'where do I come from?' I was born here in Australia, you idiot."

"Which country your ancestors come from?" I ask.

He cannot answer. Either he doesn't know, or he realises that he is a descendant of someone who also migrated to this country. He starts hitting me all over my body. I am not well-built, so I feel pain every time my body is hit. He punches me in the stomach, because I have my arms in front of my face to protect my head. I hold my breath, with the air inside my stomach. He hits my stomach again and again. I just hold my breath, not making a sound. After a few more hits, he stops. He yells at the top of his voice, "Tom, you're such an expert."

I hope he will stop harassing me now.

༄

"I'll be leaving the School after Grade Eight and won't continue on," Dennis says.

"Why?" I ask, shocked by his announcement. I will miss our close friendship.

"My father is starting a Chinese takeaway shop. It won't do enough business to employ anyone at the start, so I need to work there full-time. My mother, older sister and younger brother are still in Hong Kong. We need to build up the business until there is sufficient income for my father to sponsor them to join us here. Eventually the business will be mine, so there is no point for me to study any further. Anyway, I quite like the idea of being an owner of a Chinese takeaway business."

"I wish you luck, Dennis. I must say I dislike the idea of working at least twelve hours a day, seven days a week, at a Chinese restaurant. While I have a chance, I'll keep studying. Hopefully, it will lead me to a professional career. Besides, I don't have an option because I'm on an overseas student visa and have to carry on with my study."

SIXTEEN

TWO TRIUMPHS

Mr. Rogers is the home class teacher of one of the two Sub-Junior classes. I am pleased to be in his class, Sub-Junior Gold. Eight subjects are offered in the Sub-Junior year: English, Latin, Mathematics A, Mathematics B, Geometric Drawing, Physics, Chemistry and History. Christian Doctrine is not an examinable subject for the Junior Public Examinations.

Our class studies only seven subjects. We don't do Latin, unlike the other class which is full of bright students studying all eight subjects. The majority of the students in my class have the same belief—that it will be difficult to get a good grade in Latin—and fear failing it in the Junior Public Examinations, so we all choose the stream that skips Latin.

Although I have now been in Australia for nearly three years, I still have difficulty with English. William Shakespeare's work is now my challenge. The play is *The Merchant of Venice*. My understanding of it is limited.

I don't write regularly to my mother. Since arriving here, I have written to her at least three or four times a year. I send her birthday cards together with a pound note, and I send a five pound note for her, Leung-gong and Leung-por on Chinese New Year.

I write, at the start of my Sub-Junior year, specifically to ask her to get hold of a Chinese version of the play and send it to me. Because I need it urgently, I ask her to send it by airmail instead of surface-mail. After reading the Chinese version, I have a better understanding of the story-line, but it doesn't help me with my analysis of the literary merits of Shakespeare's work.

After my lack of academic success back in Hong Kong, I have to work hard for everything. I have learnt perseverance, persistence and the discipline of a good work ethic. I am now in pursuit of a better future. I stay up late to study after work. I have fallen into a routine of sleeping, going to school and working, but I am happy with myself because I have an income and, surprisingly, my grades at school are gradually improving.

Mr. Rogers is again my English teacher, and he patiently corrects and explains my mistakes. English is still a struggle. I have little trouble handling the two Mathematics and Geometric Drawing subjects, but I don't understand Physics, Chemistry or History. I try to learn off by heart and regurgitate what I remember during examinations, as I did in Grade Eight. I also pay a great deal of attention to what the teachers say about preparation for examinations.

I try to guess the likely examination questions and focus on them.

◎◎

SATURDAY, 22ND AUGUST 1964

Today, Father, we move into our new home at Plimsoll Street, Greenslopes. With the help of our fellow worker, Wai-Kee — who works as a carpenter during the week and in the snack-bar section of the Greenslopes Spare Room Restaurant on Saturdays — we pack his utility vehicle with our little furniture and personal belongings, leaving the rental property at Orpen Street, Greenslopes and heading for our new address.

Ah-por purchased this property a month ago, for £3,250. Before the settlement, she borrowed £500 from Mr. Mee Lee, and she asked me for the £450 I had saved for my future education. She promised she would pay me back, but she has to repay Mr. Mee Lee first. She has been working seven days a week for the last sixteen months, and now she has turned her dream of home ownership into reality.

Wai-Kee stops his vehicle in front of the house. Looking at the front elevation from the street, the house reminds me of a picture I drew when I was in Primary One. There is a door in the middle, and a window on either side of the door. A concrete pathway leads from the front boundary chain-wire fence to a few concrete steps and a landing in front of the front door. The house could have been built in the 1950s. The external wall is clad with painted weather boards. There are signs of peeling paint. The roof is made of concrete tiles, with no sign of coloured coating. The tiles are dark grey, due to the built-up mould and dust embedded in the concrete.

The house is a rectangular box. The front section is the lounge and the large main bedroom. The back section consists of a dining room, kitchen, bathroom and second bedroom. The dining room and combined lounge form an L-shaped room. Next to the dining room, the kitchen has a back door to a flight of timber stairs leading to the backyard. The kitchen sink, with a built-in cupboard, is below the window sill in the back wall. Placed in the middle of the side wall, the cast-iron gas stove, with four gas rings and oven, is similar to the one we had at Gloucester Street. There is nothing else in the kitchen.

The bathroom features a vanity basin on the door-opening side of the room and, on the opposite side, a bath-tub and toilet. The floor is terrazzo, with a few cracks showing. Two walls above the bath-tub are lined to head-height with six-inch square plastic tiles in a checker board pattern. Next to the bathroom, the second bedroom has a built-in wardrobe. There isn't much room left after putting in a single bed and a small four drawer dresser.

A floral patterned carpet in the lounge and dining room nearly matches the floral wallpaper. The main bedroom is also wallpapered, but in a different style and pattern.

The floor in the kitchen, main and second bedrooms is linoleum, and shows early signs of cracking, in line with the timber board flooring underneath.

The house is built on concrete stumps on ground that slopes from front to back. A tiny room directly below the second bedroom serves as a laundry. There is nothing inside except a twin concrete laundry tub sitting on two cast-concrete stands. A hot-and-cold-water combination-tap is screw-fixed onto a timber noggin between two studs.

On the other side of the house, and directly below the dining room, is a single garage on a dirt floor. It is neither long nor wide enough to accommodate a 1964 EH Holden. Besides, there is no driveway. It would be difficult to drive up and down on soft, wet ground.

It is more appropriate to call the place a cottage than a house, but Ah-por is so proud. We fled China with nothing. Now, at age sixty, she has something. This little house is a symbol of her financial success and her triumph over adversity.

☙❧

I too, triumph. I achieve the unimaginable by becoming Dux of Sub-Junior Gold. After the announcement, a strange feeling haunts me. I should be happy and proud. But fear creeps in. *I was never a scholar, and now I have achieved academic success that I never imagined possible. Perhaps I am not as unintelligent as I thought. Do I really have the potential to be a scholar?*

Deep down, I know I can't sustain the performance for long. My achievement is the result of two factors: my memory served me well, and I managed to pick the right examination questions. I would have been a complete flop if I had gambled on different questions, or if my memory had failed me.

School Speech Nights are for parents and families to witness their children's successes at school and on the sports field. All the prize books, trophies and pennants are on display on stage at the Brisbane City Hall. Proud parents and families gather around the recipients and indulge in a brief, glorious fantasy. I am proud and excited by my academic achievement, but I am alone, with no family congratulating me. There is no point in telling Ah-por of my achievement, because I know there won't be any praise or encouragement from her. She believes that I've already had sufficient education. She would prefer that I go into the restaurant business rather than pursue an education.

Recipients receiving academic and sporting awards are told by Brother Harding to behave while queuing up for the awards. We don't want to embarrass ourselves in front of so many parents. Books are awarded to students for academic excellence and trophies for sporting achievements. Recipients were invited to choose their books prior to the awards evening. I know I'll be happy with the book *History of the World's Art* that I selected for my award.

Hearing — from back stage — the applause for recipients, I am so excited that I am afraid I might cry. My heart pumps fast. Although I queue up calmly and patiently, waiting for my name to be called, my body is saturated with perspiration.

The Archbishop of Brisbane, the Most Reverend Patrick O'Donnell, is giving out prizes, one by one. Perhaps it isn't the book prize, but rather collecting it on stage, that makes the experience so unique for me. I can see and hear the applause, but it is not from my family.

Would you have come to applaud me, Father, if you had lived? Would you have been proud?

The recipients are to sit with their families after receiving their prizes. Because I don't have anyone to sit with, I hide in the toilet to wait until the ceremony is finished. I sit there, thinking that my success could be just a fluke and I really don't have the ability to be a constant success academically.

Achieving Dux of the class gives me a sense of joy, pride, and self-confidence. But as one of the students from the brighter Sub-Junior class said to me, "What's so great about being the Dux of a dumb class?" I know I won't be able to repeat the achievement in my Junior year. Yet, having proved my capability, I put tremendous pressure on myself to continue to do well. How will I maintain the momentum? It isn't going to be easy to sustain such a performance.

Although thrilled, I shrink from the moment of truth, because I don't want to be the top of the class any more. Having reached the top, it would be a disgrace to fall.

How am I going to handle the situation if I cannot keep myself up there?

By the time I arrive home, Ah-por is already asleep. I know she is not happy with me for taking a night off work to attend the School Speech Night. There is no point in showing her my book prize.

༺ঙঙ༻

After working through the whole of the Christmas and New Year period at the Greenslopes Tenpin Bowling Alley, I am glad to be back at school for a physical rest. It is my Junior year. In November, all Junior students in the State are required to sit for the Junior Public Examination set by the Queensland Department of Education. The result for each subject is to be graded an A (first class pass), B (second class pass), C (third class pass) or N (fail). I need at least a C pass for all the required seven subjects to gain entry to the Sub-Senior and Senior years. More importantly, I am conscious that without a 'pass' grade for English in the Senior Public Examination, I won't be able to gain entry into University. To fulfil the requirements of all the Faculties of the University of Queensland, Senior English is essential.

I wonder who will be our home class teacher for the Junior year. Before the School assembly, at the beginning of the new academic year, I run into Mr. Rogers. We exchange greetings.

"Hello, Tom. How was your holiday break?"

"Good, thank you." I am embarrassed to tell him that I only had Christmas Day off. I even worked Mondays, because the busiest period for the Bowling Alley is the six-week summer break, when all the school students are on holiday.

"Are you carrying on to Senior after this year?" he asks.

I nod. "I need to. I am on an overseas student visa."

"What do you intend to study at the University?"

"I'd like to build things—roads and bridges or perhaps buildings."

"Civil engineers build roads and bridges. Civil engineering is what you need to study."

"Yes, civil engineering."

"Do you know you need a Junior standard in a language other than English in order to get into engineering?"

"I don't understand. Why?" I can't believe what I am hearing.

"It is one of the entrance requirements of the University, unless you do a course that doesn't require a Junior standard language."

"I do Chinese."

"I'm afraid Chinese is not an established subject in the Junior Public Examination."

I am at a complete loss to know what to do or say next.

"Let's go and find Brother Harding to see what he can do."

I am devastated. Head down, I worry about what might happen next. I worked hard the previous year to establish a routine of work and school work. But now?

Better to know the situation now than discover it at the end of the year.

"Well, Tom has to do Junior Latin this year," Brother Harding says.

"Are there any other alternatives?" Mr. Rogers asks.

"No. The only foreign language taught at this School is Latin."

Now I have to cram two-years' work into one year. It all seems too hard, but what other option do I have?

꩜꩜

Junior Latin is taught by Brother Harding, and I catch up my Sub-Junior Latin with Brother Purcell after school — for a half-hour, on a one-on-one basis. I seem to have forgotten all I learned back in Grade Eight. Besides, Grade Eight Latin was elementary — only an introduction to the subject. I remember 'amo': I love; 'amas': you love; 'ama': he, she or it loves; 'amamus': we love; 'amatis': you (plural) love in plural number; and 'amant': they love. I don't understand the language and I can't follow what is taught in class, because I am a year behind. I can't pronounce the words, so I use homophones of Chinese words into Latin, as I did back in Grade Eight.

I have absolutely no concept about the language, grammar or sentence structure. I simply recite the words off by heart. It is bad enough trying to cope with English, but now I have to do Latin as well.

My brain is going to explode! I wish I'd done Latin in the brighter students' class last year in Sub-Junior, so that I could cope with it better this year. But if I'd done that, I wouldn't have achieved Dux of the dumb class.

I fail. My first term Latin examination mark is 38%. I improve and manage to achieve a low pass — 59% — in my second term.

With the Public Examination getting closer, there is no way I will have time to prepare properly. I've heard people say, often, that you can achieve anything you want in life if you simply believe in yourself.

How am I supposed to believe in myself, Father, when all I have received most of my life is negative remarks? How am I supposed to think positive when there is nothing positive to think about? It is difficult not to have negative feelings. I want to succeed, but I don't know how to make it happen.

Everything is getting too difficult. I want to be free from studying and working altogether. I am tired from all the studying and working, and with the added pressure of the end of the year Junior Public Examinations, I am worried about my future. I fear failure. Do I have the strength to keep up with the work and study commitments through Sub-Senior and Senior?

♋

Despite bringing me to Australia for a better future, my grandmother offers no support or encouragement. She takes no interest in my education. At the same time, she has never put any pressure on me to excel in school, and never complained about me not working hard enough at my schoolwork.

Perhaps she thinks I am not the academic type? Perhaps she is right—that owning a Chinese restaurant would be a better option? But I won't entertain Ah-por's idea of owning a restaurant business. I like to build things. Becoming a carpenter seems to be a very attractive alternative.

Mr. Paul Neill started teaching at St. James's the same year as Mr. Rogers. Mr. Neill is the home class teacher for the other Grade Eight class. Although he has never taught me, he always shows a keen interest in my work and is never short of words of encouragement. I guess Mr. Rogers must have told him about my background, and he empathises with me.

"Let's go and find out whether you can be a carpenter," he says. "Meet me after school today."

At three-thirty, we leave the school grounds. I have no idea where he is taking me. We catch the tram to the top of the city and hop off at the tram stop just before the Victoria Bridge, at North Quay. A four storey sandstone building faces us.

"This is the Treasury Building. The Department of Education is in here somewhere."

I am not sure if he is mumbling to himself or to me. I just follow him wherever he goes. We troop in and out of different offices, and he stops and asks people questions that I can barely hear. After ten minutes of wandering around the building, we must have located the right place, because Mr. Neill asks a girl behind a counter a few questions, and she tells us to take a seat. She disappears. A minute later, she reappears, leads us towards a room, and signals us to go inside. A man sits behind a desk. He rises, extends his hand to Mr. Neill, and introduces himself.

"Please sit down," he says. "What can I do for you?"

"My name is Paul Neill, schoolteacher at St. James's Christian Brothers' School. This lad, Tommy Kwok, a student from the school, wants to be a carpenter. We're here to find out how he can get into carpentry," Mr. Neill says.

"The minimum age for any trade apprenticeship is thirteen. Is he over thirteen?" the man asks.

"Yes, he is over thirteen years old."

"The minimum education requirement is scholarship level. Does Tommy have that?"

"Yes. He'll sit for the Junior Public Examinations in two weeks' time."

"That's good," the man says, sizing me up. "Do you think he is capable of doing all the physical work—like heavy lifting—that a carpenter needs to do? There's a lot of heavy lifting, you know."

"I think he can. He is only a lad and he'll get stronger as he grows."

"Carpentry is a four year apprenticeship. Tommy will need to work under a qualified carpentry tradesman for the practical side of the trade and attend Technical College for theory."

"I am sure he'll be okay with that."

"Has he lined up anyone prepared to give him an apprenticeship?"

"No, he hasn't. Does the Department line apprentices up with tradesmen?"

"No, we don't. Your lad will need to find someone willing to take him on as an apprentice. Oh, by the way, is he an Australian citizen or a British subject?"

"Are you, Tommy?" Mr. Neill asks.

"I am not an Australian citizen. I was born in China and was a resident of Hong Kong, not a British subject. I am on an overseas student visa."

"I see. If that's the case, Mr. Neill, he can't be an apprentice. Students on overseas student visas are only able to study full-time at school or University."

"Why can't he study to be a carpenter? It's still study. When he's finished the apprenticeship, he can go back home to be a carpenter."

"No. The trade apprenticeships are for local lads only, not overseas students. That is the rule."

"That seems a bit ridiculous. Not all overseas students are scholars, and I'm sure some of them, like Tommy here, would prefer to learn a trade instead of getting a university degree."

"Overseas students are private full-fee paying students, unless they are on scholarships from their own Governments. Besides, all the apprenticeships are jobs for the local lads. Overseas students are not permitted to work," the man explains.

"Are you sure of that?" Mr. Neill asks.

"Yes, I'm sure. They are the rules. Sorry, there is nothing I can do to change those rules. Tommy just has to carry on doing his Senior and then university."

"Thank you very much for your time," Mr. Neill says. They shake hands, and we walk out of his office.

"Sorry, Tommy. You just have to keep studying."

"Thank you Mr. Neill. It seems I have to do more study to achieve Senior." We part, catching trams to different destinations. When I see him at school the next day, he smiles at me with discreet empathy.

SEVENTEEN

DOWN CAVENDISH ROAD

Four weeks before the Junior Public Examinations start, all the lessons for each of the subjects are complete, and there is nothing new to be learned. For the next two weeks, we are to revise what we have learned during the last Sub-Junior and Junior years and practise as many of the past examination papers as we can. During the last two weeks, we have mock examinations every day, using the previous year's examination papers. These mock examinations are carried out under strict examination conditions. There will be no more school after that, except on the examination dates.

‏🦀🦀‎

I am pleased to see my name in the newspaper showing the Department of Education, Queensland Junior Examination results. I have gained A's in geometrical drawing & perspective and mathematics A and B; B's in chemistry and physics (without fully understanding these two subjects), a C in English (where I thought I had done better than just a pass) and also a C in Latin, which I passed by sheer memory. It is a relief to know I have passed English and Latin.

With a C pass in English, I doubt that I can improve much more to pass at the Senior Public Examination. I have no confidence that I'll pass the subject, but at least I don't have to worry any more about Latin. I have a C pass, which is sufficient to satisfy the requirement to study Civil Engineering at the University of Queensland, provided I pass all the required senior subjects.

Students who complete Junior at St. James's have to say goodbye. As St. James's offers only up to Junior, they must now enrol at a new school to do their Sub-Senior and Senior years. Most classmates who are continuing on will enrol at St. Joseph's College. The School is located at Gregory Terrace, Spring Hill. Locally, it is known as 'Gregory Terrace' or simply 'Terrace'. It is one of the nine Queensland private Greater Public Schools that are exclusive and expensive. There are high costs for school fees, school uniforms and sporting gear.

St. Joseph's is further up Spring Hill from St. James's. Taking into account my forty hours work a week, a more expensive school and more time getting to and from school, I realise I'll be better off enrolling in a nearby school instead. Cavendish Road State High School is the logical choice. I hope I might be accepted as an overseas student, because it takes less than half an hour to walk from home, at Plimsoll Street, Greenslopes, to the school at Holland Park.

Two weeks before the new school year starts, I wait outside Mr. Churven's office. He is the Principal of Cavendish Road State High School. My heart pumps fast. If I am not accepted into this school, I'll have to go to Terrace.

Mr. Churven introduces himself and invites me into his office. "Please take a seat," he says. "Is there anyone else coming with you?" he asks.

"No." I reply. He is probably surprised that I have come without my parents.

"Before we start, what is your full name?"

"Tommy Looshang Kwok." I spell out my name slowly and he writes it down.

"Are you Chinese?"

"Yes."

"Date of birth?"

"16th December 1947."

"That makes you eighteen—nineteen at the end of the year. And you want to enrol at this school? Which class do you intend to enrol in?"

I tell him I finished Junior last year, so I wish to enrol in Sub-Senior at his school.

"How did you go in the Junior Public Examinations?" he asks.

"I gained A's in geometrical drawing & perspective and mathematics A and B; B's in chemistry and physics; and C's in English and Latin."

"Not a bad pass."

After going through the list of subjects on offer at School, he says, "I will allocate you to the appropriate class depending on what you intend to do after Senior."

"Civil Engineering at University of Queensland."

"I will put you in either the A or D class. To do Engineering, you need to pass English, the two mathematics subjects and the two science subjects: physics and chemistry. To be in the A class, you need to study a language, or you may prefer to study geometrical drawing and perspective, which is an industrial class subject."

"University of Queensland requires only a pass in a Junior language to study Engineering."

"If that's the case, you'll be in Grade Eleven D when school starts."

I ask Mr. Churven about school fees. I'm relieved to hear him reply that Cavendish High is a state government school, so no fees apply. I had to pay fees at St James. It's pleasing to consider how much I will save.

"Go and fill out the enrolment form and hand it to one of the school office staff," Mr. Churven says, smiling. "Welcome to Cavendish Road, Tommy. See you in a couple of weeks."

This is my fourth new school. It won't be easy to settle in.

∽∾

Established in 1952, Cavendish Road State High School is a co-educational school catering for grade eight to senior — grade twelve, the final year of high school. The last time I attended a coeducational school was my primary school, back in Hong Kong. Since then, I've been to two all-boys schools. In my primary school days at Hennessy Road Primary School, boys played with boys and girls played with girls. We seldom mixed except for class activities. I am apprehensive about striking up a conversation with any member of the opposite sex, especially a female classmate.

Wearing my new school uniform, I walk around and try to familiarise myself with the school grounds. The school has a number of new two storey classroom buildings, a sports oval under construction, and a large concrete-surfaced area for students to play basketball.

I look for a familiar face, but to no avail. It looks like I am the only Chinese student in the school.

The first bell rings about eight-forty. All students stop their pre-class activities and assemble on the concrete paved areas. This must be a school assembly, to be addressed by the school principal. I ask around until I find the grade eleven D class — an all boys' class.

Although my communication skills are improving, I am still reluctant to strike up a conversation with new classmates. I can't structure sentences together without sometimes using incorrect tense. I mix up gender and leave out prepositions. Students at St. James's thought that I talked funny — not 'joking funny' but 'stupid funny'. Combined with my Chinese accent, this makes it difficult for others to understand me.

After fifteen minutes of Mr. Churven's address, each class starts to walk towards their respective classroom. Our class follows Grade Eleven C, which is a coeducational class. The boys in that class seem to be politely letting the girls walk first.

The girls tuck their skirts up as high as possible around their waists, as if they are wearing mini-skirts. This exposes their legs, whether they are shapely or not. When we reach a flight of open stairs, a boy in front of me, yells, "Don't look up."

"Don't look up." Voice after voice echoes down the line.

The boys can't resist the temptation to look up, and I follow suit. I can't see anything peculiar on the ceiling, but one of my classmates points at the girls. The boys are looking up underneath the girls' skirts. Girls in front, on the stairs, are busily pulling their tucked-up skirts down from the waist. One girl shouts, "You guys are disgusting." I look up, feeling embarrassed to be dismissed as one of the disgusting guys.

"Let's see what colour your undies are," a boy calls. The boys laugh. I remain silent.

When we reach our classroom, our Form Master, Mr. Maher, is already inside. He addresses the class and informs us where each of our classes will be held. He warns us not to take more than five minutes to walk from our homeroom to the other rooms for lessons.

Mr. Maher briefly introduces each of the subjects, leaving the details to the subject teacher. English consists of two parts. Part one covers composition, comprehension and grammar. Part two covers the study of one Shakespearean play, two novels and a substantial selection of poems.

Mathematics I is the study of Algebra, Geometry and Trigonometry, while Mathematics II is calculus and mechanics. Physics and Chemistry cover both theoretical and practical work. There are two parts in Geometrical Drawing and Perspective. Part one is plane and solid geometrical drawing. Part two is perspective.

Mr. Maher draws up the weekly timetable on the board and asks us to make a copy. Every Wednesday, after big lunch, is devoted to physical activities and sports. The first period on Friday mornings is allocated to religious studies. He lists all the religious denominations on offer for that period. Anyone, who doesn't belong to any of the denominations listed, needs to spend that period at the library. Because Buddhism is not on the list, I'll be spending that period at the library. I'm pleased to have a little free time to study.

Mr. Maher finishes addressing the class in the first period. For the rest of the day, other teachers turn up to brief us about the content of their subject. The school day finishes at three o'clock, which gives me time to do some homework before I start work at five.

To find out how much more time I can save by catching the bus instead of walking back home, I catch the bus that travels along Cavendish Road. When I am about to take a seat near the front, I hear students sitting at the rear of the bus yell out, "Tom, sit back here. The front seats are for the girls." I look up to see some of my classmates at the back. A few girls are seated at the front and near the middle of the bus. I walk toward the back, not understanding why they wanted me to sit at the back when there are no other Cavendish Road girls coming on board.

Soon, the bus stops in front of a private all-girls' school, Loreto College. Now, I understand why the boys want me to sit at the back. The front and middle seats are unofficially reserved for the Loreto College girls.

Boys throw comments at the girls, hoping to start a conversation.

"Hello beautiful. How's school today?"

"Hi Sally, you look terrible. What's the matter?"

"Will you be on the bus tomorrow?"

"What are you doing this weekend?"

The girls pretend not to hear. Boys seem to enjoy teasing the girls. I can't decide whether the girls are annoyed by the comments, or whether they enjoy being the centre of attention.

The bus doesn't save me much time, but I enjoy the banter between the Cavendish Road boys and Loreto girls. Maybe I will catch the bus again.

On Saturdays and Sundays, I sleep until nine-thirty in the morning. It's a welcome change from the usual rising at seven. I feel deprived of sleep during the week, so I welcome the chance to catch-up. But I must be at the bowling alley by ten, for long twelve-hour work shifts.

Ah-por is still in her bedroom as I walk out the front door. Although we work at the same place, we seldom leave the house together. Even when we do, within a minute or so I am well ahead of her. Her old legs can't take the hills the way my young legs do.

༄༄

One Saturday night, I set the alarm clock for eight o'clock. On Sunday morning I am going to meet Karen Strutton's family. The Struttons live in the last house on Plimsoll Street. I normally wear my work clothes on weekends, but I put on fresh, clean clothes because I don't want to smell like hamburger and fried potato chips. I change as quickly and quietly as I can, hoping to sneak out the front door without Ah-por knowing. I don't need the Spanish Inquisition this morning.

I have just stepped out of the bathroom when her bedroom door creaks open. "Where are you off to so early in the morning?"

"Karen invited me to meet her family."

"Why?"

I step nervously from side to side as she probes my eyes, looking for lies. "I don't know why," I reply truthfully.

"You are not going somewhere else and using that as an excuse, are you?"

"It's eight-fifteen. Where would I go this early on a Sunday morning except church?"

"Well, don't be late for work. Make sure to be there by ten o'clock."

I stride toward the front door without replying.

"Do you hear me?"

☞☜

The Greenslopes Spare Room Restaurant has two sections — snack bar and dining. Twenty-year-old Karen has been working at the snack bar for about three months. Because Ah-por and I work in the restaurant's kitchen, Karen and I don't talk often, except to exchange a few words now and then when she brings in dirty dishes and glasses for washing. In our brief interactions, I learn a few facts about the newest member of our crew. A secretary during the week, she works Saturday for extra money. She's saving for an overseas trip to Europe. She also tells me that she dreams of becoming an air-hostess. She certainly has the look: perfect hips, bust and waist proportions. Her boyfriend, George, hangs around all day Saturday, waiting to take her out when her shift ends.

Karen can't believe I work in the kitchen after school from Tuesday to Friday and all weekend. "When do you take time off to have a bit of fun and to go out with friends?" she asks.

"I don't have the time. My grandmother needs me here to interpret. And she can't do all the work in the kitchen by herself."

"All work and no play make Jack a dull boy." Karen senses that I don't understand. "It is a saying that means that without time off from work, a person becomes both bored and boring," she explains.

It dawns on me that I am Jack. Working forty-hour weeks and going to school has, indeed, made me a dull boy.

"Hey, since we live in the same street, why don't you come around to my place one Sunday morning and let me introduce you to my family." She whizzes back to the snack bar, leaving me no chance to argue. Even though I agree, I have no intention of going. She is probably being polite, or she feels sorry for me. Tom, the boring boy. I decide to give her a few weeks. She will probably forget about the invitation.

She doesn't forget. She persists with her invitation. At every new invitation, I am able to find an excuse, because I prefer to sleep in. Also, I don't want to explain to Ah-por.

Eventually, Karen puts pressure on me by saying, "Tom, I told my parents last night that you're coming to meet them tomorrow morning about eight thirty. Don't let me down. Please?"

I consent, wishing she hadn't made such a commitment on my behalf.

☙❧

It is less than a five-minute walk from our place to Karen's. This is my first meeting with an Australian family in their home.

What am I supposed to say to them? Will they be able to understand my English? Why is Karen so keen to introduce me? How should I behave, so as to not make a fool of myself?

My mind keeps telling me that I can still back out. I can simply turn around and go home. I keep walking forward.

Karen's timber house sits on the corner of Plimsoll and Wylma Street. On sloping ground, half of its width is a couple of feet off the ground and the other half is on high concrete stumps. The area underneath has been excavated to adequate height to house their small sedan car.

The front garden is immaculate, with various types of flowers blossoming. The manicured lawn is like carpet. I have no idea of the names of the flowers, but anyone who walks past can see the owner has taken great pride in maintaining the garden. There is no garden at our place, and the lawn is dry, patchy and full of weeds. I am no green thumb, and even if I had time, I wouldn't have the patience to produce a garden and lawn like the Strutton's.

I unlatch a small single gate and walk up the concrete path leading to a flight of stairs to the landing in front of the entrance. I want to turn back, but I know that if I don't go through with this, Karen will never let me hear the end of it. I take a deep breath and ring the doorbell.

A young female voice calls, "There's someone at the door." The door opens.

"Hello. You must be young Tom? I'm Karen's mother. We've been expecting you. Pleased to meet you." She smiles widely, extending her hand.

My hands are all clammy. We shake hands. I don't know what to say except, "Hello, Mrs. Strutton".

"Karen, Tom is here," she calls, looking inside. "Please come in," she says, turning back to me.

"Thank you." I step inside. *Where should I go next?* I stand just inside the front door.

Karen comes to greet me. "Hello Tom. Good to see you. I'm glad you could make it this time. Come and follow me into the kitchen. We're having breakfast."

Mrs. Strutton leads the way.

"Dad, I would like you to meet Tom. He is the Chinese boy I've been telling you about—who works in the kitchen at the bowling alley. Tom, this is my dad."

"Pleased to meet you, Tom." Karen's dad extends his hand in friendship.

"Hello, Mr. Strutton. Pleased to meet you too."

"Please, just call me Fred in future."

In Chinese culture, it is disrespectful to call someone of an older generation by their first name, so I am reluctant to accept his request. He insists. I feel uneasy calling him by his first name. Perhaps, it is the way in western culture. I still have so much to learn.

"Lou, come and meet Tom," Fred calls. A younger girl enters the kitchen. "This is Karen's younger sister, Ann-Louise. We call her Lou."

"Hello, Lou. Pleased to meet you."

"Come and join us at the table," Mrs. Strutton says. "We're having bacon, scrambled eggs, grilled tomatoes and toast. Would you like to have some, Tom?"

An invitation to have breakfast with a family I have just met for the first time is unexpected.

"Oh, no, thank you. I've already had breakfast," I lie.

"Are you sure? Why don't you join us for a little bit?" she asks again.

The grilled bacon and toast smell so good my mouth waters. I wish I could build up the courage to accept her invitation. I have to watch the time. If I stay and eat, I might be late for work and have to put with Ah-por's nagging all day.

"Yes, I am sure. Thank you, Mrs. Strutton."

"How about a cup of tea then?"

"How would you like it?" she asks when I accept.

"With milk and two teaspoons of sugar please. Thank you, Mrs. Strutton."

I take a seat at the table. Fred asks, "Which school do you go to?"

"This is my first year at Cavendish Road State High School. I did my junior last year at St James's Christian Brothers School at the Valley."

Karen is quick to reply, "I went to Cav Road and finished my senior three years ago. You must be in sub-senior this year."

"Lou is also in sub-senior at Brisbane Girls Grammar School," Mrs. Strutton says.

The Strutton family are welcoming, and they put me at ease. We make small talk about school and work. Eventually, conversation turns to my family background. They are curious about my place of birth, when I arrived in Australia, and why I have to work so much. My life, to date, was short, but they listen with open hearts and minds. There are sympathetic remarks.

"Sorry to hear about your father."

"I feel sorry for your mother."

"Life must be hard for your grandmother in China."

"It must be difficult for you while you are growing-up."

"How can you cope with all this?"

All eyes are on me. I am the centre of attention — something I have rarely experienced. Tears well in Mrs. Strutton's eyes as I share my story. She reaches for a tissue to dry her eyes. Karen and Lou stare into their teacups. Fred smokes his cigarette. There is silence as my story sinks in. The quiet becomes uncomfortable. I think perhaps I've said too much and bored them. I sneak a peek at my watch. Half-past-nine. It is time to go to work, and perfect timing to escape an awkward situation.

"I'm sorry. I have to go now. Thank you Mrs. Strutton for the tea. It was nice to meet you all." I start toward the front door.

"It's nice to have met you too. Any time you need help or advice, you come and see me. I'll see what I can do, okay?" says Fred as we shake hands.

"Okay, Fred. Thank you."

"Please drop-by any morning while you're on the way to school. You're always welcome here. We're interested to know how things are going with you. I'm sure life will turn out better for you," says Mrs. Strutton, hugging me. I feel awkward, but gently put my arms around her for a few seconds.

"See you, Tom," says Lou.

"I'll walk Tom to the front gate," Karen says. "My mum and dad like you," she adds as we walk. "They really mean it for you to drop-by to let them know how you're getting on. Will you promise me you'll do that?... See you next Saturday, Tom. You take care."

Two hours ago, I didn't want to meet the Strutton family, but after their warm reception, I am glad Karen introduced her mum, dad and younger sister to me.

৩৩

After our first meeting, and over the next few months, I drop in to see the Struttons on occasion. Fred was a lieutenant in the Australian Army during the Second World War, but he seldom mentions his army experiences. After his honourable discharge from the army, he studied accountancy and property valuation. He worked for the Queensland Government in his thirties. After years of service, he was promoted to a senior position at the Queensland Agricultural Bank.

The Struttons show interest in my well-being and seem to care about my future. They always make me feel welcome in their home. I experience Australian family life, chit-chatting around the kitchen table while they are having breakfast. Walking to school provides the perfect opportunity for a short drop-in. Eventually, I become a regular visitor, popping in at least every two or three weeks.

My relationship with the Struttons develops so that, on a few occasions, I address Mrs. Strutton as 'mum'. She doesn't object. In fact, it makes her chuckle.

৩৩

Breathing is a little easier a week after I start at Cavendish Road State High School. The school days are shorter. Walking to and from school each day means life is not nearly as hectic. I have enough sleep every night. I now rise at eight in the morning, which still leaves me plenty of time to get ready and to get to school before nine. I even have time to change from school uniform to working clothes before starting work at the bowling alley. In the past, I was always conscious that my school shirts absorbed the kitchen's odours.

Although deep down we respect each other, the relationship between Ah-por and me is never cordial. Conflict is normal between us, because both of us are strong-willed. Sometimes, lack of sleep, fear of failure and concern about the future causes me to be on edge with her. It is like walking on eggshells. There is also the generation gap. She doesn't realise it is tough for me during examination periods. She hasn't even let me have time off to study for examinations. She is afraid that I might use the excuse of an examination to go out for a good time. I never would, because I am concerned about the prospect of failure. I understand her point of view, because she can't do all the work by herself, and she depends on me to translate in the kitchen.

My social life is practically nonexistent. I hardly ever attend any social functions — not even those organised by the school. At my age, other teenagers are out on Friday and Saturday nights at the local dance club or movie theatre, playing sports on Saturday and Sunday, or going to the beach with family. A few of my fellow Grade Eleven D students ask me, occasionally, to join them at the movies or to go out somewhere to have fun. They don't understand when I say, "No, I can't afford it". They think I don't have money to spend on outings, but really I simply can't afford the time. It is also still important to keep quiet about my working life. And I don't want them to think me odd and interested in nothing but money.

I avoid participating in talk about weekends and term breaks. I can't say, "Because it was a wet weekend, people decided to stay indoors and spend the time tenpin bowling, so the alley was busy and we ran out of bread rolls for the hamburgers." Or, "Because it was a cold night and a lot of people preferred hot food at the alley, I had to cook endless extra serves of hot chips." Had I been eager to tell them about my life, by the end of the long summer holidays I might have said: "The only day I had off was Christmas Day. I'm glad to be back at school for a rest."

My teenage life is simple, with a set routine — school, work and sleep. I am not unhappy missing out on a social life, because I am not used to going out with others. I am quite content with my monotonous life. I don't have unrealistic expectations of myself. Although I struggle to cope under the weight of examination stress, I've never had high hopes of doing well. All I want is a good enough pass to matriculate. Education is the only means for me to break the drudgery of working in a kitchen. I've convinced myself that, somehow, I will better my life.

My hard-earned money goes straight into my education, because it is my priority. It is far more important to me than material things. Friends go to picture shows, buy records and have the latest gadgets. Apart from my school uniform and work clothes, I don't buy clothing. It would be a waste of money to buy something I would never have the opportunity to wear.

Paying for my own schooling and saving for tertiary education is not easy. Australia changed from imperial to decimal currency on February 14th, 1966. University fees are now quoted in dollars. For a private overseas student, a four-year civil engineering degree costs at least a thousand dollars per year. Books, extra tuition, and transport, are extra. And living costs also, unless I live with grandmother, who won't charge me board.

Now older and more mature, I take full responsibility for my self-sufficiency. Having a steady wage for the last three years has given me a sense of financial independence. I enjoy greater freedom, without being extravagant in my spending. I have never felt that I had a balanced life, with physical, mental and emotional needs met. I don't have positive family interactions or family support, and I lack constructive and supportive friendships. I don't blame anybody. I recognise my circumstances and accept my fate. I make a conscious decision not to let my past dictate my future. I want to become the person I believe I was meant to be.

Although there are no tears, there is still a sense of trepidation.

Who am I meant to be, Father? Is it possible for me to overcome challenges and achieve my life goals?

ᏬᏬ

During the last couple of weeks in August, a Chinese man turns up at the bowling alley to see Mr. Mee Lee for a third time. He doesn't seem to be a friend of Mr. Mee Lee, because each meeting lasts no more than fifteen minutes. This time, the Chinese man seems happy when he leaves.

"He is looking for a job," Mr. Mee Lee explains to grandmother and me as we are about to walk out the back door. Ah-por waits to hear what else he has to say.

Is my job on the line after nearly three-and-a-half years of working here?

"I've decided to have him working here for four days a week—Monday to Thursday. You can work three days, Friday, Saturday and Sunday," he says to grandmother.

"What about my grandson?"

"He still has the job. Nothing is changing for him."

"When are we starting this new work arrangement?"

"The week after next."

Walking home, Ah-por says, "Fancy a man has actually pinched a job from an old lady. He should be ashamed. Perhaps he's just too lazy to work for the whole week." I sense Ah-por is upset about the arrangement, and I don't blame her. She has given Mr. Mee Lee nearly three-and-a-half years of loyal service without a single day off.

"I don't want you to work under him. I'll tell Mr. Mee Lee tomorrow that you'll quit the job after next week."

I can't believe what I'm hearing, but maybe my grandmother is right. I should quit, as a matter of principle. After I quit, Mr. Mee Lee will have to employ someone to take over my cooking duties, because this Chinese man won't be able cope with cooking meals, making hamburgers, and all the deep-frying.

Ah-por also quits working at the bowling alley kitchen a week after my resignation in mid-September. She starts working as a kitchen hand at the Oriental Restaurant in the Valley. Her working hours are shorter — eleven in the morning to eight at night. She is normally home an hour later, after catching the tram from the Valley back to Greenslopes.

A week after leaving the bowling alley kitchen, I land a weekend job for six weeks at Cathay Café, which has changed hands since I worked there back in 1961. I also secure a full time job at the Seahigh Restaurant in the city for six weeks over the Christmas and New Year period. I don't start until December, so I have six weeks to kill.

For a while, I am able to socialise with my classmates at weekends. Inviting them back to my place is out of the question. As soon as we moved to our Plimsoll Street home, Ah-por laid down the law that there would be no inviting anyone into the house. Not that it bothers me. I don't have many friends, and I don't have time for socialising. I've never had time to get into mischief, because my forty-hours-a-week job kept me fully occupied. I haven't been subjected to too much peer pressure. Fortunately, I have never got into drinking alcohol, smoking, gambling or any other bad habits. I keep myself on the straight and narrow. If I hadn't been working such long hours; I might have ended up in trouble.

Despite having been here for over five years, my conversational English still isn't good enough for social gatherings with my classmates. My cultural background and customs are different from theirs. There is nothing in common for us to talk about. I'm not into any of the sports the Australian kids like. I don't know any of the pop music by the Beatles, the Rolling Stones or any other music group. I don't fit in to the Australian teen culture and way of life.

⌒⌒⌒

1966 is the first year that I am able to attend an end of school year party with my fellow students. At the party, there are six boys from my Sub-Senior class and six girls from the Junior class. One of the girls plays host at her parents' house. After an hour of chit-chatting, listening to the latest hits, eating party food and drinking non-alcoholic drinks, someone suggests we play a game.

Six boys and six girls sit alternatively in a circle on a concrete pavement. In the middle of the circle, there is a bottle. It doesn't take me long to figure out this party game. Each of us takes turns to spin the bottle. When the bottle stops spinning, and the top points at someone of the opposite sex, the pair go around to the side of the house, where it's dark. If the bottle points at a boy, he spins again until it points at a girl. She will be his kissing partner. As it's the first time I've played this game, I don't know what I am supposed to do with the girl at the dark side of the house.

It is also the first time I hold a girl's hand. We stand there, in silence, and gaze into each other's eyes. She closes her eyes, as if waiting for something to happen. She is beautiful, with a well-proportioned body. Because she isn't wearing a bra, I see her erect nipples underneath her blouse. With my eyes closed, I land a kiss on her cheek. For a few seconds, the blood rushes to my face so intensely that I feel like an iron that is getting hotter and hotter. But she seems disappointed with my performance. She opens her eyes without smiling, and quickly re-joins the circle.

When the bottle spins again, one of my classmates picks this girl. Instead of taking her away from the crowd, he starts fondling her in the circle, as if they are alone. They are kissing and caressing. In the background, there is cheering and clapping from the others, urging them on. There is no resistance from the girl. With her eyes closed, she is surely enjoying the experience and the attention.

I thought such behaviour was for grown-ups, and I thought it could only be seen in the movies. I am embarrassed by the promiscuity of the Australian boys and girls, and by the physical contact. Although curious, I am concerned that I could be doing something I shouldn't. But I know what to do with the next girl!

"Come on you two, that's enough," someone yells at us. Somehow, we don't want to let go. Our cheeks close together, I feel her heavy breathing down my neck. Because she also isn't wearing a bra, I feel the softness of her breasts pressed hard against my chest. I have no doubt that she can feel my bulging manhood inside my trousers. As an eighteen-year-old, I have never touched someone of the opposite sex, let alone held one so close and tight. This behaviour is frowned upon in Chinese culture.

I cherish the experience. It was something I daydreamed about over Christmas as I worked in the Seahigh Restaurant.

EIGHTEEN

THE YEAR OF THE GOAT: MY LAST IN SCHOOL

My Sub-Senior results spiral downward, examination after examination, and now, in my Senior year, my prospects of passing don't look good. My self-esteem is low and my confidence is deteriorating rapidly. I am not as focussed as when I was in Junior.

I search for reasons for the drop in my school performance. Perhaps the public school system is not as strict and disciplined as private schools. Some teachers are only interested in the few brighter students in the class. The majority struggle with their school work and just drift along. A handful of students show no interest whatsoever in class. The classroom atmosphere is distracting. There are a lot of disruptions from those who are only filling in time so they can claim to have obtained a Senior standard of education.

ᏃᏃ

Chinese New Year, 1967, falls on Thursday, 9th February. It is the Year of the Goat. Ah-por is busy in the tiny kitchen, preparing food for our New Year Eve reunion dinner. With permission from the restaurant owner, she finished work in the afternoon, so as to have sufficient time to prepare the food.

My brother and I get together only once or twice a year. Although there are only three of us in the Kwok family, this New Year is the first time my grandmother, my brother and I manage to have the reunion dinner without school or work interfering.

My brother finished his Senior last year, and he still works for our little aunt at the dim sim factory. He also now has his driver's licence and has bought a second-hand car.

Ah-por has gone to a great deal of effort to prepare the dinner, and she enjoyed doing it. Perhaps she feels happy because her two grandsons have now grown up and are financially independent. Also—after years of hard work and saving—she is now the proud owner of this small, two-bedroom timber house. I hope she hasn't forgotten that she still owes me the money I had saved for my tertiary education.

Standing at the doorway between the kitchen and dining room, I ask her, "Do you need any help?"

"No. Just set the table ready for dinner. When is your brother, Lu Kee, going to be here?"

"I told him to be here at six. It is quarter-to-six now. He shouldn't be too far away. You're cooking too much for three people."

She is excited about this evening's gathering. She seems to have a talent for Chinese cooking. Perhaps it is because of the way she was brought up, in a Chinese village where women stayed at home, learning to cook, sew and look after the household. She told me that ever since she was a teenager, she has been put in charge of cooking for special occasions. She can prepare dinner for twenty to thirty people with ease.

"Have you thought about what we have been talking about lately?" Ah-por asks.

"Yes."

"Have you discussed it with your brother?"

"Let's not go into that again. You know I don't want to be in the Chinese restaurant business."

The relaxed look disappears. She throws her hands in the air. "What's wrong with having a restaurant business? Look at the money the owners can make. It is a good business to be in."

"I want an education. I'll be finishing Senior this year and I'll be able to go to university to study for a degree."

"What happens after you get your degree? Get a job and earn a salary. If you and Lu Kee start a restaurant now, work six years in the business, you'll be much better off financially than spending the next six years getting an education. I can't see the logic of your thinking. One can't make good money by working for someone else."

I explain, again, that Lu Kee and I are still on overseas student visas, and we are not permitted to have any type of business here unless we have permanent residency.

"I know that," she replies. "I'm going to open up the business and sponsor both of you here." She grins, as if she has won the argument. She busily stir-fries the sliced meat in the wok, and says, "Can you see what I'm trying to do?"

"Yes. I want to get an education while I'm still young. We can start a Chinese restaurant any time — now, in a few years, or ten years from now. It doesn't matter. I just don't want to miss the opportunity to get an education."

She declares that finishing Senior is enough education, but I protest, again, that I don't want to be in a restaurant business for the rest of my life. I need something more mentally stimulating.

Now she tries the silent treatment. She keeps cooking on the hot stove. She isn't impressed with my response. Having finished stir-frying meat in the wok, she takes the wok to the kitchen sink to wash and clean it, ready to cook the next dish. Through the back window in the kitchen, she sees Lu Kee walking up the back stair. She quickly unlocks the screen door to let him in.

"Have you two been busy cooking? Look at all this food. How can we eat all that? There are only three of us."

"It is okay," she replies. "It is Chinese New Year tomorrow. We need to celebrate the coming of the New Year with plenty of good health and prosperity."

A soup and five dishes are on the dining-room table: chicken and dried scallop soup, crispy skin-fried chicken, spicy salt king prawns in their shells, steamed coral trout with ginger, shallots and soy sauce, stir-fried shredded beef with vegetables, roasted pork with plum sauce. These are all her specialities.

"Let's eat," she says.

It is a pleasant dinner, with many symbolic dishes appropriate for the New Year. There will be plenty of leftovers. We toast one another for good health and happiness for the coming year.

Although she hasn't mentioned anything about opening a Chinese restaurant business during dinner, I know it is just a matter of time before my grandmother brings up the subject with Lu Kee. I have no intention of voluntarily bringing it up for discussion.

"I'm seriously considering opening a Chinese takeaway, then sponsoring you two to stay in Australia to work in the business. What do you think?" she asks Lu Kee at last.

My brother is silent. He shows no enthusiasm about her suggestion either. In Chinese culture, it's considered best to have one's own business. Working for someone else is never going to make you wealthy. Chinese believe jobs are for working-class people, and no one will ever get rich on wages. It is not surprising that Ah-por is keen for us to have a business.

I am compelled to say something, "Ah-por, I'm going to continue my education. If Lu Kee decides to take on the business, I'll help out, but I'll only work after school, the weekends and school holidays, just like I'm doing now."

"That sounds okay," she replies. "Lu Kee, are you going to take it on?"

"No. I'm not going to have a restaurant business. I'm thinking of going back to Hong Kong."

His announcement shocks me. I sense our grandmother is deeply disappointed. She dips her head. There is nothing for her to say. I am impressed that a sixty-one-year-old Chinese woman still has the drive and ambition to own a business, but without our co-operation, her dream is not going to become a reality.

☙☙☙

Ah-por has been my grandparents and my parents rolled into one, the crucial figure in my life. She nagged a lot and we argued a lot, but deep down, we respect each other. She was a stern disciplinarian and always insisted that whatever I did, I must to do it properly. Excepting for a brief period of crisis, when she foolishly gambled on casket tickets, she was always careful with her money, and never squandered it. She is also a very warm and human person. She is intelligent, and not afraid to make hard decisions. I have inherited some of her characteristics. Living with her has taught me the value of hard work and not to take anything for granted. Therefore, I am able to cope with all of life's challenges. Her teaching has strengthened me and given me a 'never-give-up' spirit.

I received no praise—only criticism—from her. As far as she is concerned, I am not capable of doing anything right. It was never her way to praise me, in case I might become too big-headed. Despite all the frictions between us though, we have developed a caring relationship. There was perpetual confrontation between us, but we overcame it, if for no other reason than that she is my grandmother. The Chinese tradition is to respect one's elders, right or wrong.

I am unable to communicate with Ah-Por. First, there is a huge generation gap of over forty years. I can't confide in her about anything, because she lives in the old customary way, as if she is still back in China. As an individual with intelligence, I want to do my own thing, but she always looks at me as her little grandson. She could never understand my moods during my adolescent years.

I was deprived of a teenage life. I never had the chance to really let go without feeling some sort of guilt. But despite numerous fights and arguments, I don't intend to leave home and let her live on her own. My conscience would not let me do that. I would feel guilty.

She has never discussed what I would like to do in life. As far as she is concerned, having one's own Chinese restaurant is the ultimate success. Having worked in restaurants since my arrival in Australia, I have become tired of it. I can't see myself continuing that line of work for the rest of my life. I have an opportunity to get an education, and I want to give it a go. Ah-por, however, insists that I won't become wealthy by working for someone else. To be wealthy, one must own a business, no matter how small the business might be. I understand her thinking, but I can't agree. More to the point, I don't necessarily seek wealth. I seek security, comfort and personal satisfaction. In Australia, I believe there are many opportunities to achieve my goal.

༄༅༅

In May, my senior year classmate, Eugene Simpson, suggests that we should try to get a casual job at the *Sunday Truth* newspaper on Saturday evenings. I never get around to asking him how he found out about it. With Eugene leading the way, followed by his younger brother, Ernest, who is in the class behind us, we take the tram from Greenslopes to Fortitude Valley and walk a short distance to the *Sunday Truth* newspaper building on the corner of Brunswick and McLachlan Streets. We arrive at six-thirty.

"We can't get inside unless we get the job," I say, pointing at a sign on the wall that reads, "NO UNAUTHORISED PERSON ALLOWED BEYOND THE ENTRANCES".

"There must be two entrances. I guess one is here in Brunswick Street, and the other is around in McLachlan Street."

By about seven o'clock, a crowd is building up and there must have be at least fifty people waiting at each entrance. The three of us have no idea what is going on.

"Shouldn't we be queuing up or something?" I ask.

"Obviously not. There is no line, and everyone seems to be just hanging around near the two entrances," Ernest replies.

"This is bloody hopeless. Like back in the 1930s, during the Depression. A man gets a job by the luck of the draw," Eugene whines.

"Hi, Guys. I'm John. I couldn't help but overhear. Are you trying to get night work here?"

"Yes," says Ernest. "This is my older brother, Eugene, and he's Tom. What are we supposed to do?"

"There isn't any rule. I've been working here, on and off, for the last three months. There are two foremen on duty every Saturday evening. No one knows which one is going to do the picking or from which of the two entrances," John explains.

"Why do they do that? Wouldn't it be easier for them to get a team of permanent workers?" Eugene asks.

John explains that they need about sixty people for the night. Forty are classed as permanent, because they've been coming for quite a number of years and turn up practically every week. They need another twenty men—called 'floaters'—who come and go and are very unpredictable. Besides, the foremen want to keep them on their toes so that they don't get too complacent. If any of the floaters don't perform well on the night, they won't get picked again.

"Can't see the logic behind it," I say.

"All the so-called permanent workers, including myself, already have full-time jobs during the week and we work here for a little bit extra. How many people would want to start work from seven-thirty on a Saturday evening and finish at half-past-four on Sunday morning? It upsets the rhythm of daily life. You'll see once you start. You can wipe the whole of your Sunday off. You will see later, that most of the floaters are made up of guys on the dole, alcoholics, and the homeless. It doesn't surprise me that there are even some drug addicts here. What are you boys doing here?"

"I'm trying to make some money to put myself through school and, hopefully, university. My friends need some pocket money," I reply on behalf of the three of us. "If you don't mind me asking, what's the job about?"

John sucks the cigarette that hangs from one side of his mouth.

Eugene replies that a friend of the family told him that the *Sunday Truth* was looking for casual workers for their Saturday evenings. "So here we are," he says. "We haven't a clue what the job is. Is it something to do with carrying newspapers?"

John explains patiently that during the week, on Wednesdays, the *Truth* prints all the advertisements first. They're stacked underneath the benches. The *Truth* prints the Sunday newspaper on Saturday evening, and into the early hours of Sunday, for distribution all over Queensland.

"Our job is to insert all those pages of advertisements inside the newspapers prior to delivery and distribution," he says.

"Sounds simple enough," I remark.

John continues, "Thirty men do the carrying while the other thirty do the inserting. Each man does half-an-hour carrying and rotates with a man behind the bench for half-an-hour of inserting. There are fifty copies of the newspaper to each bundle. You need to carry a bundle of the newspapers from the printing press to the working bench and then carry the bundle with the advertisements to the dispatch."

After puffing on his cigarette, John continues, "After our seven-thirty start, we have a forty-five minute break, at quarter-past-midnight, starting again at one o'clock. You can get something to eat across the road at the fish and chip shop. It'll be open until one-thirty." John points at the shop across Brunswick Street.

"Thanks for all the information. I've been wondering where we could get something to eat at midnight," Ernest says.

John urges us to make sure we get something into our stomachs during the break. The first session is okay, getting all the lightweight newspapers for north Queensland ready to be shifted up there by plane. After the break, they use the normal paper. A bundle of fifty copies, together with the inserted advertisements, weighs about fifty pounds. This is the time when all those permanent guys start their wrangling games. They'll make newcomers spend more time carrying and less time inserting.

"It will feel like an eternity until knock-off time at half-past-four in the morning," John warns. "Well, good luck! Hope you all get jobs. I'm going to get a pack of cigarettes."

"We have to think about how we're going to get in," Eugene says.

Ernest has an idea. "How about, instead of hanging around together in a group, we spread out? I'll stand here at the corner. Tom, you stand at the Brunswick Street entrance and Eugene at the McLachlan Street entrance. One of you signal me once the picking starts and I'll wave and signal about which entrance to get to quick."

"Good thinking!" I exclaim. "It's quarter-past-seven. Let's get in position now. Hurry."

The crowd starts moving closer and closer to the entrance. The person behind me is breathing down my neck. Soon, we are standing very close and tight, like sardines in a tin. We all try to catch the foreman's eyes, to ensure we don't lose eye-contact when the time comes.

Some of the people around me appear not to have washed for days. I gasp in a breath of fresh air whenever I can. Cigarette smoke and alcohol is emanating from several of the queueing men, making a cocktail of foul odours that makes me nauseous.

What am I doing here, surrounded by all these people?

I wish the foreman would hurry up and pick all the men he needs for the night.

At last, I see Ernest signalling me to go to the McLachlan Street entrance. Thank goodness.

"You, you, you," the foreman says, pointing. "You ten stay, the rest of you — thanks for coming. There are another ten workers being picked at the Brunswick Street entrance."

We've missed out. After listening to that chap's talk, I'm not sure I want the job any more.

"I don't know how much we are going to get for the night's work. Let's assume it is about ten dollars. We need to spend a dollar something for food and drink. Sharing the taxi fare to go home after work will probably cost us another dollar-fifty each. That leaves eight bucks. So it works out a dollar an hour, and that's not bad. I reckon we should come back next week and give it another go," I say.

Ernest and Eugene agree. We are walking around the corner toward Brunswick Street when a voice calls us from behind. It is the other foreman, "Where were you? I've been looking for you guys. I wanted to give you a start tonight. See how hard you can work."

"We thought all the pickings were at the McLachlan Street entrance tonight," Eugene says.

"Will you be here next week?" the foreman asks. "Come back next week. I'll give you guys a start. I'll recognise him." The foreman points at me. It pays to look different sometimes. He recognises me because I'm the only Chinese here looking for work.

The main problem working at the *Truth* is that it upsets the normal daily routine of my life. I finish the shift about five o'clock in the morning on Sunday. By the time I get home and spend time in the bath, it is almost six in the morning when I finally get into bed. I have to clean myself from head to toe, because every exposed part of my skin, nostrils and hair is covered with a fine film of black ink vapour. The noises of the printing presses are so loud that we can't hear ourselves talk, even if we shout at one another from just a foot apart. Even lying in bed, I can still hear the noise of the printing presses rattling in my head, as if I've been brainwashed. After a while, I manage to relax and doze off, but before long the sounds of mowers start to echo around the neighbourhood. It is impossible to sleep.

Although I wake at two in the afternoon, I still feel tired. I don't feel like doing anything, let alone studying. It takes until Wednesday for me to feel normal again.

I mention my predicament to Eugene and Ernest. I discover they feel the same way. We agree that to be in bed at two seems all right, but to not get to bed until six in the morning upsets the rhythm of our bodies. The job at the *Truth* only lasts three months. Our final shift is the last weekend in July. I secure a job at the Seahigh Restaurant for the August school holidays.

♋♋

In the last term before the Senior Public Examination, my results are worse than before. If it had been the Senior Public Examination, I would have failed to matriculate. My goal to get a university degree is fading. I am losing heart. Doubts chew away at my confidence. A constant fear of failure plagues me.

To concentrate on preparation for the public examinations, I decide not to find another job after I finish working at Seahigh Restaurant for the two week August school holiday.

As preparation for the Senior Public Examination, which is set by the University of Queensland, we spend the last term revising what we have learned for the last two years and working on past examination questions. At the Junior Public Examinations, I relied on my memory to get reasonable results. At the Senior level, I doubt that I can depend on my memory without a true understanding of the subjects.

ॐॐ

A week before we start our Senior Public Examinations, during a closing address to all the senior classes, the student guidance officer says, "Half of all you senior students will be in the workforce after matriculation, whether you pass or fail. Of the remaining half, some of you will gain apprenticeships in trades, some will get into Teacher Training College, and some of you will continue on to get a tertiary education at the University of Queensland or the Queensland Institute of Technology. Whether you take an academic, a professional or an industrial course, on behalf of the Queensland Education Department and myself, I wish you all the very best of luck in your examinations and future endeavours."

There doesn't seem to be much pressure on everyone to succeed in this examination. All the senior students have a similar attitude. If they can't get in to do this or that, they will just get a job. If I fail to matriculate, it could mean going back home to Hong Kong. I might be branded a failure and a disgrace to the family.

I have mixed feelings. I am glad school is finally over, but I am worried that I have now lost the security of being at school. I had hoped I would matriculate and be able to extend my overseas student visa. I don't think many of my fellow Grade Twelve D students intend to go on to further study.

At the end of the year, all senior students, in particular the male students show their delight at walking out of the school gate for the last time. Some of them tear up their school shirts. Others throw them into the rubbish bins. Some mutilate them with scissors. One student even burns his with a cigarette lighter. A small crowd gathers to see it burn. Perhaps they are trying to let off steam after twelve years of schooling, or they might be trying to prove that they are no longer schoolchildren.

Walking out of the school gates, I reflect. Academically, I should have done better during the last two years. I have other regrets too. I was never into sport. During the Wednesday afternoon sporting sessions, I felt intimidated by the other students. They were taller and much heavier than me. I was in the school open soccer team when I was in Sub-Senior, but I was always in reserve. I played on the field no more than twenty minutes over a couple of games. I wasn't wanted in the team because I never turned up at training after school, due to my work commitments. In my senior year, I invented some personal health issues to avoid participating in physical activity, and I spent sporting afternoons in the school library, studying.

There were army, air force and navy cadets at our school. They wore their respective cadet uniforms every Friday for after-school training and activities. I intended to sign up as an Air Force cadet, but changed my mind when I was told that I should have joined in Grade Eight. I wasn't too keen to mix with those thirteen-year-old students. In any case, I wasn't able to stay back on Friday afternoons for the activities.

With no academic brilliance or sporting prowess, or outstanding contribution to outside school activities, I was never a prefect nor a leader of any sort. But a few months before the end, I did make a small contribution to the school. It was on the Friday before the 1967 school fête. After the principal made his usual address at school assembly, he called me up to talk about my offer to run a Chinese food stall. I didn't know what to say. There I was, in front of the entire school, looking down on a sea of students. All their eyes were fixed on me. I was completely frozen and not able to utter a single word.

Those few frozen seconds seemed like an eternity, until the principal came to my rescue by whispering in my ear to tell everyone of my offer. I muddled through, making a speech to the whole school, telling everyone that I intended to raise some money for the school by selling Chinese food. If they wanted take-away, I invited them to bring a billy-can, because the stall would only provide paper plates and plastic forks. There was laughter all around.

The stall was in the home economics classroom, which had preparation benches and a stove. I spent hours that morning, chopping and preparing. Although the classroom wasn't ideal for preparing and cooking a large volume of food, between eleven-thirty and one-thirty, six female Home Economics students and myself managed to produce chow mein (with a choice of either chicken or prawns), sweet and sour pork, and fried rice. Trade was brisk, and even some of the teachers came and enjoyed my cooking. Parents and teachers couldn't believe that a senior student was capable of producing such a large quantity of delicious meals during a two hour lunch period. They couldn't know that I had been slaving in a kitchen after school, weekends and school holidays, for all of my high school years.

The Chinese food stall was a huge success. It was one of the top money-spinners of the school fête that year. Before this event, I was just a quiet Chinese student in senior 1967. Afterwards, every teacher and student in the school knew my name and acknowledged that I cooked delicious Chinese meals at the school fête. I became an instant celebrity.

For my personal memento of the school, I managed to get nearly all of the teachers at Cavendish Road State High School — including the Principal, Mr. Churven, Deputy Principal, Mr. Mayze, and the Principal Mistress, Mrs. Godfrey — to sign my autograph book.

NINETEEN

CHRISTMAS CHALLENGES

"Hello Mr. Lee, this is Tom Kwok here," I say on the phone.

"Yes, Tom?"

He obviously remembers me from my work over the August holidays, when most Brisbanites were going to the Royal Queensland Show.

"I finished my final examination paper this afternoon. I'm on school holidays now, so I'm ready to start work."

The Seahigh Restaurant was on the verge of changing hands. When I was introduced to the future owner, he promised me a job for two months over the Christmas and New Year period, and I was keen to get started.

"Oh. Sorry Tom, I don't need you anymore."

What happened to good old-fashioned promises?

I protest inwardly while thanking him. My panic at being unemployed is, I suppose, not his problem.

I hang up the phone, deeply disappointed. *Why hadn't he let me know earlier? Maybe I should have checked with him a month earlier.*

After my anger and disappointment subside, I realise there is no point being upset. I am not going to sit around and wait for someone to give me a job. I devise a simple plan—hit the road and knock on doors. Having worked at various Chinese restaurants and the Greenslopes Spare Room for nearly five years, the logical step is to target the Chinese restaurants in Fortitude Valley and the City. But there are no vacancies in any. They all seem to have enough hands for the Christmas and New Year holiday period. I am too late.

On the way back home to Greenslopes, I decide to call into the Greenslopes Military Hospital. My next-door neighbour, Mr. Bill Gamack, a veteran of two World Wars, has taken ill. I fill him in about my day of fruitless searching. Although he can't do much about it, he lends a sympathetic ear. I feel much better after letting out my frustration. He wishes me luck.

୬୬

I have never ventured outside the Chinese restaurant community for work before. Despite having a senior education standard, I have a great fear of speaking English. I worry that people will misunderstand me, due to my accent. I still struggle to pronounce unfamiliar English words. Nevertheless, I resolve to build up courage to start asking at the city's Western restaurants for a job.

"Do you need anyone to work in the kitchen?" I ask one restaurant manager.

"No, not in the kitchen. But we do need someone to wait on tables. Do you have any experience as a waiter?" he asks.

Surely it can't be that difficult taking orders and putting meals on tables. Although I haven't actually worked as a waiter, after working at the Greenslopes Spare Room for three-and-a-half years, I know what to do. But because I have no experience, he will not employ me.

"I am looking for a job during the Christmas and New Year period," I say to the next restaurant owner I approach. "Any job... kitchen hand or waiter."

"We already have enough people working in the kitchen. I might have a job for you as a waiter. How soon can you start?"

"I can start tomorrow," I reply, with a touch of excitement.

I've done it. I've landed myself the job as a waiter.

"Your shift will be from five to ten o'clock. I want you to come at three tomorrow afternoon to do training, and we'll sign you up as a causal worker. You won't be paid for those two hours of training. Is that okay?"

I wasn't concerned about not being paid for the two hours of training. I was glad to have a job.

"I want you to wear a white shirt, a pair of black or dark grey trousers and leather shoes. Any problem with that?"

I don't have a white shirt, but I'm happy to go and buy one now. He assures me my dark grey school trousers will be satisfactory. I promise to be there at three next day.

"Wait... Wait, Tom," I hear the owner call. "Do you have any experience serving drinks?"

"No."

"If that's the case, I can't give you the job, because my waiters need to know how to serve drinks. Sorry."

"Show me and I'll learn."

"Sorry, Tom."

A minute ago, I had a job. Now I'm back to square one.

Five more days of unsuccessful searching follows, so it is time for me to take stock and try something different. I decide to try my luck at the largest grocery store in the city—Woolworth's Food Fair. I believe the store employs casual staff during the school summer holiday period—usually high school students sixteen years old or older.

"May I help you?" a teenage girl behind the candy bar counter asks.

"I'm looking for a job."

"I don't think Woolworths needs anybody at the moment. But wait a minute, I'll check with the section manager."

"What sort of job are you after?" the section manager asks.

I explain that I have just finished my senior year, and I am looking for a casual job during the summer holidays.

"Sorry. The store selected its casual employees during the month of October and they started work in late November. We have enough casuals and you're too late. Applications open next October."

My next step is to try my luck with five retailers in the city: Bayards, Penneys, Allan & Stark, Trittons and

McDonnell & East. I walk into Bayards and approach one of the sales staff.

"Sorry! We don't employ casuals. Only permanents."

Next stop is Penneys, and I lie to one of the sales staff. "I'm looking for a permanent job."

"Sorry, there are no permanent positions vacant, but we are looking for a casual," he replies. I can't backtrack, because he might sense that I lied about looking for a permanent job. It wouldn't reflect well on me. I go to Allan & Stark and ask the same question of one of the staff.

"Sorry, there is no job here."

I only need someone to give me a chance. I walk down George Street and head toward McDonnell & East. This time, I am going to see the manager. He will not only know of any positions vacant, but he will have the authority to hire me. I remind myself to be polite and humble, and I take a deep breath.

"Do you need any assistance?" one of the sales staff asks.

"I'd like to see the manager."

"What about?"

"I'm looking for a job."

"I'll see if he's available." He walks toward the offices at the back of the store, quickly returning with a smile on his face and pointing at one of the offices at the back. "You can go and see him. His office is on the left."

I knock on the open office door and a middle-aged man looks up and invites me in. "You're looking for a job? What sort of job you are looking for?"

"Any job."

"We do need a cleaner, but it's a night-time job to vacuum the carpet and to clean and polish the vinyl floor after the shop closes. It takes about five to six hours to do the whole store."

"I'm happy to give it a go.'

"Have you worked as a cleaner before?"

"No. However, I've been working in kitchens and I did a lot of cleaning there."

"But this is different. The cleaner needs to know how to operate commercial cleaning equipment such as a vacuum cleaner and a vinyl cleaner and polisher."

"It shouldn't take me long to learn to operate your equipment."

"Sorry, we need someone experienced. The cleaner has to work on his own at night and must know how to operate the equipment."

So I even need experience for a cleaner's job? How difficult would it be to operate cleaning equipment? I thank him for his time.

Not too far away from McDonnell & East is Trittons. I use the same technique and ask to see Trittons' store manager. He looks at me and, by the look on his face, he is considering something carefully as he sizes me up and down. After a minute or so of silence, he says, "There is a vacancy in our storeroom".

Is it my lucky day after all?

He continues, "A storeman's job requires some heavy lifting and you're of very small stature. I don't think you would have the physical strength to handle the job. I wouldn't want to see you getting hurt. Sorry, I don't feel that giving you the job is the right thing to do."

I have to admit he is right. I am a very small guy, and not really built for any physical work, particularly heavy lifting.

Preoccupied with job hunting, it must have been over a week before my next visit with Mr. Gamack at the hospital. He tells me he is getting better, but still there is no definite date for his release.

"I still haven't found a job," I confess, downhearted. "I've tried all the Chinese restaurants in the Valley and the City, a dozen or so Western cafés and restaurants, Woolworths Food Fair, Bayards, Penneys, Allan & Stark, Trittons and McDonnell & East. I just can't understand it. Christmas and New Year is the busiest time and I didn't expect any trouble getting a casual job. Maybe I'm too late applying."

"Never mind, Tom. Let me congratulate you on your persistence. Don't give up. Keep trying and you'll find a job soon."

Mr. Gamack seldom talks about his experiences in the two World Wars. Life must have been very hard for him, fighting in the First World War as a teenager and again in the Second World War, when he had to leave his wife and young children behind in Australia. What I have been through over the last two weeks is insignificant compared to his experience. This thought not only motivates me, but also gives me the inner strength to carry on searching.

"Mr. Gamack, I won't give up. I'll keep soldiering on to battle rejections, fear, despair and frustration. I believe every rejection is a step closer to getting that job."

"That's the spirit, little mate."

All the rejections haven't dampened my spirit. As long as I keep to my schedule and keep knocking on doors, something is bound to happen. It's just a matter of time. As long as I try, I'll be satisfied that I have done my duty for the day, even if a job eludes me.

"It's getting late — nearly half-past-eight — so I must let you rest. I'll come and see you in a few days' time, if you are not home before then."

After nearly two weeks of disappointment, I make a decision to be positive, starting from the moment I wake up each morning. I determine to start each day by telling myself that someone will give me a chance that day.

I get off the tram at South Brisbane and find my way to the Peter's and Paul's Ice-Cream factories in West End. There's a sign across the front gate of both factories: "CLOSED FOR THE FESTIVE SEASON, MERRY CHRISTMAS AND HAPPY NEW YEAR".

It won't be a happy New Year for me if I don't find a job soon.

My next attempt is at the Coca-Cola factory in James Street, New Farm. I meet with the same disappointment. It finally dawns on me that most of the manufacturing factories are probably closed for four weeks during the Christmas and New Year period.

There are quite a number of small manufacturing factories around the back streets of Fortitude Valley. Some of them are closed for the festive season, while others are still open for business.

"Looking for a job?" asks a small factory owner.

"Yes, just for the Christmas and New Year holiday period. I'm prepared to do anything, so long as it is not too physically strenuous."

"Yes, I see what you mean. You're not a big guy. Maybe tidying up the workshop and cleaning the factory floor?"

"I'd be happy to do that."

"Why are you just working during the holiday period?"

"I finished my Senior Public Examination two weeks ago, and I'm waiting for the results to come out. If I matriculate, I'll be going to University next year."

"Oh. I see. Well, well." He seems troubled by something. "With your Senior standard education, you should be aiming for something better. I only got to scholarship standard. With your intelligence and high standard of education, I wouldn't give you a job even if I had one. I'd be ashamed to offer you a job as a cleaner."

No matter how hard I try to convince him, he refuses to give me a chance.

☙❦❧

"Yes, I'm looking for someone to do the deliveries. Are you familiar with the Valley and city areas?" says the owner of a small manufacturing business in Fortitude Valley.

I have no car and no driving licence, although I have a learner's permit. The only means for me to get around is by catching the tram from Greenslopes to the city, and then from the city to wherever by tram, bus or train. Having to depend on the public transport system isn't an efficient way to hunt for a job.

"Yes. I've lived in Spring Hill and New Farm for a couple of years," I reply hopefully, "and I'm fairly familiar with the city."

"Do you have a driver's licence?"

"No, not yet, and I don't have a car, but I've been taking driving lessons. I took the driving test a week ago but failed it. I'm happy to take the test again as soon as I can arrange it."

"Sorry, Tom. I need someone who already has a driver's licence. I can't let you drive the van with a learner's permit. There's no one with a licence to sit next to you while you drive."

"How about you give me a chance to get my licence within a week? If I fail, you can hire someone else."

"Sorry, I need someone to do the deliveries right away. There's no guarantee that you'll pass next time, and I can't afford to take the chance."

After another unsuccessful day, my hope of getting a job is fading. I have lost three weeks of income that I expected to have by now, and the chance of getting a job three weeks before Christmas is very slim. I decide to pay Mr. Gamack another visit, to give him an update on my job hunting venture. Besides, I need a sympathetic ear.

After nearly a month in hospital he is much happier, and he tells me that he'll be out of hospital in three days. Before I have a chance to tell him about my job hunting saga, he hands me an envelope.

"This is a letter of introduction from John, who was in the next bed. You haven't met him, but you probably remember he was here when you visited me last."

"Yes, I remember there was a man lying in the bed next to yours. He was asleep and I didn't get to meet him."

"He was here only for three days and was released from the hospital yesterday, or maybe even the day before. I can't remember."

"What is this letter of introduction about?"

"John — I can't even remember his surname — is a World War II veteran. He is a travelling sales executive with Geo. Pickers & Co. Pty. Ltd. in Newstead. I told John about your background, and how hard you've been trying to find a job. John was impressed with your attitude and determination, so he's taken the initiative to write the letter of introduction. Hopefully, it'll get you a job with Pickers."

"Thank you very much. I'm not afraid of hard work, as you know. I'm willing to do anything to earn some money. For the last three weeks, I've been walking around the streets in the City, West End, New Farm and Fortitude Valley and I'm running out of ideas as to what to do next. I hope this letter of introduction will help me to get a job at Pickers."

"You've nothing to lose, son."

"Thanks again, Mr. Gamack. I'll go and see them tomorrow."

Already my mind is busy planning my route — up early, catch the tram to the Valley and then change trams to Newstead. "I wish I could thank John."

"You might meet up with him at Pickers. You can thank him then."

"Okay, you take care. I'll see you when you're back home."

TWENTY

‖‖

OPPORTUNITY KNOCKS

To get to Newstead, I have to change trams at the Valley to either Clayfield or Ascot and get off at the tram stop before Breakfast Creek. Despite having a letter of introduction in my top shirt pocket, I am not hopeful of getting a job, due to all the knock-backs over the last three weeks. I turn up at Pickers, just to satisfy myself and Mr. Gamack that I tried.

I walk up to the second floor office and hand over the letter of introduction to the receptionist behind the counter. She studies the name on the envelope and says, "Wait here for a minute please, while I get the manager."

A middle-aged man holding the letter appears behind the counter. He reads the letter and looks at me. "You're looking for a job here?"

I nod. He sizes me up again, his face expressionless. There is no way I can tell what is in his mind. I wonder what John, the travelling sales executive, has written in that letter.

"Come and follow me," he finally says. I follow him down the stairs and through a side door into the showroom. He turns his head left and then right, until he spots another middle-aged man with grey hair. He walks toward him and mumbles something I can't hear. Then he turns to me and says, "This is Mr. Scott, the showroom manager. He'll give you a job. When can you start?"

"I can start straight away... today." No one has told me what sort of work I'll be doing. I guess it must be cleaning.

"Good. You can start now. After lunch, come up to the office to sort out some paperwork to get you paid at the end of each week. Okay? Mr. Scott will take care of you."

"Thank you very much. I'll see you after lunch." The manager leaves me with Mr. Scott. "Where do you want me to clean first?" I ask him.

"Who told you that you were going to be a cleaner here?" Mr. Scott asks.

"No one. Looking at this large showroom, I assumed there must be a lot of dusting and cleaning to do."

"No, you are not going to be a cleaner here. You are going to be a sales assistant."

"I don't have any experience in sales."

"That's all right. I am going to train you. Anything you don't know, you just ask me. Don't be afraid to ask. Do you understand?"

"Yes. Anything I don't know, I will ask you."

"The showroom opens at eight-thirty and closes at five, Monday to Friday," he continues as he shows me around. "On Saturdays, it opens at the same time but closes at one o'clock. I'd like you to get here a little bit before opening time. You have half-an-hour for lunch and you can have a cup of tea or coffee at any time in the morning and afternoon provided it's not busy. Do you have a car?"

"No, I don't, and I'm still working on my driver's licence."

"Will you have any problem getting here around quarter-past-eight?"

"No."

"Here's a copy of the catalogue for all the goods we sell here. When customers come in and want to buy something, you just look up the catalogue and ask me where to find it in the showroom. Sometimes the stocks might be low, so you need to go around to the storeroom to see either of the two storemen. They will tell you where to find the stock to refill. When you get a chance later, go around to the storeroom and introduce yourself to the two storemen and the storeroom manager."

"There is nearly an acre of floor space, so there must be tens of thousands of items of merchandise. How am I going to remember them all?"

"Ask me. There will be another older guy, Peter, and a young fellow, Andrew, starting next week. They have worked here casually in previous years during the Christmas period. I'm normally here by myself, but if it's busy the two elder daughters of the owner, Mr. Pickers, come down from the office to give me a hand with the customers."

"I see. What about a man called John, who's the travelling sales executive? Does he work here? I'd like to thank him, because it was he who wrote the introduction to get me this job."

"No, he doesn't work here at the showroom. He's a travelling salesman. He drops in occasionally to say hello. I seldom see him."

Each day is a blur. I don't even remember how many questions I ask Mr. Scott. Whenever a customer walks into the showroom and asks me for an item, I feel completely useless. I have to ask Mr. Scott first. There must be hundreds, if not thousands, of camping items on display in the showroom. They range from tents of different sizes and makes, to portable gas burners and gas bottles, portable iceboxes, fold-up furniture such as tables and chairs — again in all sizes and makes — cooking utensils and cutlery, gas lanterns and torches, sleeping bags, air mattresses and air pumps, beds in the form of steel stretchers and foldaway double-bunk beds, shoulder carry bags of different sizes and makes, ropes and poles... and the list goes on and on. I've never gone camping, and I know absolutely nothing about it. When customers ask me about the best places to go camping, I feel embarrassed to be completely ignorant about the subject. I have no doubt that — though they say nothing in my hearing — the customers wonder why the company employed me.

On the fourth day, I slowly get out of bed, dress, and force myself to walk out the front door. As I drag my feet down Plimsoll Street, towards the tram stop on Logan Road, I give myself a pep-talk. For three weeks, no one gave me a job. I should consider myself fortunate to have this one. If

I hadn't visited Mr. Gamack at the hospital, and if he hadn't told John, the travel sales executive, about my predicament, I would probably still be walking around the city looking for that elusive job. I should be happy and grateful.

By Friday, Father, I will have worked at Pickers for a whole week and it will be the weekly pay day. I might as well stick it out for another couple of days and get a full week's pay.

Perhaps, they might sack me tomorrow, because they may have discovered how useless I am. If I quit the job tomorrow, I'll be back to looking for a menial job. With only two weeks before Christmas, there'll be few chances to score a job. More importantly, all the people at work are really good to me and, of course, Mr. Scott is exceptional. He is patient, and has never raised his voice when explaining things to me, even though I usually ask more than once.

With this in mind, I decide that if they are not happy with my performance, they will advise me that my service is no longer required. I will have no regrets because, deep down, I know I am not capable of doing this sales assistant's job.

Two weeks pass. My salesmanship skills, and my confidence handling customers, are improving day by day. I now have a better knowledge of the merchandise, because I have been spending time, at night, studying the catalogue. Since the older guy, Peter, and the young fellow, Andrew, started two weeks ago, I don't need to bother Mr. Scott as frequently. I now have Peter and Andrew to ask. Peter, who is already retired, has been working here for the last few years. He has come back for a few weeks, during the Christmas and New Year period. I am not sure what Andrew usually does, but I know this is his second year working here, so he too could be useful.

Generally, the showroom quietens down after half-past-three. There aren't really enough customers to keep the four of us fully occupied. I remember Ah-por's advice — keep busy; don't stand around talking with others; find something to do. So I re-stock the shelves with merchandise between three-thirty and knock-off time. Re-stocking the shelves also gives me an opportunity to familiarise myself with the location of items. It saves time running to the storeroom for the item while serving customers. When all the re-stocking is done, I dust the goods on the shelves and sweep the showroom floor.

After opening my third weekly pay packet, I notice there are a few extra dollars inside.

"Mr. Scott," I say, "I think the office has overpaid me this week. What should I do?"

"Go and ask Sam up in the office. He is the accountant and paymaster."

After checking with Sam, I tell Mr. Scott, "There is no mistake in my payment. Sam told me that my hourly rate increased due to my birthday on the 16th of this month. Because I've turned twenty, he has to pay me a higher rate."

"Happy birthday to you! Why didn't you mention it to us so that we could have a birthday cake with you?" He shakes my hand.

"It's funny, because 16th December, 1947 is not really my birthday. My actual birthday is 7th January, 1947. My birthday is the 16th December in the Chinese calendar, but that falls in the year 1947 in the Western calendar. Somehow, someone has mixed up the Chinese and Western calendar and registered my date of birth as 16th December, 1947. As a matter of fact, I'm nearly a year older than is shown on my documents."

"So, on paper you are a twenty-year-old and in actual fact you are nearly twenty-one?"

"That's right."

෨෨

It is a miserable, rainy day. The weather has been like this for several days and I feel depressed. According to the forecast, it is going to be like this for the next few days too. It is near dark by the time I get home after work. I put my hand inside the letter box, grab whatever is inside, and run straight inside the house.

Although I walked home from the tram stop under an umbrella, the bottom section of my trousers and shoes are damp, and I feel chilly. My hands tremble as I open the stamped Government envelope. It is a conscription registration form.

Although it's a cool day, I break into sweat. I unfold the form and lay it on the table and start to read it: name, date of birth, sex, occupation and so on. Why is it necessary for me — an overseas student — to be registered? I'd heard that it is a Government requirement that every twenty-year-old male, irrespective of whether he is an Australian citizen or a foreigner, must be registered for conscription. Fighting a war in Vietnam is something I never contemplated when I arrived in Australia six years ago. My brother escaped being conscripted. Now it is my turn to worry.

෨෨

It is about half-an-hour before closing time at Geo. Pickers. The four sales staff gather around for a chit-chat. It is a good opportunity for me to ask some questions about the Vietnam War and conscription.

"Why are Australians fighting in Vietnam?" I ask.

"Let me give you some background," says Mr. Scott, who seems to be very knowledgeable about world affairs. He proceeds with a long dissertation on the history of Vietnam and the course of the war.

"Since not every twenty-year-old is selected to go, what is the selection process?" I ask.

"It's by ballot. A ballot was introduced in 1965 by the Government," Mr. Scott continues. "There are twelve months in a year, and each month has twenty-eight to thirty-one days. I think how it works is by pulling a month out of a barrel, followed by a date. Whoever was born in that month and on that date is conscripted."

"I'm an overseas student. Why should I be picked?"

"The Government can soon fix it by letting you become an Australian," Andrew says.

"I've been thinking that if I get picked, I'll join the Australian Air Force."

"No, you don't get to choose. If you are conscripted, you'll be in the army," Peter says.

"I reckon the Government will let you be naturalised and then pick you to train as a spy," says Andrew.

"You can't be serious."

"It makes perfect sense. The Government trains you as a spy and parachutes you into the enemy's territory in the North, and you send the information back to the South. If the North finds out that you are a spy, they'll execute you. If you manage to escape back to the South, they might think that you are from the north and they'll shoot at you. Doesn't matter which side you are on, you'll die on the battle field."

"Look at the size of him," Peter points out. "Five-feet-eight tall and weighs about hundred and twenty pounds. Am I right?"

"As a matter-of-fact, I'm only five-feet-six and weigh about a hundred pounds."

"You won't be able to survive the training. Just carrying fifty pounds of gear will kill you before you complete the training. You might as well go and enjoy life while you can, because you're going to die soon," Peter says.

᭡᭡᭡

"I might have to go to Vietnam," I tell Ah-por.

"Why?"

"There is a war going on there. The Australian Government is sending troops over to help the Americans fight."

"What war in Vietnam?" Although my grandmother has been in Australia for over thirteen years, she still can hardly understand the English language, let alone what is going on around the world.

"Fighting the Communists," I answer.

"Oh, no! Not again. We fled China because of the Communists. They took everything from us. We had nothing when we fled to Hong Kong. We could have lived a comfortable life back in China if it wasn't for the Communists."

"I know."

"Lucky your little aunt married an Australian Chinese. She managed to sponsor me out here in 1954. Since then, I've worked hard and saved enough money to bring you here on a student visa. I cannot understand why a Chinese boy like you has to go to war. How come you got picked?"

"No, Ah-por, I haven't been picked yet. I'm only up to filling in the registration form."

"Why? You're only an overseas student and you're not even a new Australian!"

"I don't know. All I know is that every twenty-year-old male who currently lives in Australia is required to be registered. I have just turned twenty. I need to fill this registration form in."

"You could get killed over there."

"So be it. If the Australian Government lets me become a naturalised citizen, it's my duty, as an Australian citizen, to fight and protect this country. We're not invading Vietnam. We're fighting to stop the invasion of Communists. Maybe it is payback time. After all, it was the Communists who ruined us back in China."

"Are there any alternatives?"

"I don't know. I don't even know how people get selected to go. A guy at work seemed to think that I would definitely get picked. The Government needs people who look like Vietnamese to train as Australian spies, he said. After the training, they'll drop me in North Vietnam to spy on the Communists and relay the information back to the South."

"Our family has lost everything due to the Communists. I don't want to lose you, Loo Shang."

"I'm frightened too, Ah-por. I'm told that not every twenty-year-old is picked to go. Only one in every twelve. I might be lucky."

It seems like an eternity, waiting for the Government's response. The anxiety of not knowing is taking a toll on my health. I can't eat or sleep. I constantly worry about the worst case scenario: getting killed on the battlefield.

I look in the letter box. There is a stamped Government envelope inside. I tear it open. My service is not required. I am overjoyed at the good news. A huge load has lifted.

After the excitement had subsided, I feel guilty. My family fled with nothing when the Communists took control of China. I dread to think there could be a possibility of Australia also ending up in the Communists' hands. I feel guilty because, after all, I won't be helping combat a possible Communist invasion of Australia.

TWENTY-ONE

DEVASTATING DISAPPOINTMENTS

FRIDAY 22ND DECEMBER, 1967

Father, it's the night before the Senior Public Examination results. Since eleven o'clock, I've been lying in bed twisting and turning, unable to sleep. I'm excited, anxious and worried. A good result will enable me to matriculate and gain entry to a tertiary engineering course.

English is my weakest subject, but hopefully I'll gain at least a score of 3.

I doze and wake. It is still dark outside. A quick glance at the alarm clock confirms that it is only three o'clock. It will be another four hours before I can get hold of a copy of the newspaper to check my results.

After years of struggling to balance my school work and earning money to put myself through high school, I am tired—already burned out before reaching the age of twenty-one. I twist and turn, trying to go back to sleep, but my mind is too wide awake.

Some senior students probably have their results already. It is a tradition that the keenest go to the newspaper printery—at the Newspaper House in Queen Street—for the dispatch of the first newspaper at midnight on Friday. I am waiting till morning, when I will buy a newspaper at the local grocery shop. Students living in the metropolitan and surrounding areas are to receive their official results through the post next Monday. But this year, Christmas Day and Boxing Day public holidays fall on Monday and Tuesday. Therefore, students won't receive their official results until Wednesday, 27th December. Country students will have to wait an extra day or two before getting theirs via the post.

I know that if I fail to matriculate, it could mean the end of my stay in Australia. My student visa could be cancelled.

I get out of bed at half-past-six, feeling tired, but with adrenaline pumping. I hurry to the local grocery shop around the corner. The newspapers are bundled up, lying on the footpath in front of the shop entrance. I consider doing the wrong thing—somehow untying the rope to get at a copy of the newspaper out to check my results. But I contain my anxiety and wait until the shop owner turns up, then pay for my copy.

Weeks before the commencement of the examination, each candidate was supplied with a card showing his or her examination number, which must be retained until the examination is complete. Only the candidate's number is to be published, together with his or her results. I check my number first, and then my results. I can't believe what I read: "1 in English, 4s in chemistry, mathematics I and II, 2 in physics, and 5 in geometrical drawing and pPerspective".

To study the Diploma of Engineering at the Queensland Institute of Technology, I need a total score of 20, with a minimum 3 in English. My total score is 15. It is a bad dream! A nightmare!

I want to wake up, Father. It has to be a mistake.

My result in English is devastating. A score of 1 means 'Very Unsatisfactory'. The result is far worse than I had ever contemplated. If I had scored a 3 in English, with a 4 in mathematics I and three of my other subjects, excluding physics, I would have had a total of 20 points — sufficient to gain entry to do a Diploma in Accountancy or Business Studies or Public Administration at the Queensland Institute of Technology. Those courses might not be of my liking, but at least I'd be studying at tertiary level.

It should have been the happiest time of my life, but I am choked by frustration, anger and disbelief. For some students, the release of their matriculation results will mark the beginning of a bright future. For me, it signals disappointment and fear of the future.

This is a real test of my ability to cope with setbacks. I have experienced many disappointments in my life so far. Now, facing yet another, I am unsure how many more I can take before cracking up and becoming mentally unstable.

I have never been shaped and encouraged by parental influences. I wonder, with the proper nurturing, encouragement and assistance, how far I might have gone to reach my potential.

My grandmother doesn't understand my predicament, or maybe she doesn't want to understand. As far as she is concerned, as long as I am in Australia, I won't die of hunger. I am no scholar. Perhaps she is right that I should have given up study years ago, and tried to find a way to own a Chinese restaurant.

My overseas student visa is due to expire in five months' time. It needs to be extended after 31st May, 1968 if I am to remain in Australia as a student. One solution is for me to repeat Senior, with the hope of getting better grades in all the subjects. I am not keen on repeating because, with my below average English standard, there is a possibility that I could fail again.

So what is the next step?

I drag myself to work, but my mind is not in it. It is the most anxious and traumatic time of my life.

"What's the matter, Tom? You look so down and out. Are you sick?" Mr. Scott asks.

"Yeah, you don't look too good!" Peter adds.

"No, I'm not sick. I failed to matriculate to get into University. My student visa expires at the end of May next year. I don't know whether the government will extend my visa."

"You should repeat Senior next year. I think the Immigration Department will extend your visa," Mr. Scott suggests.

"I really don't want to repeat Senior. If I fail English again next year, I'll be back to square one and still unable to matriculate."

"Listen, you only have to repeat English and Physics. I know a private tutoring college that has a good reputation for getting students through the Senior Public Examinations, but it costs a bit," Mr. Scott says.

"No, no, there are other ways," Andrew says.

"What? Another of your devious schemes?" Peter teases.

"Hey, when one is desperate, one has to try anything," Andrew replies with a cunning grin.

"I don't want to do anything illegal and make matters worse than they are now," I say.

"You just disappear. Ha ha ha!" Andrew says.

"What do you mean 'just disappear'?"

"You leave the city and go to work in country towns. Australia is a big country. You become an illegal immigrant. It'll take a few years before the Immigration Department finds you. You work and save up all the money. Then, you either give yourself up to the Immigration Department—they might let you stay—or wait until the Department finds you and deports you back home."

Andrew's comments remind me of when I worked at Greenslopes Spare Room Restaurant and the Department Immigration Officer, together with the Commonwealth Police, were rounding up all the illegal immigrants.

"It is illegal. It's the wrong thing to do. I don't want to get caught and deported back to Hong Kong."

"Don't listen to Andrew. He's being silly. You repeat Senior next year and I'm sure the Immigration Department will extend your overseas student visa for another year," Mr. Scott says.

"Wait. There is another way." Andrew interjects.

"What devious scheme have you come up with now?" Peter asks.

"Why don't you find an Australian girl, marry her and settle here?" Andrew suggests.

"You're not serious, are you?" Peter asks.

"He doesn't want to repeat Senior and he doesn't want to disappear. It's a way to stay in Australia."

Mr. Scott advises me not to listen to him. Peter says he's being stupid.

"I read in the newspaper, not so long ago, that an overseas guy found an Australian girl and paid her a sum of money to get married. He got a marriage certificate, a legal document, saying they were legally married. The Immigration Department couldn't send the guy back because he was married to an Australian girl. After a period of time, this guy paid the Australian girl more money to get a divorce. He got to stay in Australia," Andrew says.

"I think what I'll do is contact Mr. John Murphy of the Department of Immigration to see what he has to say about my situation," I say.

"That's a good idea. Talk to the Immigration people and they might have a solution for you," Mr. Scott says.

ॐॐ

SATURDAY, 23RD DECEMBER, 1967

Father, next Monday is Christmas Day. Although the showroom is open till one o'clock, everyone at Pickers is already in the holiday mood. The showroom will close for the festive season today and will re-open for business on Tuesday, 2nd January. Everyone is greeting each other with a Merry Christmas and a Happy New Year. I guess that the peak period of the business is over. After the break, it's unlikely that Pickers will need four salesmen on the floor. Because I'm the last casual they employed, I guess that I'll be the first to be let go. I've resolved to start looking for a job after Boxing Day.

"Goodbye Mr. Scott. Thank you for all the help you've given me for the last three weeks. Without your help and patience, I might have quit in the first week. I wish you and your family a Merry Christmas and a Happy New Year."

Mr. Scott returns the greeting. "But who has told you that you're not coming back after the break?" he asks.

"I guessed that the peak period for the business is before Christmas and after that it will be quiet and you probably don't need me anymore."

"I have some good news for you. We want you back on Tuesday, 2nd January. We'll still be fairly busy in the New Year period because a lot of people are still on annual leave and some people leave their camping trips until after Christmas. Does this suit you?"

I am ecstatic.

"Thank you very much. I'm more than happy to come back. I thought that I'd have to start looking for a job after the public holiday. I didn't like my chances. I'll be back for sure."

∽∽

Three times I've picked the phone up to dial, Father, and three times I put it down. I am worried about how Mr. Murphy from the Department of Immigration is going to react to my dismal Senior Examination results. My hands shake each time I try to dial. Although it isn't a hot day, sweat is pouring off my forehead and back. I need his advice.

After taking a deep breath and steadying my hands, I build up enough courage to pick up the phone a fourth time. This time, I dial the number.

"Good morning, Department of Immigration, Marilyn speaking. May I help you?"

"Mr. John Murphy, please."

"John is on the phone. Would you like to hold?"

I wait. I still vividly remember the first time I saw John. It was when he turned up, together with the Commonwealth Police, at the Greenslopes Spare Room Restaurant kitchen to round up illegal immigrants. The following year, when I was in my Junior year, he became the Immigration Officer in charge of all overseas students studying in Queensland. From then on, I had to meet with him at least twice a year to go through the progress I was making in my studies and any issues that the School Principal might raise regarding my school work. He then wrote a report to the Immigration Department. Over the last three years, I have met with John a number of times. He is a pleasant and understanding man.

At last, I am connected.

"John Murphy speaking."

"Good morning, Mr. Murphy. This is Tommy Kwok."

I have to repeat my name before Mr. Murphy recognizes it.

"You don't sound too good. What's the matter?"

"I did badly in the Senior Public Examination."

"It can't be that bad, can it?"

"Yes. I only scored 1 for English, which is a compulsory subject. I need a minimum of 20 points to gain entry to study at the Queensland Institute of Technology. I only have 18 points for my top five subjects, including English. I got 4s in Chemistry, Mathematics I and II, 5 in Geometrical Drawing and Perspective, and 2 in Physics. But because the Physics examination was too difficult for Senior students, every student has been up-graded and now I have a 3. But it's still not enough."

"Instead of talking on the phone, how about you come and see me. What about next Friday, 29th December, at ten o'clock? Is that okay with you?"

Relieved, I put the phone down. Although my future is still uncertain, my hands aren't shaking any more, and I have stopped perspiring.

ೲೲ

On Friday, I am half an hour early. Being late for my appointment with John would be a bad start, so I prefer to wait for him. Soon, he appears behind a counter that has a number of small timber screens dividing it up, like bank teller compartments. This allows us to talk in private.

After we exchange greetings, I tell him, "I'm working for Pickers and it is closed from Christmas Day until New Year's Day, so I have eight days off. I can't stop worrying about my future."

"My wife and I don't go away at this time of the year," he tells me. "We take holidays during the quiet period. We had all our grown-up children home for a Christmas dinner, which was nice. Now, you told me on the phone, a few days ago, that you didn't do well in the Examination. You've always had trouble with English, haven't you?"

"Yes, but I was hoping to get a 3 in English. I got only a 1."

"Why don't you repeat Senior next year?"

"I've thought about it. I don't really want to repeat Senior unless I can be certain that I can get into either the University of Queensland or the Queensland Institute of Technology the year after. If I fail English again next year, I'll end up wasting a year."

"I can understand your concern. Have you thought about going down to Sydney? There are more Universities down there. You might find one that will accept you without a pass in English."

"Mr. Murphy, you know how hard I've been working for the last few years. I've put myself through high school and managed to save about three thousand dollars for my University years. I need a thousand dollars each year to cover fees, books and transport for four years. I'm living with my grandmother, so at least I don't have to pay board. The amount I have in the bank is enough for three years, and once I'm at university I'll earn another thousand dollars to cover the fourth year. But I don't have enough to cover the cost of living away from home."

"I'm fully aware of your situation, Tommy. You probably worked too many hours and your school work suffered."

"I didn't have much choice. I needed the money. If I move down to Sydney, I'd be lucky to survive for eighteen months."

"Okay. You don't want to repeat Senior and you don't want to move down to Sydney. So what do you have in mind?"

"I know my poor results won't get me entry to either the University of Queensland or the Queensland Institute of Technology (QIT) as a full-time student. But I might be able to get into QIT as a part-time student to study for an Associate Diploma in Civil Engineering."

"Will QIT accept you as an Associate Diploma student?"

"I don't know yet. As an overseas student, I'm supposed to study full-time. My student visa expires in five months' time, on 31st May, 1968. Before I approach QIT, I'd like to know whether the Immigration Department will allow me to stay and study part-time."

"I know you have been trying hard all these years since you arrived here in 1961. Don't worry. We'll work something out. Take a seat and I'll be back soon."

After a few minutes, Mr. Murphy signals me back in front of the counter. He hands me a letter and says, "This is a letter stating that this Department has no objection to you enrolling at QIT for the Associate Diploma in Civil Engineering (Part-Time)."

I am ecstatic. "Thank you Mr. Murphy. When I send my enrolment form to QIT, I'll write to ask for special consideration to allow me to study only some of the first year civil engineering subjects while I repeat my Senior English and Physics."

"Give it a try and let me know how you get on. Good luck, Tommy."

"Thank you. I'll let you know." We shake hands. As I depart, I think that Mr. Murphy is my guardian angel. I feel optimistic that QIT will accept my enrolment just for the two subjects, say Engineering Drawing IA and Engineering Materials IA. I don't have to wait long for their answer.

Queensland Institute of Technology
16th January 1968

Dear Sir,
Your application for special consideration
for entry to the Diploma in Civil Engineering
is acknowledged.

The Admissions committee has decided that you must repeat your Senior English and Physics, and acquire a grade of 3 or better in English, and a 4 or better in Physics, bearing in mind that a total point score of 20 is essential when these subjects are associated with your 1967 Mathematics I, Mathematics II, and Chemistry results.

Yours faithfully
(Registrar)

My world collapses again.

ᏋᏋ

Work at Pickers has resumed. What Mr. Scott said at the end of last year has proven correct! In January, business is just as brisk as it was in December. Mr. Scott and I are run off our feet. I am surprised there is no sign of Peter or Andrew. Curiosity gets the better of me. I ask, "Mr. Scott, are Peter and Andrew still on holiday?"

"No, they finished up before Christmas."

"So they're not coming back?"

"No. We kept you."

I am pleased but mystified. Mr. Scott continues, "The office people have been keeping track of your sales since you started with us. Your first two weeks were a bit slow, which is understandable, but since then you've been selling a lot, especially tents and camping accessories. They are curious to know how you do it."

"I don't know what you mean by how I do it. Do what?" I ask.

"Sell tents. You've sold more tents than anyone else, including me. How do you do it?"

I still don't know what he means, but I do my best to answer. "I simply try very hard to satisfy the customer. To find out exactly what he needs, I ask lots of questions."

"What do you mean you ask the customer a lot of questions?"

"Half of the customers who walk in here know exactly what they want. The other half are not so sure. It's this group that needs a bit of assistance."

Mr. Scott prods me for further information. "Let's say a customer comes in and wants to buy a tent but is not too sure what to buy. What do you do then?"

"I walk him to the tents display area and let him see the various sizes of tents available. I ask him how many people will be sleeping inside the tent. He then gets a feel for what he needs. Then I ask him what the weather could be like at the place where he's going to camp. His answer enables me to make a suggestion about whether to choose a canvas tent or a calico one. My next question is how often he thinks he'll go camping. If his answer is quite often, then it's better for him to buy a heavy-duty, waterproof canvas tent. If he is a first-timer or a novice, I suggest buying a cheaper tent to try out, rather than outlay money on an expensive one that could end up sitting in his garage for many years to come. After he's decided which tent to buy, I go through the camping accessories in the catalogue. I use it as a check-list to find out what other accessories he might need—like gas burners, ice-block containers, sleeping bag, fold-up beds, tables and chairs, cooking utensils and so on."

"So that's what you do? You're a born salesman, Tom."

"No, I don't think so. I just try to provide a service to satisfy the customers' needs and help them to make up their minds."

"Well, good on you," he says.

৩৩

After my disappointment with QIT's response subsides, I realise that applications for enrolment in QIT's Certificate Courses are still open. I have until the end of January to apply. The Certificate Course in Engineering, which runs for two years full-time and two years part-time, requires only Junior passes in English, mathematics A, mathematics B, chemistry and physics. I have these. This seems to be the solution. If I manage to get a good pass in my Certificate subjects, I'll be able to upgrade to the Diploma course. Perhaps 1968 won't be so bad after all.

৩৩

I pick up my last weekly wage, after my tenth week at Pickers, with mixed feelings. I've grown to like the place and the people, and I will miss them.

"Tom, Mr. Pickers wants to see you before you go," Mr. Scott says.

"Why?"

"I don't know. Maybe he just wants to say goodbye to you and wish you luck. Go up to his office now and see if he has time to see you."

I had met Mr. Pickers a number of times in passing, and each time he stopped and made small talk. He has shown some interest in me, which flatters me, especially considering I am only a casual employee. I learn that he started life from humble beginnings. During the Second World War, he started mending army tents. From there, he built up a huge business in camping equipment and the manufacture of tents. Now in his early sixties, he is still energetic and running the business. He takes care to ensure that his staff are happy in their work.

I knock on his open door. He is sitting behind his desk, head down, reading a document. He stands and extends his hand for a warm handshake. I have never experienced a face-to-face meeting with the owner of a big business before, and I feel overwhelmed. I'm afraid I might make a fool of myself. I can't understand why a big boss like him would want to see me.

"Thank you for working here during the Christmas and New Year period," he begins.

I thank him for the opportunity. "The staff have been helpful, considering I didn't know anything about the business and had absolutely no sales experience."

"Mr. Scott, and all the others who've been dealing with you, told me you are very hard working. I have seen, with my own eyes, that you always keep yourself busy—even cleaning the shop-front windows when the showroom is quiet. You are a very quick learner. You said yourself you knew nothing about the business when you came here, and now you can serve the customers with ease. I'm impressed with your work ethic and attitude. Congratulations."

My face warms and my heart races. I have never had such an accolade before. I don't know how to respond to his praise, and I look down to hide my discomfort.

"I have a proposition for you," he says. I don't understand what he means by 'proposition', so I frown. He seems to sense that I don't understand, and explains. "I know you didn't do well in your Senior Public Examinations. I am offering you full-time employment here."

I am dumbfounded. I thought that he wanted just to say goodbye. It never crossed my mind that he would offer me a permanent job. He has caught me off-guard, and I don't know how to respond to his kind gesture without offending.

"What sort of a job?" I ask.

"You've been with us for two-and-a-half months already. For the next nine months you will be in the showroom with Scotty, so that you can fully familiarise yourself with every piece of merchandise on display. This will also give you more time to deal with customers. After a full twelve months in the showroom, we will put you in the factory for six months so that you can learn how the tents, horse rugs and other canvas goods are manufactured. Then you'll spend the following six months in the office. After two years, you'll have all the training you need to become a travelling salesman for the Company. It's a position like

John's, the man who wrote you the letter of introduction. Like the other travelling salesmen, you will have a territory to look after. Your territory would cover the whole of Queensland, Papua New Guinea and the northern part of New South Wales. It would take you three months to go around your territory, and then you would have one month off. Then you'll go around again. You'll go around three times a year."

"Do I go around the country-town shops and sell the merchandise?"

"No, you'll go around to the cattle and sheep stations and farms and collect the orders. You don't need to sell too much because the market is already established. You just have to visit every station and the station people will tell you what they want. You'll take their orders and phone them through each night, and then your job is done. It's up to us, down here, to deliver the orders up to them."

He tells me the customers will order tents, rugs, tarpaulins, canvas goods, camping accessories and many other things. The company will supply me with a car, and I will stay in motels.

"The company pays for your motel stay and all meals," he says. "You don't have to spend any of your own money at all. And on top of your salary, you'll receive a percentage commission for your effort. The commission will be as much as your salary, if not more."

My enthusiasm fades when he tells me he would expect me to stay with the company for at least five years. I realize that, by then, I will have saved a lot of money. A career in sales is not what I envisaged, yet the offer is tempting.

"I'm on an overseas student visa and am not permitted to have permanent employment in Australia," I tell him, playing for time.

"The Company can sponsor you and make application to the Immigration Department to change your overseas student visa to a work visa."

It is comforting that Mr. Pickers has recognised my talent and hard work; that he has decided not only to sponsor me, but also to offer me the potential to earn a good income. It is a golden opportunity, but professional salesman is not the career I want for the rest of my life.

"Mr. Pickers, you are very kind. I have just found out that I can use my Junior Public Examination results to enrol at the Queensland Institute of Technology to do a Certificate of Civil Engineering at a technician level. I failed to matriculate, so I can't do the professional engineering course I wanted, but the Certificate course will do fine. The first term starts next Monday. I appreciate your kind offer, but I'd really like to give engineering a go."

"Good. Then Tommy, I wish you the very best of luck in your engineering study. Just keep in mind, if you can't manage the course, there's always a job open for you here." He stands to shake my hand.

Mr. Pickers offered me a permanent job today, Father. He said I could apply to change my student visa for a work visa, and the company would sponsor me. It sounded as though I might make excellent money. He even offered me a car, and all my living expenses would be paid, plus I'd earn commission. It's not what I want to do, but it took great courage to turn him down. It really was an amazing opportunity. And I was quite overwhelmed to hear him say there was always a job open for me with his firm if I want it.

CHAPTER TWENTY-TWO

I ACHIEVE MY GOAL

In February 1968, my brother, Ah-kor, stops working at Golden Dragon Products and moves into Ah-por's house in Greenslopes to live with us. He doesn't tell me the reason for leaving the factory. Perhaps he is tired of the work and has decided he needs a change. He has been working there, and living with Sai-goo's family, for nearly ten years. I don't know how he managed to find a job in a joinery factory in Bulimba. Being his usual quiet self, he doesn't talk about it, and I don't bother to ask.

The joinery factory is owned by a Chinese man and manufactures laminated particle-board cabinets and cupboards. Occasionally, Ah-kor brings home some off-cuts. We are to save them so that, hopefully, we might eventually have enough to match them up and make small shelves to store things.

My bedroom isn't big enough for two single beds, and we both dislike the idea of a double-bunk. Ah-kor says he doesn't mind sleeping on the large fold-up lounge-chair in the lounge room.

He goes to work early, well before I leave for QIT. Ah-por is the last person to leave the house for work, and she doesn't get home until nine at night. Ah-kor and I have dinner at home, and Ah-por eats at work.

"Loo Shang, I don't like your cooking," Ah-kor says one evening.

"All right, Ah-kor. Let's come to an agreement. You do the cooking and I'll do the washing-up."

We settle into this arrangement, and I find myself enjoying at last being close to my brother.

It is five weeks into the term when Ah-kor hands me a letter he retrieved from the mailbox. It is from QIT. I have attended all the lectures since the commencement of the first term and am pleased with my studies to date.

Queensland Institute of Technology

19th March 1968

Dear Sir,

Your application for enrolment in the full-time Certificate Course in Engineering is acknowledged.

It is regretted that State Education Department policy does not permit your application to be accepted.

Yours faithfully
Registrar

I can't believe what I am reading. I need to talk to Mr. Murphy again.

ᥰ᥉

It seems to take an eternity to secure an appointment, and I arrive at the Immigration Office tense and fearful. Mr. Murphy's warm greeting and kind smile does little to ease my anxiety.

"Everything sorted out with QIT?" he asks.

"No." I am aware that my distressed tone alarms him. I am trying hard to hide my distress. "Please read these two QIT letters. They give the reasons for my rejections in both courses."

He scans them quietly. "Oh. I see," he says. He sounds concerned and caring. "I wonder why QIT wouldn't let you do the Certificate in Engineering."

"I guess as an overseas student I'm not supposed to take an Australian's job. This Certificate course requires two years full-time and two years part-time. During the two part-time study years, students must obtain employment in suitable engineering work."

I pause a moment. He is nodding thoughtfully.

"I remember when I finished Junior," I continue. "Mr. Neill, a St. James's school teacher, took me to the Education Department to find out whether or not I could do a carpentry apprenticeship. They said apprenticeships were only for local boys because they are employed as apprentices for the four years training. Overseas students are not allowed to have full-time employment."

"So, what are you doing now?" he asks.

"I'm working at my aunt's dim sim factory to earn some money. I'm not studying anything at the moment. I might have to consider repeating the Senior English and Physics after all."

He is silent, but his expression tells me he understands my reluctance. I've discussed my preferences with him before.

"Geo. Pickers, where I worked during the holidays, offered to sponsor me to stay in Australia," I tell him proudly. "They wanted to train me to become one of their travelling sales executives, but they expected me to stay in that position for five years. I was reluctant to accept the offer because I believed once I became a salesman, I would remain a salesman for the rest of my life. I don't really want to do that."

"I understand," he says, leaning forward to reach in his tray for a form. He hesitates, studying it thoughtfully for a moment before passing it to me. "Stick with what you believe is your career calling, Tom," he urges. "Here. Fill this in."

"What is it?"

"It's an Application for Permanent Residency."

I am overwhelmed. *What do I feel? Confusion, relief, ecstasy, gratitude...?* But I can't help fearing that my application might be rejected. This is quite irregular, according to my understanding of the rules.

"I thought I'd have to wait until five years after I finished my tertiary education before I could apply?"

"You've been here since 1961. That's seven years. Have a go."

"Do you think I have a chance?"

"You can only try."

⧖

WEDNESDAY, 29TH MAY, 1968

I'm again in the Immigration Office, Father, waiting for an appointment with Mr. Murphy. It is just two days before my overseas student visa expires. He told me to bring my Hong Kong Certificate of Identity, the equivalent of an Australian Passport.

Again after greeting me warmly, Mr. Murphy gets down to business.

"Did you bring your Certificate of Identity with you, Tommy?"

"Yes."

He takes it, peruses it briefly, then stamps one of the pages with a circular rubber stamp with black ink.

"Congratulations, Tommy Kwok," he says, smiling broadly and passing the Certificate back. "You are now a Permanent Resident of Australia."

The stamp reads: "DEPARTMENT OF IMMIGRATION – PERMITTED ON 29 MAY 1968 TO REMAIN IN AUSTRALIA – BRISBANE."

I am lost for words. My heart is dancing.

"We know your family background." Mr. Murphy says. "You have tried hard to cope with study and work to put yourself through school. Now you have the freedom to do whatever you like, without the threat of being sent back to Hong Kong. I hope you won't betray the trust I have in you. Do drop by one day and let me know how you're getting on. All the very best in your future endeavours."

I stare at the stamp again, overflowing with joy. It occurs to me that failing to matriculate was, perhaps, a blessing in disguise.

☞☞

Father, I am now officially a permanent resident of this country. It's hard to believe. I don't have to worry about my overseas student visa expiring; about failing English; about working after school and during holidays. The psychological burdens I have carried for so long have fallen from my shoulders.

I ponder the reasons for my good fortune. Perhaps it is because of Mr. Murphy, who is aware of my family's tragic background and might sympathise with my circumstances. He has given me a chance to start a new life here. Maybe it is because of Fred Strutton, who told me that a month before my overseas student visa was due to expire, he had spoken to the head of the Immigration Department in Brisbane and put in a few good words for me. Maybe it is due to the Government phasing out the White Australia

Policy and opening the door to more Asians settling in the country.

Maybe it is the combination of my circumstances and the dismantling of the Policy. Whatever the reason, I am extremely grateful. I am free to pursue my choice of career. I never again have to fear being sent back to Hong Kong.

I made up my mind not to take up Pickers' offer to be trained as a travel salesman, Father. It was a kind offer, but I have chosen, instead, to enrol at QIT to do the Certificate of Engineering next year.

Until the new term starts in February, I'm back working at Golden Dragon Products. Sai-goo encourages me to seek something better than working at their factory full time. She is pleased that I have chosen to continue my studies.

In the months following Mr. Murphy's granting of residency status, I apply for several jobs. One of the applications I submit is for is a cadet technician position with the Brisbane City Council.

In mid-November, 1968, a letter arrives. It reads:

```
Brisbane City Council,
Department of Works
15th November, 1968.
Dear Sir,
I refer to the recent application submitted
by you for a position as a Cadet technician
in this Department and would request that
you call for an interview at Room 216,
```

Second Floor, City Hall, on 20th November,
1968 at 2:10 p.m.

> Yours faithfully
> Chief Engineer and Manager

My mind races as I contemplate the meaning. I am about to have my first real job interview.

Apart from my school uniform and a couple of business shirts, that I bought when I started work with Pickers, I don't have the right clothes for such an important occasion. *Should I spend some of my savings to buy a few new clothes, knowing that the money could be wasted if I miss out on the job?*

I buy myself a new long-sleeved shirt—light blue in colour — a matching tie, and a new pair of trousers. It is the exact outfit worn by the male mannequin displayed in the shop window.

I have been to many job interviews, but this one is particularly nerve-wracking. I am so anxious that I arrive an hour early. I allow myself plenty of time to find Room 216. Introducing myself to the secretary, I advise the purpose of my visit, then sit patiently in the waiting area until she returns to lead me past the counter, toward one of the offices inside.

Two middle-aged men sit side by side behind a desk. Each has a copy of my application. They introduce themselves, but I don't register their names. My nerves have taken over my hearing. The one wearing glasses is from the Department of Works. The other is from the Department of Water Supply and Sewerage. The guy from the Works Department offers me a seat.

"Would you like a glass of water?" the Water Supply guy asks. Although the room is reasonably cool, he must have noticed sweat on my forehead. After a drink of water, I feel better. My mouth is not as dry.

"We're putting on eight cadet technicians next year. Four are for the Department of Works and the other four for the Department of Water Supply and Sewerage," he explains, and pauses to wait for my nod in response. "If you are successful, which Department would you prefer?"

I hesitate. I don't know the functions of either Department. I don't like the sound of the word sewerage, because I guess it has something to do with toilets.

"I'd prefer to work in the Works Department," I answer. "What is the Works Department?" It is embarrassing to have to ask such a question.

"The Works Department mainly carries out roadwork, bridge work, storm water, and kerbing and channelling."

A relieved sigh escapes my lips. I have picked the right Department.

"Would you like to work in our Design Office or out in the field?"

It seems that the interview is now just between me and the Works Department guy.

"I don't know. Will you explain to me what design office work is and what field work is?"

"Working in the Design Office means that you will be working at City Hall in the Works Department Design

Office, drawing up plans for construction work as a Cadet Design Office Technician. Field workers are attached to a district depot, supervising construction and maintenance works as a Cadet Construction Technician."

"I'd prefer to work in the field." I answer, suppressing my fear of giving an answer that might, in some way, reduce my chances.

The Works Department guy turns to the Water Supply guy, "Do you have anything you would like to ask Tommy?"

"No."

"You sat for your Junior Public Examination in 1965. That's three years ago. You had a good pass with three A's, two B's and two C's. Last year, you did the Senior Public Examination. You didn't do too well. One 5, three 4s, one 3 and a 1 in English."

My heart is pumping and blood rushes to my head. *Should I respond to his remark? Was it a statement or a question?*

He lifts his head and looks straight into my eyes, as if waiting for my response.

"Yes," I reply. *Have my poor Senior results just caused me to miss out on the job?*

Although the technician position only requires a Junior pass, my Senior Public Examination results may not be good enough to compete against other applicants with better results. I start to feel uneasy, and I wish the interview would end. I can't wait to go to the toilet to relieve myself.

"You were born in China on 16th December, 1947. That makes you twenty-one next month?"

Does that make me too old for the position?

"Although you didn't have a good Senior Public Examination result, you had good Junior results. To qualify as a Cadet Construction Technician, you only need a Junior pass. Your Senior standard is an added advantage."

His tone is thoughtful. He pauses for a moment, then continues, "In your application, you mentioned that you've been working since 1963. This is also an added advantage."

I can't believe that working in restaurant kitchens and being a sales assistant with Pickers could have a positive impact on this job application.

"I am sure you are aware that the Cadetship requires you to enrol at QIT for the five year part-time Certificate of Civil Engineering course?" he says. "In your case, because you prefer to work in the field, you need to take the Construction Technician stream."

"Yes," I reply, struggling to suppress excitement. "I understand the academic requirement of the Cadetship. I'll enrol at QIT next year."

I am starting to feel more comfortable now. Strangely, my Senior result, although poor, seems to be an added advantage in his estimation. But his next statement sends my hopes plummeting.

"Brisbane City Council is part of local government. Employees at all levels of Government need to be either British subjects or Australian citizens. Are you either a British subject or an Australian citizen?"

"I'm not a British subject. I was only a resident in Hong Kong," I admit, adding hopefully, "But I am a permanent resident in Australia."

"Sorry. If you're neither a British subject nor an Australian citizen, we can't offer you the position."

My heart sinks. I refuse to give up. I am compelled to muster every ounce of courage to ask, "If I become an Australian citizen, will the Council offer me the position?"

"We are unable to indicate one way or the other if the job would then be offered to you. We have to complete all the interviews first, before we can make any recommendation."

I'm sure he detects the tremor in my voice as I ask, "Before you reject my application, is it possible for you to give me some time? I'd like to go to the Immigration Department to see whether they can do something for me."

The man from the Department of Works agrees to hold off until I get back to him. "Best of luck with the Department of Immigration," he says. "See you later this afternoon."

❧

The distance between City Hall and the sandstone buildings housing the Department of Immigration Office, next to Anzac Square in Adelaide Street, is about half a mile. After a brisk ten minute walk, I arrive huffing and puffing.

"Tom Kwok," I tell the receptionist. There is an urgency in my tone as I tell her, "I need to see Mr. Murphy please."

She picks up the phone and dials a number. I am silently praying that Mr. Murphy is still in the office and might be able to spare me a few minutes.

"Take a seat," she says. "He will be with you in a minute."

I look at my watch. *Time is ticking away! How long will the two Council guys wait for me.*

"What's your problem now?" Mr. Murphy asks after we exchange greetings.

"I just had a job interview with the Brisbane City Council." I go on to explain my dilemma.

"What sort of job is it?"

"It's a Construction Technician Cadetship with the Department of Works."

In response to his questions, I assure him this is what I want to do. "I'll need to enrol at QIT next year to study for a five years part-time course in the Certificate of Engineering. I have to be a citizen of Australia in order to qualify for the job," I tell him, embarrassed at the despair in my tone.

He disappears through a door behind the counter. I look up at the clock. Nearly four o'clock. *How long will I have to wait? Will the two Council guys wait for me?*

The minutes tick away. Each movement of the minute hand sounds an ominous warning that time is fast running out. I am pacing... sweating... taking deep breaths to try to calm myself. I chastise myself for my impatience.

At last, Mr. Murphy returns to hand me a document. "Take this letter to the Council," he says. His broad grin tells me he is pleased with himself. "It states that you'll be naturalised at Brisbane City Hall on Australia Day, 27th January 1969."

"You better go quickly, before they finish up for the day," he adds.

Mr. John Murphy is like my guardian angel. His Department approved my student visa application back in Hong Kong. It extended my stay after the first five year visa. It granted me permission to study a part-time Diploma course in Engineering at QIT. It gave me permanent residence status. And now, naturalisation might enable me to gain employment with the Council. I am overwhelmed with relief and deep gratitude. Making haste back to the Council offices, I dare to believe that my future might finally be secure. I have a real chance, now, to achieve my goal.

ᗡᗡᗡ

Look, Father! I've done it!

I am gazing at the heavens, waving a letter I have just received. My heart is thundering. I can't remember when I have been so thoroughly ecstatic. Perhaps when permission to enter Australia was first granted? Or when Mr. Pickers offered me a permanent job? Perhaps when Mr. Murphy advised that I'd been granted permanent residency? Perhaps when I received the letter inviting me to an interview?

No, Father. As joyful as I felt on those occasions, my delight at those victories doesn't even come close to my feeling of triumph seeing the words on this page.

TOM KWOK

Brisbane City Council

Department of City Administration

5th December, 1968.

Dear Sir,

In response to your application for a position on the Council's Staff, I am pleased to inform you that you have been appointed as a Cadet Construction Technician, on probation, in the Department of Works.

The terms and conditions of your employment will be those prescribed by the Municipal Officers' (Brisbane City council) Award and the Council's Ordinances, and confirmation of your appointment will be subject to your satisfactorily serving a probationary period of three (3) months. In this position you will be paid a commencing salary at the rate of $1,582 per annum; being the rate applicable to the 3rd Year of the Cadet Scale.

Will you please report for duty at 8:30 a.m. on Monday, 9th December, 1968, to Mr. J. Carter, Acting Secretary, Department of works, 2nd Floor, City Hall, Ann Street Entrance.

Yours faithfully
Town Clerk

♋♋

JANUARY 27TH, 1969: THE AUSTRALIA DAY HOLIDAY.

Australia Day is the official national day of Australia. Celebrated yearly on 26th January, the date commemorates the arrival of the First Fleet from Great Britain at Sydney Cove in 1788, and the beginnings of the first British settlement. With community festivals, concerts and citizenship ceremonies, the day is celebrated in townships and cities around Australia.

Australia Day is the day on which, customarily, qualifying immigrants take an oath of allegiance and are accepted as new citizens of Australia. Today, I — Tommy Kwok — am to become an Australian.

The naturalisation ceremony will take place at the City Hall in Brisbane. The Lord Mayor, Clem Jones, will give a welcoming speech, and afterwards we will all hold up our right hands and swear allegiance to Her Majesty Queen Elizabeth the Second, her heirs and successors, and swear to observe the laws of Australia and fulfil our duties as Australian citizens. Then one by one, we will walk up onto the stage to collect our Certificate of Naturalisation as an Australian Citizen from the Lord Mayor. After we return to our seats, a man representing all New Australians will thank the Australian Government for giving us a new lease of life in this great country. We will all cheer and clap and wave small Australian flags. We will shake hands and congratulate one another.

This is the achievement of a goal I have worked for eight years to fulfil. It's an end, and it's a beginning.

⏳⏳

The next milestone is confirmed in a letter from the Department of City Administration, Brisbane City Council. It is dated March 11, 1969. It reads:

```
Dear Sir,
    Further to my letter of the 5th December
1969, wherein you were advised of your
appointment as a Cadet Construction
Technician, on probation in the Department
of Works, I am pleased to inform you that,
as your work and conduct are reported to
have proved satisfactory, action has been
taken to confirm your appointment.

                          Yours faithfully
                               Town Clerk
```

After three months, my job is giving me a sense of achievement and satisfaction. I now have the certainty of a permanent appointment in a job of my choosing. I want to stand on top of Mt. Cootha and shout. I want the whole world to know how happy and how lucky I am.

Everything happens for a reason. Now looking forward to a positive future; whenever I face another obstacle, I'll look at it in a positive way.

I can't change the way I was brought up or the way I have lived my life to date, but I have no regrets. It was character building. It has moulded me into the person I am today. I have the strength to cope with adversities, and I am in control of my own destiny. Finally, I find myself living without fear. From now on, I will enjoy the fruits of my hard work, and celebrate the life experiences that shaped me.

സ്കൈ

THE EVENING OF 11TH MARCH, 1969

I feel the urge to write my father a letter. I want to thank him for my birth. I want to thank him for his guidance. After conveying my gratitude, I tell him:

> To ensure my longevity, your mother gave me a girl's name, Loo Shang. She sought to trick the evil spirits. 'Loo' 潞 —literally means 'waterway', which has the element of water. Some Chinese believe that the best name contains the five elements—fire, metal, wood, water and earth. 'Shang' 珊 is a girl's name meaning a 'jewel, like coral'. In ancient China, coral was considered one of the seven treasures. Wealthy people exhibited their coral to show off their wealth. Loo Shang 潞珊 may mean 'the waterway to get coral'. Because coral is very valuable, Loo Shang can be interpreted as 'the way to get riches'.

Despite his passing before my birth, my father has always been with me. I wasn't aware of it in my early years, but he was my guiding spirit—always giving me strength and taking care of me from above. I believe, from now on, I can take care of myself.

In Chinese culture, the rice bowl symbolizes food, a full stomach and an income. A broken rice bowl means the loss of employment: no income, no food and no full stomach. An iron rice bowl means a bowl made of iron, which can't be broken. The iron rice bowl, the cradle-to-grave employment system of the Government, is the envy of many Chinese, because it is a guarantee of employment for life.

I close my letter to my father with the words:

I may not achieve great riches, but I have achieved my goal. I now have an iron rice bowl. Thank you, Father, for giving me life. You may now rest in peace.

END NOTE

After staying with Brisbane City Council for nearly five years, I resigned my position as Work Supervisor in 1973, to pursue a career in the commercial building industry.

To gain a competitive advantage in the workplace, I realised I needed further education. After completing a Certificate in Civil Engineering in 1974, I continued studying, gaining a Diploma in Accountancy five years later. I then enrolled at Queensland University of Technology (QUT) for a Graduate Diploma in Project Management, graduating with Distinction in 1992. The following year, I earned a Master of Built Environment. I won the inaugural QUT Construction Management PhD Research Scholarship in 1994, and became a Doctor of Philosophy in 1999.

For thirty years, I worked at a number of major commercial building companies involving the construction in high-rise office buildings, 5-star hotels, hospitals, a major shopping centre and the re-development of Central Railway Station. Then, for a couple of years, I did free-lance consulting work in the construction industry.

Between 1995 and 1998, I was a part-time Lecturer at QUT. From 2003 to 2007, I was employed as a Professional Practice Coordinator, supervising final year students' practical work experience in the building construction industry. In 2008, I was engaged as a Construction Management Lecturer. I continued in that position for the next three years, until my retirement in 2011.

I met my wife, Puis Shim, at a friend's wedding ceremony rehearsal in 1971. Three years later, we married. We are proud parents of five children, Joon-Yee Bernadette, Hing-Wah Matthew, Wai-Ming Ann-Louise, Gee-Wai Michael and Ho-Doug Nicholas. All five are university graduates and all have excelled in their respective professions.

Ah-por, my grandmother, retired from her job as a kitchen hand at the Oriental Restaurant in 1970, at the age of sixty-five. Soon after, she sold her little cottage at Greenslopes and bought a small unit in Nundah, where she passed away peacefully in her sleep seven months short of her eightieth birthday. Despite her ordeal in China and struggle in Australia, she enjoyed reasonably good health throughout the latter part of her life. She was happy knowing Lu Kee and I grew up to be decent people and made good lives for ourselves.

I returned to Hong Kong at Christmas 1970, staying with my mother and her parents in their old home in Wanchai. When I returned again in the New Year, 1973, I promised to bring my mother to Australia soon. Early in 1974, I sponsored her to immigrate to Australia. She lived with her mother-in-law in Greenslopes. In 1981, she moved in with my family, and she lived with us until she passed away from stomach cancer, aged eighty-five. For thirty years, she watched her five grand-children growing up under the same roof.

ᔕᔕ

Lu Kee went back to Hong Kong in 1968 and stayed for about twenty months before going to the US to further his studies. He has lived there ever since. I travelled to the US at Christmas, 1972, to meet up with him and other relatives — our father's younger brother and half of our mother's siblings, who had migrated to the US earlier.

Since 1992, Lu Kee has visited and stayed with my family in Brisbane for a couple of weeks once every two to three years. Our mother was overjoyed to see her two sons and the grand-children together.

Lu Kee is still an Australian. He was granted a 'Green Card' to work in the US. During a recent visit, he indicated that he intended to retire in Australia one day. I am waiting to see when 'one day' might be.

ACKNOWLEDGEMENTS

Before embarking on writing my memoir, I enrolled in a number of short writing courses. Most, if not all of the assignments, were pieces of my life story. I thank the tutors, Tony Aldridge, Michael Pyne, Ernest Nash, Kathleen McGregor and Patti Miller, for their comments and feedback.

My gratitude also goes to the members of the Fairfield Writers' Group for their support and constructive criticism during the very early stages of writing this book.

I am indebted to my friends, who provided advice and encouragement, especially Bruce Thomas, Bob Spence, Jim Lam, Alie Blackwell, Tina Bridge, Joe and Sandy Sheridan and Helga Parl. Their corrections and comments were all extremely helpful.

I am appreciative of Elsie Brimblecombe who copy edited an early draft of the manuscript. I also thank Lesley Synge for her very useful structural editing and to Sophia Barnes for her invaluable input and experience in editing.

Heartfelt thanks goes to Lauren Daniels for giving me frank suggestions to improve my story.

A huge thankyou goes to Lorraine Cobcroft who suggested taking an entirely different approach to the story line. I really appreciated her honest opinion and I felt completely comfortable entrusting my story with her. With her expert knowledge and skills, she deftly pulled my draft apart and reassembled it. The finished product is impressive and one that I am very proud of.

Thank you also to Peter Cobcroft, the designer of my book cover, for his creativity and wonderful design work.

Writing is a solitary process. I thank my wife, Puis Shim, for giving me all the space that I needed to write.

And to our five children, Joon-Yee, Hing-Wah, Wai-Ming, Gee-Wai and Ho-Doug, thank you for your encouragement and cheering me on to write this book.